Bringing the Devil to His Knees

Bringing the Devil
to His Knees

The Craft of Fiction and the Writing Life

Edited by
Charles Baxter and Peter Turchi

Ann Arbor

THE UNIVERSITY OF MICHIGAN PRESS

2004   2003   2002   2001   4   3   2   1

A CIP catalog record for this book is available from the British Library.

Library of Congress Cataloging-in-Publication Data

Bringing the devil to his knees : the craft of fiction and the writing
    life / edited by Charles Baxter and Peter Turchi.
        p.   cm.
    Includes bibliographical references.
    ISBN 0-472-09774-1 (acid-free paper) — ISBN 0-472-06774-5
(pbk. : acid-free paper)
        1. Fiction—History and criticism.   2. Fiction—Authorship.
    I. Baxter, Charles, 1947—   II. Turchi, Peter, 1960–
PN3321 .B75   2001
809.3—dc21   00-12899

The editors would like to thank Ruth Anderson Barnett,
who provided generous and expert organizational and editorial assistance,
and the writers at Warren Wilson College, whose book this is.

Everything I have written up to now is trifling compared to that which I would like to write and would write with great pleasure. . . . Either I am a fool and a self-conceited person, or I am a being capable of becoming a good writer; I am displeased and bored with everything now being written, while everything in my head interests, moves, and excites me—whence I draw the conclusion that no one is doing what is needed, and I alone know the secret of how it should be done. In all likelihood everyone who writes thinks that. In fact, the devil himself will be brought to his knees by these questions.

—ANTON CHEKHOV, in a letter to Alexei S. Suvorin, 27 October 1888

Contents

CHARLES BAXTER AND PETER TURCHI

Introduction

As anyone who has tried to do so very well knows, a person—with the best of intentions—can learn the basics of how to write a story from a book of do's-and-don'ts and still be unable to write a good story.

This sad (perplexing, dismaying) fact may have something to do with the particular book of do's-and-don'ts the person chooses, but it has more to do with the gap between rule-governed activity and actual practice in the creation of fiction and with the bewilderment any artist faces in the practice of an art. Acquiring a basic competency in an art or craft is a necessity but will get its practitioner almost nowhere, if we define a "destination" as the completion of a beautiful or solid piece of work. Competency must be allied, must give way, to good judgment, energy, and creativity, which is only to say that anything that is completely rule governed will probably be formulaic, and anything that is merely competent and which lacks passion or vision is not worthy of more than a glance.

Knowledge does not necessarily lead to excellence in execution or creativity in the solution of an aesthetic problem. Knowing the rules, such as they are, and being able to implement them to create a beautiful result are two very different ways-of-knowing, and the gulf between them is large. A how-to book can suggest norms, but it cannot show anyone how to exercise judgment, and that is why teaching—or coaching—creative work is sometimes a hit-and-miss affair. For this reason also, rules for art that may not result in a living piece of art are sometimes referred to as "academic"—useful but perhaps not essential. All this is a terrible tragedy because it means that not everyone can master an art even after learning all the rules, and it is also a great blessing, because it means that everyone who truly practices an art cannot quite tell you how to go about it. Consequently, the book that you hold in your hands does not contain a set of rules but something quite different—what we might call a set of approaches.

The practice of an art is not a complete mystery, to be sure, but its uncertainties need to be unraveled with tact and caution and humility. In the justly famous letter by Chekhov that provides this book its title, he also wrote:

Only the individual who has never written and never dealt with images can say that there are no questions in his sphere, just a solid mass of answers. . . . You are right to demand that an artist take a conscious attitude to his work, but you confuse two concepts: *resolving a question* and *posing a question correctly*. Only the second is required of the artist. In *Anna Karenina* and *Onegin* not one question is resolved, but you are quite satisfied solely because all the questions in them are posed correctly.

In these essays, then, you will find writers considering the questions they ask themselves, questions about craft and about the knowledge and practice that enables a writer of fiction to transcend mere competence. Many of the essays suggest that a practical writing pedagogy might well be approached most effectively through metaphors, one of the only figurative means we have to describe the judgments that are involved, word by word, sentence by sentence, in the creative process. What such metaphors produce is a way of guiding the crucial strategic decisions that arise at every moment in the production of a work of fiction.

This collection is a companion volume to *Poets Teaching Poets: Self and the World,* edited by Gregory Orr and Ellen Bryant Voigt. The essays here, like the ones in that book, emanated from the first low-residency graduate program in writing, which was established at Goddard College in Vermont in 1976 but soon moved to Warren Wilson College in North Carolina, where it has grown and its practices have evolved over the past twenty years. As the editors of that earlier volume observe, in American higher education, the norm in advanced creative writing seminars is to have a mentor guiding a group of less-experienced writers in critiques of their own work, week after week, in workshop format. "The low-residency model," they write, "sought a supplement and an alternative to this method, within a pragmatic semester structure designed for adults: two weeks on campus to initiate six months of independent tutorial through correspondence."

The editors of *Poets Teaching Poets* go on to note that the term *low-residency* fails to suggest the instructional advantages of that intense period of conferences, workshops, seminars, and lectures:

Tutorial requires a low student-faculty ratio, which in turn brought together a greater number of practitioners in each genre than is possible in wholly residential programs. Tutorial also needs its correction: a variety of aesthetics, team teaching, and a mixture of new and returning faculty every term. And it was faculty, not design, that provided the crucial element: innovation does not *always* attract, as it did in this case, the serious and the gifted.

Both volumes of essays began as a series of craft lectures. These lectures became an increasingly significant feature of the program following its move from Goddard to Warren Wilson in 1981. The essays that now follow from those lectures more often than not include readings of literary texts, with analyses that do not function as interpretations so much as professionally guided tours to an understanding of decisions made by the writers concerning subject matter, form, tone, and identity. They were delivered to an audience of students and peers, and they often created and stimulated discussions, controversies, and counterarguments. This is as it should be, as it must be, whenever artists who are in the thick of the practice of their art gather together to offer explanations and justifications of how they go about their work. An artist without strong opinions is likely to cave in to the first pressures that she or he encounters, and good arguments are the product of the clash of strong opinions. Not every argument poisons the well; some clear the air.

The essays in this volume are divided into three categories. The first includes those considerations most often gathered under the catch-all category of formal techniques. These essays comprise two on the subject of voice, one voice being that of Chuck Wachtel, the other that of Steven Schwartz; Richard Russo's essay on point of view, with particular attention to the question of omniscience; Joan Silber's comments on "weight"—the sense of a subject's importance—in short fiction; and Charles Baxter's notes on inflection. Susan Neville considers mindful villainy as a necessary aid to plot, and Jim Shepard warns against the dangers of epiphany. Here, too, we encounter Debra Spark's help on "getting in and getting out" of a story and Ehud Havazelet's observations on Chekhov and form.

A number of the essays begin with a metaphor for the acts of the imagination that result in fiction or the process of fiction making. In this category we find Robert Boswell's meditation on architectural spandrels; Peter Turchi's equation of cartography and fiction writing; C. J. Hribal's commentary on the need for scene setting as the answer to a form of readerly hunger, allegorized wittily as "the scene beast"; Karen Brennan's observations about fictional perseveration and confabulation as seen through the difficult and harrowing recovery of her daughter from a brain trauma; and Antonya Nelson's intricate (and serious) reading of the joke form as an analogy, or base, of storytelling itself.

The last category sees all these activities from a slightly greater distance, where overall aesthetic strategies begin to touch other realms, particularly the social and political; no purely formal writing tactics can be separated from other matters of equal or greater importance. Here Pablo Medina addresses the issues of politically charged identities in "Literature and Democracy"; Michael Martone asks how the (conventional) ruination of a story might provide its (paradoxical) salvation; Kevin McIlvoy writes letters, as an editor, to a writer who is safely if uneasily dead; Margot Livesey suggests ways of approaching truth itself, in "How to Tell a True Story"; and Judith Grossman reminds us that there are, after all, readers to keep in mind.

None of these essays presumes to tell the reader how to write. The reigning tone here is that of experienced writers making an *offering* to their students and peers of what, by painful trial and difficult error, they have had to learn themselves in order to do their own work. The reader will encounter some faiths and beliefs but very little arrogance. As a result, the essays typically contain a quality of hard-won knowledge that cannot prescribe but can often suggest directions and strategies for those who are still so transfixed by the myriad and sometimes infinitesimal difficulties of what they are doing that they cannot see the overall layout of the field on which they labor.

Reading these essays is a lesson in both the self-sacrificing humility and the discipline of art. In a passage written by Proust (and much beloved by Randall Jarrell) these disciplines and artistic obligations are spelled out in clear detail:

> All these obligations which have not their sanction in our present life seem to belong to a different world, founded upon kindness, scrupulosity, self-sacrifice, a world entirely different from this, which we leave in order to be born into this world, before perhaps returning to the other to live once again beneath the sway of those unknown laws which we have obeyed because we bore their precepts in our hearts, knowing not whose hand had traced them there—those laws to which every profound work of the intellect brings us nearer and which are invisible only—and still!—to fools.

This book does not mean to provide—cannot provide—a set of answers. At best it will be suggestive (in the best sense), informative, and inspiring. Instead of blind self-assurance, the authors offer possibilities, assuming that whoever reads this is interested in writing as a life activity over the long haul and knows better than to believe there is an easy route to a destination worth reaching.

PART ONE   *Techniques, Devices, and Strategies*

RICHARD RUSSO

In Defense of Omniscience

Part of the problem with trying to teach anybody anything is that we who know how to do it forget what it was we didn't know. Having arrived at understanding for ourselves, we forget what the problems were, what we were confused by, what was getting in our way. It's like teaching someone to drive a stick shift. It doesn't seem that complicated after you've been doing it for ten or fifteen years. You don't think about it anymore. Your left foot knows where to find the clutch, when to depress it, when to let up and how fast, how much gas to feed with the right foot, when to slip the shift out of one gear and into the next, where the various gears are, where your eyes should be when all this happens (on the road, not on the diagram they give you on the ball of the stick, not on the floor beneath the dash where the clutch was the last time you looked, before it moved, so that you can no longer locate it).

My father, who taught me how to drive a stick shift one summer afternoon when I'd come home from the university to work road construction with him, was one of the world's worst teachers in that, once he'd mastered any difficulty, he no longer considered it to *be* difficult. Difficult was how he characterized anything he *hadn't* mastered. Driving a stick, he told me that afternoon, was something any goddamn idiot could do. Half an hour later he had to pick up his carelessly thrown down gauntlet and admit he was wrong. There was one goddamn idiot who couldn't seem to learn, no matter how loudly instructions were bellowed at him. My father couldn't seem to grasp that I was wired in parallel, that, when my left foot came off the clutch, my right instinctively left the gas. Part of it, too, was that he'd started me off at the foot of a steep hill, his reasoning being that I would encounter hills eventually, and he didn't want my instruction to be deficient in this regard. Finally, the gearbox was slippery, and I kept locating reverse by accident, grinding the transmission frightfully. I can still remember my father's frustration at this, it seemed to him, most unnatural of mistakes. "Jesus Christ," he complained. "Can't you *feel* it?"

This is the problem in a nutshell. Once you've learned how to do something, you do it by feel. In familiar situations the wrong thing *feels* unnatural. Right feels right, wrong feels wrong. Easy. The timing, the hill, the slippery gearbox, once mastered, become familiar, and we forget what it's like to lurch along the road, other motorists swerving into the passing lane when they come upon us and recognize us for what we are—novices—sailing by, honking derision, often flipping us the bird. We forget that to be a novice is to be in unfamiliar situations pretty much all the time.

Omniscience, my friends—you see I've finally sidled up to my subject—is a slippery gearbox, and most apprentice writers prefer to drive the more "automatic" prose transmissions: first person literary, close third person. And these work perfectly well in most situations, getting writers where they want to go. Some authors will write through entire careers without ever tackling true omniscience and will write very well indeed. Ah, but the stick is a wonderful thing, and there's nothing quite like it once you've learned, and in this essay I'll try to explain why.

First, some background. A surprising percentage of the literary novels being published today are told from an omniscient point of view. I confess that I have not done anything like a scientific study. I have simply been struck by a disparity that I believe would be borne out by formal research—that professional writers are far more likely to opt for omniscience than are novice and apprentice writers. In lieu of statistics, here's some compelling anecdotal evidence. When I teach Introduction to Fiction Writing to undergraduates, one of the exercises that I and many other writing teachers employ to teach point of view is to have students write the first page of a story from several different points of view (not character viewpoints but literary points of view). When I first started teaching, I went over the various broad options for telling stories: first person literary, dramatic monologue, close third person, effaced, omniscient and, grudgingly, stream of consciousness/interior monologue. After explaining how they all were supposed to work, I told students to pick three. Or pick four, depending on how ambitious I was feeling. Until I noticed that, when the assignment came in, everybody avoided omniscience. Everybody. Beginners are drawn to the flashy, on the one hand, and the simple, on the other. They all want to try the seldom used dramatic monologue form because, I suspect, one of the two or three novels they've read is *Catcher in the Rye,* a book richer in technique and style than substance. Beginners are even drawn, despite my warnings, to stream of consciousness, which they see as a license for incoherence. They like the effaced point of view because they don't have to enter their characters' thoughts and close third person because it seems to answer that old workshop question, "Whose story is this?" and they enjoy literary first person because they like the sound of their own voices or the idea of mimicking other voices. Full-blown omniscience? No takers. They don't see the margin in it.

But these are, after all, beginners. Surely more seasoned apprentices would not share the beginners' prejudice. To find out, I consulted the 1990 Residency Worksheets of the Warren Wilson MFA Program, which contained the fiction of thirty-five talented, intelligent writers, most of whom have been writing long enough to have become discouraged for whole months at a time. Out of thirty-five, how many, gentle listeners, would select the voice of choice of Henry Fielding and nearly the whole eighteenth century, the point of view most suited to the wide canvases of the nineteenth-century Victorian novel, the point of view that has never been anything but the mainstay of storytelling in our own century, regardless of the literary movement then in vogue (experimentalism, minimalism, postmodernism, any other "ism")? How many of these stories would be told by an omniscient narrator?

By my count, four. I did not count stories that began with an omniscient paragraph before zooming in, camera fashion, to close third or limited third person. I did count stories that hadn't mastered omniscience but, rather, seemed to be striving in that direction, the omniscience unintentionally leaking away at times. Four out of thirty-five. That statistic alone may be meaningless, but consider this. In the first workshop of this Warren Wilson residency one of the stories on the worksheet concerned three brothers attending in shifts their dying father in a hospital. The story was told in the form of notebook entries, each son offering his thoughts and observations to his brothers. The story built nicely to a satisfying emotional conclusion, and the workshop consensus seemed to be that the story was successful despite some difficulties of execution. The notebook entries, more than one reader pointed out, got more interesting toward the end as the brothers became less reticent and more honest in what they wrote in the notebook. Also, it was said, the author seemed to have considerable difficulty in releasing what Steven Dobyns has referred to as the secondary information of the story—descriptions of the hospital room and hospital procedure—because these brothers would have little reason to describe a room or discuss a procedure in a notebook entry intended for their brothers, who know what the room looks like and are themselves witnessing medical "process." Also, these brothers tended not to tell us, until very late in the story, some pretty important things about themselves. They had no reason to, because they knew each other.

Since we had identified but offered no remedy to these difficulties, I asked how the author might have done the story differently to allow easier access to the needed information. Quickly, there were hands. One person suggested selecting one of the brothers, letting him be the principal storyteller who would perform that function, in addition to writing his own notebook entries. This idea (providing a close third-person point of view) was immediately rejected and for valid reasons. It would upset the balance of the story, which gave equal time to each brother, suggesting their equal importance as characters. Another hand. Why not let the dying father tell the story, let the notebooks be secondary? That would keep the relative balance by making no brother more important than the others. True, but it would diminish them and their conflicts collectively. Also, the father was comatose. This solution too was rejected. Let one of the nurses tell the story, someone threw out in desperation. The person next to me groaned. Nurses have even less reason to describe hospital rooms, and no nurse would be privy to the kind of personal information about these brothers that has to get revealed somehow.

Dead end. Impatience in the room. Could anyone, I asked, think of a natural way to tell the story that would surrender necessary information about the brothers and the setting and the situation, without upsetting the careful character balance of the story as it existed? "Well," someone said, "I *liked* the notebook entries," thus effectively diverting the subject. (And, indeed, the notebook entries were looking more attractive again, their problems notwithstanding.)

Obviously, I was hoping that someone would see an omniscient narrator as the solution to the specific problems raised by the author's chosen method, but no one saw it, not even as an option. Omniscience, I freely admit, might have towed in its wake another different set of problems. The author's notebook entries, though they wouldn't have been my choice, might still be the best choice for her. That's not the point. The point is that omniscience, for many apprentice writers, is rejected even before it's considered.

There are reasons: (1) omniscient narrators tell a lot, and telling is something that students of fiction writing have been warned against early and often; (2) omniscience is an outside, not an inside view, and the clichés of our profession seem to disapprove. Get inside your characters, we recommend. Become your characters. See through their eyes; (3) omniscience feels old-fashioned, even stilted—Henry Fielding addressing us as Gentle Reader; (4) omniscience is the most arrogant of techniques, inviting the writer to play God and placing the burden of wisdom in all matters that pertain to the story squarely on the shoulders of the author. When we're misinformed, stupid, bigoted, clumsy, we can't blame any of it on the character we've "become."

But before I examine these issues, let's, just for fun, define *omniscience* and illustrate what it achieves. I'll begin at the beginning, with examples of the three major third-person points of view I was given in my first fiction writing course:

1. Bob kissed Ellen. (Effaced. We don't know what the characters are thinking or feeling.)
2. Bob kissed Ellen, but he was thinking of Sue. (Close third person. We go into the thoughts of one of the characters.)
3. Bob kissed Ellen, but he was thinking of Sue, and Ellen was thinking of Tom. (Omniscient. We go into the thoughts of more than one character.)

Okay. Simple enough. Omniscience allows the writer to know more and reveal more. The problem is that the example is unlikely to convert many writers to omniscience. Who'd want to write such a sentence? Worse, the example doesn't begin to convey or illustrate the real advantages of omniscience. So, let's examine a couple of sentences that will. Here John Steinbeck, in *Cannery Row,* describes Dora Flood, madam of the local whorehouse: "Dora Flood is a great woman. A great big woman with flaming orange hair and a taste for Nile green evening dresses." Here we begin to see the true advantages of omniscience. First, there's the convenience of being able to describe Dora from the outside—her flaming orange hair, her Nile green dresses. It's clearly an outside view, because Dora would never see or describe herself this way. But even more important is the matter of voice. Omniscient narrators, even when they seem matter of fact, convey attitude. It's not so much the author speaking to us as it is the author in a particular pose. Here Steinbeck's attitude is sardonic, clever, distant, and yet affectionate. When in the first sentence he tells us that Dora is a great woman, the word *great,* modifying a noun, seems to convey a judgment about her character. In the second sentence, when the same word *great* modifies another adjective (*big*), we realize that in addition to learning something about the character of Dora Flood, we've also learned something about the "character" John Steinbeck has become, or the pose he has struck, to tell the story. He's copped an attitude that may or may not be the same as other omniscient narrators he uses to tell other stories.

Omniscient narration, then (at least full-blown omniscience), exhibits the following traits. It looks at characters from the outside but can "see" inside, directly into thoughts and feelings. It transcends time and space. The omniscient narrator can be in as many places as he or she needs to be and possesses knowledge of all moments—past, present, and future— and is free to reveal it. (Of course, there are varying degrees of omniscience in literature, though examining them would be the subject of another essay.) And, finally, there is always a narrator, a voice that embodies a clearly defined attitude, an authorial pose, a consistent and recognizable way of seeing and understanding. By way of illustration, consider the following passages from Jon Hassler's wonderful novel *Grand Opening:*

> The moment he set foot in homeroom, Brendan was offered a stick of gum by a shifty-eyed boy named Dodger Hicks, who had been lying in wait for a friend. Among the twenty-four boys and girls of the seventh grade, Dodger had not even one friend, the parents of Plum having warned their children away from him because his father was a convict, his mother drank, and Dodger himself stole things from stores—crayons, comic books, candy.
>
> Dodger was older and taller than the rest of the seventh grade, having taken nine years of school to get there. A poor reader, he was taunted for what his classmates assumed was stupidity and had spent every recess and noon hour of his life lingering at the edge of a game. His face was dark, his cheekbones prominent. He had a habit of nodding his head when he spoke, and of squinting and showing his long teeth when he listened. His dark hair, which hung unevenly about his ears, he trimmed himself, using a pair of small shears pilfered from art class. As he gave Brendan a stick of grape gum . . . he said he had stolen it that very morning from Kermit's Grocery, the door being unlocked and no one inside.
>
> "That's our store," said Brendan. "My mother and Dad bought it."
>
> "No kidding?" asked Dodger. He gave Brendan the rest of the pack.

After school Brendan lets Dodger tag along home with him. Dodger examines with interest all of Brendan's toys and is particularly fascinated by a boomerang that Brendan has been unable to make return. Dodger has better luck.

> The boomerang sailed up and away, spinning as it climbed, and at its apogee—incredibly high and small—it tilted almost vertical as it wheeled around and began its return flight, picking up speed and spinning faster and faster and heading straight for their heads and passing over them as they threw themselves flat and crashing through the kitchen window. At the sound of the breaking glass, Dodger was up and running. He never glanced back or said goodbye.
>
> The noise woke Grandfather, who called from his window

upstairs, "Where are we, lad, and what was that noise like a china closet tipping over on its face?" This being Grandfather's second awakening in this unfamiliar house, he was of the opinion—as he had been for awhile this morning—that he and his wife and two daughters were lodging in a tourist home en route West, retracing a trip he had made in 1921 to visit relatives. At breakfast it had taken three cups of coffee and a stern word from Catherine to convince him this wasn't a stopover in Billings.

"We live here," Brendan shouted up at him. Then softer, "And my friend broke a window."

"We live here?"

"Plum! Remember?"

Grandfather backed away from the window, smartly rapping his skull with a knuckle—usually a sign that a surge of fresh blood was making a swing through his brain and carrying off his delusions.

Indeed, one of the first things Grandfather recalls, once his delusions are carried off, is his beloved wife, long dead, and his life on the railroad:

Thirty years married and twenty years a widower. . . . Thirty years building railroad lines, then nearly twenty years as a brakeman. In those years a brakeman was exactly what his title implied. Besides throwing switches in the railyards and keeping tally of the box cars dropped off and picked up, a brakeman scurried along the tops of the cars, often while they were in motion, to turn the wheels that set the brakes. Treacherous work. He had seen a brakeman killed one icy afternoon in the St. Paul yards. His own freight was pulling out, heading west; he was standing on the rear platform of the caboose and looking off to his left at another freight pulling in. He saw the brakeman standing on a cattle car of the inbound freight. The man wore a long black coat and black mittens. He noticed Grandfather and waved, and then as he turned and was about to leap the gap between cars he slipped. Down he went, striking his head on a coupling and then dropping to the track, and the wheels of the cattle car passed over his legs, or rather passed through them, for they were cut clean off just below the hip. Grandfather, riding away, signaled his engineer to stop and he jumped from his caboose and ran through the sleet to the other train, which continued to move, wheel after steel wheel rolling over the bloodsoaked pants and coattails. Grandfather pulled the man away. He was out cold, had been knocked out before he hit the ground, thank God. Grandfather waved and shouted but the train continued to crawl through the yard, and when the caboose finally rumbled by, there on the back platform stood the second brakeman looking down in disbelief at his dying partner, whose loss of blood was so lavish it spouted like a fountain from his stumps and he lost his life before he came to.

Ah, the damn trains. The wonderful damn trains.

While I don't wish to belabor the obvious, allow me to point out some of the features and advantages of Hassler's omniscient point of view. Perhaps most important, no other point of view offers such immediate access to the story's necessary information. Dodger Hicks comes to life as a result of this access. We not only see him standing there, "a shifty-eyed boy," in time present, but we also have access to his past, to the events of his young life that have made him shifty-eyed—the fact that he has no friends, that the other children have been prejudiced against him by their parents. We know that Dodger steals things, and we know what he steals. We know not only that he's swiped a pair of scissors but that he uses them to trim his own hair, an intimate detail that powerfully suggests the realities of Dodger's life: that in his family there's no money for haircuts and that nobody cares enough for Dodger to trim his hair. Because of an omniscient narrator's ability to transcend time and space, to examine the present and the past within the same short paragraph, we learn an amazing amount about Dodger very quickly. No other point of view gives a writer such easy, natural access to the things that need to be revealed. If you don't believe it, reread the sections of *The Great Gatsby* that go into Gatsby's past, things that need to be revealed to us but that Nick Carroway has no access or only strained access to. *Gatsby* is a great novel, a transcendent novel, but the transitions into and out of the past, the explanations of how Nick came to learn such things after Gatsby's death are often tortured, sometimes simply lacking. You can see the writer struggling with the artistic implications of his choice. I have no doubt that first person was the right choice for Fitzgerald, but in the wake of that choice were real problems, including access to necessary information.

Hassler's omniscience also allows the narrative baton to be passed with great ease from one character to the next. The chapter excerpted here moves gracefully and naturally from Dodger to Brendan to Grandfather without any of the devices required by more limited and limiting points of view. Neither a new chapter nor a space break is required. Nor is any explanation needed. One moment we're told what Brendan is seeing and thinking when the boomerang comes zooming back at the boys. The next paragraph begins, "The noise woke Grandfather," and we are introduced to a new consciousness. The outside view not only gives us access to Grandfather's inner thoughts but is able to evaluate them, see them for the delusions they are.

Not being restricted by time and space also has the effect of encouraging digressions. If the spell works, we see the story of the man dismembered by the train as part of Grandfather's personal history, but more interesting is the ease with which that digression is slipped into the larger narrative. It is followed by two more train stories (not quoted here), each recalled by Grandfather and each as rich and enjoyable as the one quoted earlier. Think of them as Grandfather's stories if you choose, if you enjoy that illusion, but in reality they are Jon Hassler's stories. The author clearly knows a lot about trains and train lore, and he's chosen a point of view that will allow him to reveal what he knows in the most natural way. Omniscience means, of course, all knowing, and it favors writers who know things and are confident about what they know and generous enough to want to share their knowledge.

And, finally, Hassler's omniscience allows him stylistic freedom. Effortless though the storytelling seems, Hassler's "narrator" is having great fun with the language, and the person speaking to us (Jon Hassler? Jon Hassler in a particular frame of mind or mood?) has a consistent and recognizable attitude. When we first meet Dodger Hicks he is not awaiting a friend but, rather, "lying in wait of a friend." Friendship by ambush. Grandfather's confusion is dispelled not by fresh blood to the brain but, rather, fresh blood "making a swing through his brain." The man whose legs are amputated by the train suffers a "lavish" loss of blood. Omniscience is neither voiceless nor mechanical in its telling. Indeed, it offers as much opportunity and latitude to exercise a writer's love of language as any other point of view, indeed more than many.

Having seen some of the things omniscience can do, let's return to the kinds of objections I often hear from students when I suggest omniscience as a possible solution to a story's problems: (1) *Omniscient narration stresses telling, not showing.* True. But there's nothing wrong with telling, provided it's balanced with showing. The trick is to know when to tell, when to show. It should be remembered that we're storytellers, not story showers, and fiction writing is not film. Novels are not pre-screenplays. In a screenplay everything must be shown. There's no such law in fiction. And, often, telling the reader things is a test of what the writer actually knows, and it can also reveal what he or she doesn't know. The more limited (and limiting) points of view can offer an attractive (though dangerous) refuge. If the writer knows next to nothing about, say, law, it's tempting to tell the story from the point of view of a character who's equally ignorant. (2) *Omniscience doesn't allow you to be truly inside your characters. We don't see through their eyes.* True again. But sometimes there's nothing to be gained from being inside. The metaphor of "becoming our characters" derives, again, from the screen (and the stage). You must lose yourself in order to become your character. Great actors will do almost anything to become their characters. On a recent "Saturday Night Live" skit "Robert DeNiro" has several segments of his spine removed so he can play a shorter man. But "being" and "understanding" are not the same. We can understand murderers without becoming murderers. If being inside were the best way to understand something, we'd all major in self-knowledge, whereas few of us do, even those who seem to have taken up permanent residence in confessional mode. (3) *Omniscience feels old-fashioned.* Well, gentle reader, who gives a damn? Are we talking old-fashioned in the sense of being part of an extended, rich literary tradition? There are worse things. That which is trendy, for instance, is a worse thing. (4) *Omniscience encourages the writer to intrude into the fiction, and authorial intrusion is to be avoided. Omniscience is thus an arrogant technique.* Let's take the last point first. Poet Elinor Wilner has joked about rewriting the Bible in her poems. Pretty arrogant behavior, right? Except that arrogance is part of the equation. We aren't writers to be timid. If playing God scares you, there are other professions. And who says authors shouldn't intrude into fiction? What they shouldn't do, it seems to me, is intrude clumsily or stupidly or unwittingly. Who could object to the presence of the omniscient narrator in the following passage from Steinbeck's *Cannery Row,* in which Mack and the boys go hunting frogs?

During the millennia that frogs and men have lived in the same world, it is probable that men have hunted frogs. And during that time a pattern of hunt and parry has developed. The man with net or bow or lance or gun creeps noiselessly, as he thinks, toward the frog. The pattern requires the frog to sit still, sit very still and wait. The rules of the game require the frog to wait until the final flicker of a second, when the net is descending, when the lance is in the air, when the finger squeezes the trigger, then the frog jumps, plops into the water, swims to the bottom and waits until the man goes away. That is the way it is done, the way it has always been done. Frogs have every right to expect it will always be done that way. Now and then the net is too quick, the lance pierces, the gun flicks and that frog is gone, but it is all fair and in the framework. Frogs don't resent that.

Not content to speak for all Mankind, Steinbeck wants to speak for frogs as well.

So, then, what am I advocating? That you should write more stories employing omniscient point of view? No. At least not exactly. The real reason that apprentice writers first shy away from omniscience, then gradually gravitate toward it, is a reason few beginners suspect or could articulate. Omniscience, in the end, is a mature writer's technique. Our being drawn to it has something to do with years, with experience of life, with the gradual accumulation of knowledge and pain and wisdom. Omniscience not only invents a world; it tells us how that world works and how we should feel about the way it works. Few writers at twenty-five or even thirty are ready to assume such a mantle. Omniscience is permission to speak and to speak with authority we know we really don't have, about a world that in our century (any century?) is too complex to know. Ultimately, omniscience forces us to pretend we know more than we do, and we're afraid we'll get caught. We're afraid we won't know as much as we need to and that our imaginations will not supply the lack, for omniscience places a premium on both knowledge and imagination.

But it's a sweet, lovely, rich, generous stick shift of a technique, and it'll take you places you can't go with an automatic transmission. The first few times you try it, it'll buck you all over the narrative road and send you fleeing back to the vehicle you already know how to drive, wondering what perversity would make anyone want to make a hard job harder. But many of you will return, and those who master the technique will come to enjoy the more complex involvement with and control over the machine.

After I finished my novel *The Risk Pool,* a long first-person narrative, I began two other books,[1] one in first person, the other close third. I've since switched both into omniscient, where I hope they'll stay. I've granted myself permission to speak, taken a deep breath, and prayed that what I speak will be knowledgeable and true and wise. If it isn't, I can always go back to close third and blame the characters. I turned forty this year. I've begun to understand the attraction of telling people what frogs think.

---

[1] These novels, published after the original lecture was given, are *Nobody's Fool* (New York: Random House, 1993) and *Straight Man* (New York: Random House, 1997).

JIM SHEPARD

I Know Myself Real Well.
That's the Problem.

In graduate school for a brief miserable stretch I shared an apartment with an excitedly New Age-y kind of guy who worked with what he thought was cunning zeal to convert me to Christian Science. (He had just taken the plunge himself.) This attempt at conversion took the form of encouraging me to drink a lot and then suavely introducing into the conversation every so often the tenets of Christian Science. According to his no doubt somewhat flattened version of that theology, what was wonderful about Christian Science was how sunnily nonjudgmental it was: in his version human frailty, human foolishness, and human transgression were all attributable to a simple lack of information. People did bad things out of ignorance. Dispel the ignorance, and you effectively dispelled the bad behavior.

I've found myself wondering, lately, if that old graduate school roommate has been secretly teaching fiction writing workshops all across America. More and more I've been seeing stories in which the protagonists are whooshed along the little conveyor belts of their narratives to that defining moment of insight or clarification that will allow them to see with new eyes the essential emotional or spiritual furniture of their lives. The implication is nearly always that this moment of insight removes one of the last major obstacles on the road to personal fulfillment. What has so entrenched, as the poet Carl Phillips has put it, "this belief that to spill our difficulties is to undo them"?

Now, as I understand it, a short story, by definition, does have a responsibility, in its closing gestures, to enlarge *our* understanding, but it seems to be increasingly difficult for writers to resist allowing their hapless *protagonist* a new understanding as well—an understanding that will set him or her on the path to a more actualized life. This is, as we all know, the age of the Oprah Book Club, whose credo is that a book is useful precisely to the extent that it conjures up for us a ratification of our own particular experience and can thereby be morphed into a self-help text. It's not our task, though, to save our characters, however adorable we secretly find them. We should not, in other words, be afraid to withhold consolation.

One effect of the tyranny of the epiphany in the short story is the assumption that an enhanced level of self-awareness is inherently liberating; in other words, once we realize we're doing something self-destructive or foolish, we won't do it again. Alas, we know from the rubble of our own lives that this isn't always the case.

Certainly, Robert Stone knows it. He teaches us in every one of his works about the endless ways in which we can be intricately self-aware and yet still geniuses at self-destruction. And none of his works may handle that subject as powerfully, and concisely, as his magnificent short story "Helping."

Stone's background may have uniquely prepared him for an understanding of the limitations of self-awareness. He was born in Brooklyn. He grew up as the only child of a schizophrenic mother. (One of his wonderful remarks about that situation was that "I had to sort out causality for myself.") He was raised as a Catholic. He was given the kind of eye-opening and not altogether edifying education that only institutions like the U.S. Navy can provide. He worked as a journalist in places as remote and far-flung, and likely to generate solitary brooding, as Antarctica and South Vietnam. During the 1960s he was what we could choose to call an involved participant in the counterculture. He was in on the ground floor, in other words, with Ken Kesey and his bunch during the early days of experiments with the consciousness-expanding properties of LSD. We have to assume that he is one of the few Merry Pranksters to end up on the Yale faculty.

We would expect, in other words, someone who had lots and lots of experience with LSD to be suspicious of epiphanies. As might also follow, perhaps no one in America writes as well as Stone does about such primal and metaphysically resonant psychological states as terror, rapture, and dread. And it may be that that particular combination of states is the one best suited to confronting our late-twentieth-century world, a world in which, as he informs us in his most recent novel, *Damascus Gate,* we might come across a character who's "an aging Glaswegian skinhead, a former French Legionnaire and African mercenary who had taken up haute cuisine and was employed at one of the big chain hotels," or find ourselves in a place in which "across the valley lay the Hill of Evil Counsel, where the United Nations had its offices."

His protagonists belong to the restless, rootless, cosmopolitan side of things and are forever inquiring of wide-eyed obsessives the nature of their dreams. His protagonists understand that desire for the brilliant transforming clarification of the epiphany, because his protagonists, whether they're fully aware of it or not, are tireless in their pursuit of the numinous, tireless in their desire for some kind of transcendent ground.

In other words, like Elliot, the protagonist of "Helping," whatever they say, and whatever the odds against it, they believe in the transfigurative capabilities of a human nature that is everywhere unworthy of itself. And that possibility is not only the cause of their greatest hope; it's also the cause of their greatest torment. Without possibility, they cannot be failing themselves. With that possibility intact, their failure could not be more spectacular or profound.

There's an old George Raft movie in which George is, as he so often was, a gangster at bay, holed up with some hostages. The police surrounding his hideout bullhorn in the news that if he surrenders, they'll guarantee him a fair trial. "Fair trial?" Raft mutters to himself. "If I get a fair trial, I'm *dead*. What I need is an *unfair* trial."

"Helping" opens with what seems to be an explication of the process of just how it was that events conspired to undermine poor Elliot and to knock him off the wagon. "One gray November day," we're told, the story beginning with the storyteller's most traditional opening, Elliot went to Boston, which undermined him; then there was Christmas, which did the same; then January, which did the same; and then, finally, Blankenship, one of his most recalcitrant reclamation projects (Elliot is a social worker) and the straw that broke the camel's back.

The severity of the narrative economy does, in fact, transmit to us powerfully a sense of the bleakness, as well as the paucity of notable joys, involved in Elliot's life on the wagon: "Christmas came, childless, a festival of regret. His wife went to Mass and cooked a turkey. Sober, Elliot walked in the woods." Well. So much for December.

But from the story's very first gestures it's working to establish, in fact, *Elliot's* capacity for undermining *himself;* his capacity for poisoning everything that might help. In the opening paragraph the story's verbs quietly remind us that not only is this view of Boston the result of a particular means of perception—"The wet streets *seemed* cold and lonely," instead of *were* cold and lonely—but it's also the result of a pretty resourcefully pessimistic means of perception: "He sensed a broken promise in the city's elegance and verve." When that sentence is interrogated, we come to understand that the *city* is demonstrating elegance and verve. *Elliot,* meanwhile, is sensing a broken promise in that elegance and verve. *Sensing* here seems designed to suggest a particular and admirable sensitivity, as if Elliot picks up nuances of things that you or I might miss. *Sure, the average guy on the street might enjoy Boston right now. But I sense a broken promise in all of this. I've been promised something by the cosmos, and the cosmos hasn't delivered.*

"Old hopes," we're told immediately afterward, "tormented him like phantom limbs." For Elliot the simile is particularly apt: what's most tormenting about phantom limbs is the way the phantom pain or discomfort they generate seems to suggest their presence, while in so doing it in fact only confirms their absence. For all of his insistence on his own nihilism, Elliot continually returns to the notion of the tormenting nature of hope. Hope becomes possibility (later, in the midst of a quasi-euphoria Elliot can't quite explain, we're told that "what he was experiencing, he thought, was the principle of possibility"), and then possibility becomes promise. The broken promise mentioned in the story's very first paragraph returns just before Elliot tumbles from the wagon: "He felt in possession of a promise," we're informed, and then he spies the lights of a nearby tavern. A page or two later he brings the issue up again when he puts his own failure in context by outlining his sense of a fallen world to his wife, Grace: "First the promises, and then the rest." Hope, possibility, promise: there's a difference in the metaphysical implications of the third term in that progression. *Promise* indicates that someone or something had to have *extended* that promise.

So the story opens with its cheerless shorthand versions of Elliot's December and January. January turns out to render expressionistically the state of poor Elliot's soul, besieged by the void—it's too cold even for snow, and in the white silence he can feel a shrinking in his bones and hear the starveling deer being run down by packs of dogs—and it also seems designed to demonstrate that if there was no solace for Elliot in the city, there won't be any in the country, either. Elliot, I'm claiming, in other words, seems to be in covert control of this narrative. And the clearest indication that we should be suspicious of the simplicity of his apparent causality—*well, who wouldn't fall off a wagon, given Boston in November, a childless Christmas, January in the Shawmut Valley, and a guy like Blankenship?*—comes in the following paragraph, still on the story's very first page: "In his mind's eye," we learn, "he could see the dead leaves rattling along brick gutters and *savor* that day's desperation." "Savor"? That *savor* is startling, and should send us back to those early indications of his subtle capacity for poisoning everything. This is the same Elliot who chooses to believe that when Candace, the Quaker librarian who seems genuinely to enjoy his company and who seems to want to help him, asks him about Vietnam, she's probing him, as he puts it, "for the edification of the East Ilford Friends' Meeting." This is the same Elliot who contrives to promise himself a drink. This is the same Elliot who stages his fall off the wagon so theatrically for his wife, in their confrontation. The same Elliot who ultimately threatens melodramatically self-destructive violence against both the misfit on the social margin, Vopotnik (one of his wife's clients), and the pillar of the community, his neighbor Loyall Anderson.

In this story called "Helping" the notion of helping is treated by the protagonist with weariness, impatience, suspicion, bitterness, scorn, and rage, without the story's ever losing sight of its absolutely essential nature. Negotiating this story means learning more about the difficulty of bringing common sense and common decency to bear and the importance of doing so. This is old-fashioned, art-is-good-for-you stuff, presented without apology: the story continually demands that we consider how we can persistently—or even intermittently—come through for others, when we're persistently unable to help even ourselves.

The story organizes itself structurally around ten separate examples of helping that apparently does not help. Elliot does not help Blankenship. ("Lemme alone," Blankenship says fearfully to Elliot during their session, after Elliot has snapped impatiently at him. "Some doctor you are.") Candace the librarian does not help Elliot; liquor does not help Elliot; music, one of Elliot's few genuine joys, does not help Elliot; Grace does not help Elliot; Elliot does not help Grace; Grace relates how she was unable to help the Vopotnik child; Elliot does not help Mr. Vopotnik, when he calls, instead baiting the homicidally weird Vopotnik to come on over for some "radical problem-solving"; Grace again does not help Elliot, when she leaves him downstairs with a loaded shotgun; and, finally, the story ends on a final opportunity for helping, with Elliot outside in the snow, looking up at Grace in the window.

Naturally, both Elliot and his wife are engaged in social work for the state. Every day they experience their failure to help, at home and at work; every day they soldier on, dutifully. Elliot cannot help, at work or at home; which means he cannot be helped, at work or at home.

The hapless Blankenship, the sort of character Stone once described as "one of life's little yo-yo's," is the kind of feral and halfwitted small-timer that tends to populate Stone's fiction; the kind that makes helping so gosh-darn difficult. Not only does he have an apparently limitless number of unappealing traits; he also has developed a maddening sense of entitlement, and passivity. He's used to depending on others and not helping himself; he's used to playing the system, He and his entire family, Elliot points out to us, "made their way through life as strolling litigants."

What's particularly maddening about Blankenship, though—what makes him, finally, the last straw—is the sly and apparently purposeful way in which he literalizes the single notion that Elliot finds the most intolerable: the notion that Elliot is in no position to pretend to give advice to anyone, because in fact Elliot is no better off. Blankenship is in his office to complain about a particularly debilitating dream, an anxiety dream about Vietnam, even though he's never been there. The dream he describes, down to its details, is Elliot's dream. Such dreams are apparently just in the air. Elliot isn't even granted any special position among the suffering elect for having actually been in Vietnam himself.

Blankenship's enraging combination of duplicity and genuine piteousness—he is, after all, at that point living "in a Goodwill depository bin in Wyndham," and he comes from a family so comprehensively incarcerated that even "their dog's in the pound"—combines with the sorry spectacle of a system passing the buck to push Elliot over the edge.

Just before his fall we're provided with the can't-see-the-forest-for-the-trees method by which Elliot, either half-consciously or disingenuously, protects himself from having to confront fully, and so head off, his own self-destructiveness. This is after he leaves work early:

> Halted at the first stoplight, he began to feel the want of a destination. The fear and impulse to flight that had got him out of the office faded, and he had no desire to go home. He was troubled by a peculiar impatience that might have been with time itself. It was as though he were waiting for something. The sensation made him feel anxious; it was unfamiliar but not altogether unpleasant.

What he wants, what he's waiting for, is a drink. His inventory of his own sensations at that moment is intricate and nuanced and yet stops just short of that crucial perception. What we see here is something that's scrupulously detailed and yet myopic. At the end of that paragraph we see the avoidance even more clearly, as we see his demon justifying itself: "What he was experiencing, he thought, was the principle of possibility." Well, yes, in a sense. But what we more or less understand even then, with a certain amount of dread and unease, and certainly understand in retrospect, is that mostly he's talking about the possibility of a drink; the possibility of letting go and falling off that wagon. This is the voice of someone who knows exactly how he ticks, exactly what it is he shouldn't be doing, and goes ahead and does it anyway, a strolling spectator of his own collapse.

Confirmation of that understanding is quickly provided. He tells us on the next page that he had no clear idea of why he went to the library, and we're encouraged at first to think that he went to seek help, in the form of his friend Candace's benign solicitude. But such solicitude only makes him impatient and suspicious, and it's only when he heads back outside that "his heart, for no good reason, leaped up in childlike expectation." The adjective *good* in that sentence does at least double work: no good reason in the sense of no particular reason; and no good reason in the more traditional ethical sense as well. His heart leaps up at the drink it knows he's headed for. His heart leaps at the prospect of his own self-destructiveness. Such is the extent of his own anger and disappointment with himself and his world that that self-destruction seems to be the only thing in the story that inspires joy. The metaphysical aspects of terms like *possibility* and *promise* are here evacuated with a vengeance, as those terms are brought rudely down to earth: *possibility* means the possibility of a drink; *promise* is the promise to collaborate in his own undoing.

As Stone himself put it in his *Paris Review* interview, "There are people who have delusional systems they are really quite aware of." And as he has the protagonist of his novel *Dog Soldiers* put it, upon having decided to get into the heroin trade: "So there. . . . That's the way it's done. He had confronted a moral objection and overridden it. He could deal with these matters as well as anyone."

Elliot's decision to drink allows him to find a momentary refuge from the spectacle of inadequate attempts at helping. In the package store "he realized that the old man neither knew nor cared who he was." In the tavern "no one turned to note him when he passed inside," and the bartender responds to an alcoholic's announcement that he'd thought he'd have just one with, "Good move. Scotch?"

Which carries the reader to the confrontation at the heart of the story: the confrontation between, fittingly enough, Elliot and the well-named Grace. Coming into the house unsuspecting, she knocks over a cross-country ski, thereby not only nicely foreshadowing the story's ending, when Elliot confronts his neighbor, the skiing Professor Anderson, but helping account for Elliot's rage, then and now: "It had been more than a year since Elliot had used the skis," we're told. He's not the man he used to be. He's not fastidious about taking care of body and spirit, the way Professor Anderson is. Grace complains twice that the skis shouldn't be underfoot, since he never uses them. This enrages him. Then the moment he's been both dreading and anticipating comes, and "with dread and bitter satisfaction" Elliot watches his wife detect the smell of whiskey.

Well. It's constructive to consider in this story how often Elliot is caught watching others watch him. Examples are all over the place. A page later, while they're still arguing, we read, "He was aware of her eyes on him." The narcissistic self-indulgence of his little playlet as fallen angel is part of the point, in fact, of the whole scene with Grace—a scene, in my edition, that gobbles up six of the story's twenty pages.

That same bitter satisfaction in his role as Outlaw is what causes Elliot to feel he needs to detest so viscerally his neighbors the Andersons, a family so comically healthy and well adjusted that they bring to mind Homer Simpson's neighbors the Flanders.

Meanwhile, in the quietest of ways we see how he works to transform the world to his own disadvantage. Early on in the argument we read this about Grace, after she has absorbed his bad news: "He looked at his wife and saw that she had stopped crying. Her long, elegant face was rigid and lipless." The second sentence—"Her long, elegant face was rigid and lipless"—is notable for the transformation involved in its adjectival pairs. It's as if the first pair—*long* and *elegant*—precedes the act of will that generates the second pair: *rigid* and *lipless*. It's as if, in other words, Elliot's perceiving sensibility let slip through some of his wife's beauty—long and elegant—before his sentence's somewhat brutal agenda—rigid and lipless—kicked in.

"Helping" is rightfully famous for its depiction of a couple sunk into a long-term dysfunctional relationship that is nevertheless not without real tenderness or regard. Husband and wife are continually rolling this rock up the hill. Their desperation feels to them tedious and their tedium desperate. Like nearly all of Stone's fictions, then, "Helping" reads like a captivity narrative. And by captivity narrative I mean those narratives that constitute perhaps America's oldest literary tradition, works like Mary Rowlandson's seventeenth-century narrative about being captured by the Narragansett Indians. The protagonists of such narratives feel themselves to be sinners in the grip of a fallen world. They seek an understanding of their own degradation and come, inevitably, to understand it to be the result of both their own shortcomings and the world's ruthlessness in exposing those shortcomings. Again in mid-argument, toying with an explanation of his behavior, Elliot muses on a fragment from *Medea:* "Old friend, I have to weep. The gods and I went mad together and made things the way they are."

Perhaps because of *Medea's* influence, he says he's very sorry; he wants to make that clear. And yet in the very next sentence he can't help but note that "the delectable Handel arias spun on in the next room." We're continually reminded how much perverse enjoyment lives on, inside the suffering.

It's no longer possible for either Elliot or his wife to separate the theatrical aspects of their behavior from the more genuine aspects of their suffering. "It's out of my hands," Elliot says soon afterward. Then he shows Grace his empty hands. The gesture is both funny and appalling because of his willingness to parade his irresponsibility; his surrender. Then she demonstrates that they're made for each other; or, rather, that they've fashioned themselves, by this point, in each other's image: "I can't stand it," she tells him. "You reduce me to hysterics." And she wrings her hands for him to see. "See?" she adds. "Here I am. I'm in hysterics."

The self-parodic elements of their gestures do *not* undermine their claims of suffering. They *do,* however, undermine any hope we would have that, if only these two people were shown what they were doing and what it cost them, they would stop.

Elliot says increasingly brutal things. Grace throws a sugar bowl and screams at him. Elliot then proceeds, when challenged, to make the sort of speech that shows up in bad theater from the 1930s, like something out of a ninth-string Clifford Odets play:

> What do I mean? I mean that most of the time I'm putting one foot in front of the other like a good soldier and I'm out of it from the neck up. But there are times when I don't think I will ever be dead enough—or dead long enough—to get the taste of this life off my teeth. That's what I mean!

The speaker's covert pride in his rhetoric, a rhetoric so flamboyant it sounds like bad hard-boiled detective fiction—*I needed to get the taste of this life off my teeth*—should combine with the hyperbole of that final exclamation point to warn us about the theatricality of the speech itself. But if it doesn't, we always have Grace's wonderfully unimpressed reaction, as well, once he's finished: "She looked at him dry-eyed. 'Poor fella,' she said."

When Grace then tells him that she can't take it anymore, that she hasn't got it in her, that she'll *die,* Elliot takes Scrooge's position: "'Do what you feel the need of,' he said." In other words, he assumes the role of one of the most famous villains in our cultural tradition. When Scrooge is informed that many would rather die than go to the prisons and workhouses, his retort is, "If they would rather die, they had better do it and decrease the surplus population." And again the sentimental theatricality of the *Christmas Carol* model returns, on the bottom of the page: "The Vopotnik child will die, I think," Grace says, her syntax suddenly sounding oddly like the Ghost of Christmas Present, "This one I think will die." As the Ghost puts it, in his own story, "If these shadows remain unaltered by the future, the child will die." Grace underlines her point even later: "'If the child stays in that house,' she said, 'he's going to die.'"

What keeps Grace going, it turns out, is her sense of a divine plan. That, she tells Elliot, he can't have; that's the only part of her life he can't mess up. Elliot makes fun of that—"Sometimes," he says, "I try to imagine what it's like to believe that the sky is full of care and concern"—but we remember that it was *hope* and *possibility* and *promise* that got this whole destructive train going in the first place; we were told, and we begin to wonder if the reason that "earnest seekers like Candace" cause Elliot "great secret distress," as he confides to us when feeling cornered in the library by her, is that they remind him painfully how appealing he finds, even as he sees through, the pull of the seeker. Elliot tells himself with melodramatic fierceness during the argument that "if it had not been for her [Grace] he might not have survived. There could be no forgiveness for that." But his rage follows not an example of how she prevented him from committing suicide but a simple announcement of her faith. Her *faith,* in other words, is what he ultimately refuses to forgive.

Their self-parodic awareness of even *that* dynamic is confirmed immediately thereafter, when Grace tells him that from here on in she won't be there for him, and he answers, "I don't believe it. Not my Grace." How's that for a sneer, underpinned by genuine suffering? *At least the* possibility *of Grace will* never *leave me, because I'm one of God's children.* And she says, not having missed the point, "You make me feel ashamed of my own name."

Nevertheless, that abandonment without grace is what she threatens him with when she finally goes upstairs and leaves him alone, drunk, on the ground floor with a loaded shotgun. It's at that point, acting out his own suffering for himself and for Grace, and drunk, that Elliot starts having his epiphanies. All of the epiphanies he experiences have some merit, in terms of insight, and all of them are false bottomed, in the sense of (a) being something that on some level he already knew; and (b) not necessarily leading to any sort of transformation in his life.

His first is that he "was sympathetic with other people's tears but ashamed of his own. He thought of his own tears as childish and excremental." *Oh, I get it,* we think. *He's too hard on himself.* His second, a paragraph later, is that "He had found a life beyond the war after all, but in it he was still sitting in darkness, armed, enraged, waiting." Hmm. More news.

We note that both of these are insights that had previously occurred even to us—after all, much of the preceding talk about Elliot's tactical savvy concerning his defense perimeter, in anticipation of Vopotnik's visit, is supposed to make us understand the irony of his having recreated Vietnam here in the Shawmut Valley—and there's ample evidence that these insights have occurred to Elliot as well.

After he stands up, puts on his coat, grabs his gun, and heads out into the early-morning snow, more epiphanies. Standing in the middle of the snowfield with his shotgun, hungover and tired, dazzled by hypnogogic patterns behind his eyes, he thinks: "Fear, anger and sleep were the three primary conditions of his life. . . . Once he had thought fear the worst, but he had learned that the worst was anger."

Well, yes. As fiction writer Charles Baxter once put it, "That old insight train just keeps chugging into the station, time after time." But what does that insight produce? Following that insight, along comes Professor Anderson. And Elliot *uses* his anger and his new understanding to take some cheap satisfaction in frightening his neighbor with his potential for violence.

Like the protagonists of "The Dead" and "Araby," the most widely anthologized examples of the Joycean epiphany, in such clarifying moments, Elliot has become visible to himself. He sees how completely he's been arrayed against himself. He possesses what feels to him to be a heroic watchful wretchedness. But the "heroic" suggests how much he's still sentimentalizing his position. And the sheer number of insights piling up suggests how powerfully someone in his position—especially someone pulled, whether he likes it or not, toward the notion or possibility of transcendence—is attracted to the seemingly problem-solving premise of the epiphany. He tells us:

> Getting drunk was an insurrection, a revolution—a bad one. There would be outsize bogus emotions. There would be petty moral blackmail and cheap remorse. He had said dreadful things to his wife. He had bullied Anderson with his violence and his unhappiness and Anderson would not forgive him. There would be damn little justice and no mercy.

But in his sentimentalizing and needy state, the epiphany gates seem to be wide open, with everything pouring through. Two paragraphs later:

> He wished no harm to any creature. Then he thought of himself wishing no harm to any creature and began to feel fond and sorry for himself. As soon as he grew aware of the emotion he was indulging, he suppressed it. Pissing and moaning, mourning and weeping, that was the nature of the drug.

In this case the drug is not only the alcohol but also the desire for the epiphanic turning point, the brilliant transforming connection to larger manifestations of wisdom. *We* want that as much as Elliot does. We expect the story to provide wisdom. We expect the author to dispense it.

"Helping" provides its own cautionary moments designed to make us, in retrospect, think twice about that desire. The scene of Elliot counseling Blankenship, one of the story's first scenes, provides a model for the limitations of the author-reader relationship. Blankenship, in the role of the reader, has a look that's "disconcertingly trustful; he was used to being counseled." Elliot, *reacting* to that responsibility, finds "his voice sounded overripe and hypocritical in his own ears. What a dreadful business, he thought. What an awful job this is." Anyone who's been in a position like I'm in now—presuming to write on such matters—knows how Elliot feels.

Elliot, meanwhile, for better or for worse, hasn't stopped having his realizations. On the last page he realizes that somehow (a) Grace has gotten out in front of his gun, to the wrong side of the wire. He realizes that (b) "if he looked long enough, he'd find everything out there. He would find himself down the sight." Then he thinks, (c) "How beautiful she is." Then he thinks, (d) "At the best of times, he was a difficult, fussy man." Then "Elliot began to hope for forgiveness." Why then? Because he apparently feels he's earned it, with all those Epiphanies. He has, after all, laid it out like an equation: $a + b + c + d = e$, e being forgiveness.

But how savvy this story is, in terms of exposing the ubiquitous power of that desire, without at the same time evacuating its possibility. Elliot waves. He decides he wants her to show a hand. He decides that if she *does* show a hand, he will take that as something to build on. He will be able to put one day on top of another, as Grace said the Vopotniks, and people like them, could not do. Grace does not respond. He puts his hand higher, to signal his readiness for a Sign more plainly. And the story ends.

This moment constitutes, as I mentioned before, the story's tenth and final opportunity for helping. But not only do we never find out if the helping occurs; we also never discover just whose help is really required at that moment: is Elliot waiting for Grace's help, or, given the way he's already announced he'll interpret her gesture, is he waiting for his own?

Elliot's need—his propensity—and *our* need—*our* propensity—for the kind of closure that the overuse of epiphanies in contemporary fiction has come to provide is exposed. We don't get closure. We get an unfolding of the mystery of the self-destructiveness of Elliot's behavior but not its resolution. We get a glimpse of free will on the loose, in all its solitary and often self-defeating stubbornness.

In a fallen world humanity becomes divided between those who make things happen, those who watch things happen, and those to whom things happen—between perpetrators, bystanders, and victims, in other words—and Elliot has tried on all three roles as we've watched.

Where he ends up, when he's seeing most clearly, is not at a point of despair. Where he ends up is somewhere more like: *let's find out how bad it gets and begin from there.* But as anyone who's been in an intensely fraught relationship knows, there's something inextricably constructive and destructive about an impulse like *let's find out how bad it gets.*

Elliot is painfully aware of his limitations and failures but even more painfully aware of the imminence of a breakthrough. Which makes him instantly identifiable as a Stone protagonist. As he does in all his work, Stone finds the mist of illusions through which we move hopelessly dated, nearly criminal, and strangely moving.

Given our status in this worldview as fallen beings, delusion becomes a natural response. For Stone our delusions are dangerous, and saddening, but they also can be sublime; they're also what drive us forward and make us human.

Understandings like *that* help make us glad that stories like "Helping" exist and glad we read them. Understandings like that demonstrate to us the way even sad stories or scary stories can provide us with enormous satisfaction, mostly by making the world less lonely. This is writing as a means of invocation or, as Stone himself has put it elsewhere, a response to the silence to which we have otherwise been consigned. In this way he attends to all the broken promises that undermine us. In this way he attends to all our little festivals of regret.

I've told my students—and an alarming number of strangers and near-strangers as well—that Robert Stone is the author of one collection of short fiction and five novels, every one of which they should personally own and periodically reread. "Why?" they seem to ask in response, their expressions drifting somewhere between boredom and defiance. "What's in it for me?" This is what I wish I'd answered:

They should give their closest attention to Robert Stone's work because he writes with spectacular compassion and understanding of our status as frightened, wounded, haunted, and self-invented. He forces us to reinspect those versions of ourselves that, at our laziest and most fatuous and most hypocritical, we most cherish. He shows us how to be less lazy, not only as human beings but as writers. He asks us to reexamine those cruelties that, out of self-protection, we do not care to see. As the South African poet Jeremy Cronin has articulated it: "Art is the struggle to stay awake."

And Stone does all of this without removing the possibility of hope. He shows us how to be, and why we need to be, to use his phrase, "athletes of perception." Which makes his work sacramental in nature. I'm not sure how much we can ask of a writer, given the present state of our society, but that seems to me a pretty good day's work.

SUSAN NEVILLE

Where's Iago?

The day of the winter solstice, the day the spaceship *Mir* would fly directly over Indianapolis so that astronaut David Wolf could talk to his mother, we held our department end-of-first-semester lunch. My friend Aron knew I was thinking about this essay and the topics of misfortune, calamity, evil—for days he'd brought them up. You know, Aron said, last night I discovered the origin of the word *disaster*.

It's *dis-aster*, he said, *astral*, a misalignment of the stars.

And *religion*, he said, means to bind back, to heal. The Hebrew word is *tikkun*.

A colleague named Larry sat across from us, but we didn't talk to him. We talked about Iago and the origin of words.

For several years now Larry has been studying labyrinths, and he is in fact the kindest, most introverted person any of us knows. This day he was wearing a new sweater, a reddish brown, with other colors and textures woven through in no discernible pattern. You could lose yourself trying to trace the threads, so we didn't try, just as we always take his introversion at face value and smile and say pleasantries but make no real attempt to knock at the door and enter.

But that night, before I went outside to look for *Mir,* I got a phone call from Aron. He'd been driving away from the restaurant and turned the corner into a cluster of police cars, he said, directing traffic away from an accident. He was about to turn into the line of diverted cars, but he saw the shoes of the victim and then, as more cars turned, the pants, little by little unmasked, until finally there was the sweater.

I recognized him then, Aron told me. It was Larry. Like a lamb there in the road, he said, blood all over his face and only me left there to help get him in the ambulance and go with him to the hospital and to call his wife.

It was so intimate, Aron said, that I realized I had no idea before this moment who he was. Every day it's all "ha ha happy happy." Something like this happens to one of us, and we don't know who it was it happened to. We hide from one another, he said, all the time, as though there's something we're ashamed of.

I talked to Larry, Aron said, on the way to the hospital, in between the doctors and the nurses, until his wife came.

You know, he said, all of our literary tradition sees evil as having something to do with the inability to see outside ourselves, to see another human being as real.

And by the way, he said, you want to know where Iago is? I'll tell you where Iago is, he said. He's here, he said, and even over the phone I knew he was pointing to himself.

A year ago, about this same time, I received one of Kurt Vonnegut's famous late-night phone calls. "Susan," he said, with no "hi" or "how's the weather there?" or "how have you been?"; it was just "Susan, is it breath of new-mown hay or scent of new-mown hay?"

I think it's "breath," I said, but I told him I'd look it up and call him right back if it weren't. The line he was fact-checking was from the Indiana state song *On the Banks of the Wabash Far Away*. For some reason writers who were born in Indiana and move away often think I'll know the answer to questions like this. What town were Dusenbergs built in? I can't remember, but it was up near Fort Wayne. Where was the Conn trombone factory? In Elkhart. What was the name of D. C. Stephenson's secretary? Madge Oberholtzer. What color are the soybean fields in mid-November? I haven't a clue.

The song Vonnegut was referring to was written by Paul Dresser, Theodore Dreiser's brother. They were both—Paul and Theodore— from Terre Haute, Indiana, as was Eugene Debs, as is Larry Bird, in case you're wondering. Every one of them, until he was conveniently dead and iconic, was a source of embarrassment to Terre Hauteans, with the exception, of course, of Larry Bird.

My great-grandfather was a carpenter and stonemason; he did all of the woodwork for several of the Indianapolis buildings that Vonnegut's grandfather designed, so this whole exchange felt like some sort of weirdly historical déjà vu thing. I was so eager to be helpful that I heard myself doing that *ladadada* fast singing you do when you're trying to get to the lyrics in the song you want to remember. *La da* dream about the moonlight on the Wabash, *la da da* there comes the *what* of newmoon hay. *La da la da da da.* A ha! Here's the oak you need for that doorframe: *Breath.* It's *breath* of new-mown hay, not scent.

He was working on the galleys for *Timequake,* and the line comes up on page 166. I say this because I will probably always think of it as my most important contribution to American literature, and it will go unfootnoted.

At any rate, he said "thank you," then, and in order to say something kind, he asked how my novel was going.

It's a mess, I said, truly awful, and I tried to think of some way to change the subject.

I can tell you what's wrong with it without seeing it, he said. You're missing Iago.

Iago?

The character that bounces all the other characters around. I wasted twenty years figuring that out. Look for Iago.

Let me say here that Vonnegut has been, my entire conscious life, my hero; if this weren't true, I wouldn't have wanted to think about this topic for longer than two minutes. Even when I was a child, if something broke in our house, my parents would go to Vonnegut's Hardware Store to get the tools to fix it. Which shows you in part that it's more lucrative to be an architect than a carpenter. But more important—any child growing up in Indiana, when she feels that sense that it's an impossible place to be from, remembers Kurt Vonnegut with relief and gratitude. It's a feeling both irrational and deep, and I would gladly cover an island in flowers or write a lecture over Christmas break to express it. And I felt that he was probably right but had no idea how and wasn't going to ask. I was too overwhelmed at the time with the sense of God speaking to me from the whirlwind to follow up with "Huh?" The blueprint's beautiful, the math is elegant, I might have said if I'd thought of it, but I'm a poor architect myself, better with the materials than the design, and I don't quite get it, Mr. Vonnegut, I don't quite get how this window should be placed. Whatever do you mean, Where's Iago?

And it occurs to me now that I didn't ask questions because I wanted to hold on as long as possible to the mystery of it, which has happened. I've thought a lot about Iago, about how and why Iago might be a tool that helps create structures that are level and true, buildings strong enough to hold imaginary lives.

Iago is the image of evil in the way that Romeo and Juliet are forever the image of romantic love, so I have to talk about evil here but also have to say that I'm slightly embarrassed by the idea of talking about it. I think that even thinking about it made my hard drive crash. While there is of course such a thing as catastrophe, I wouldn't before writing this essay have called anything evil, which seems to imply a conscious malevolence in human beings, in the case of "moral evil," or the universe, in the case of "natural evil." There is no such thing as evil, I've always assumed; it's all simply a matter of tracing things back far enough until you can determine some completely understandable cause in biology or chemistry or physics. If you want to call it the force of entropy or chaos as opposed to the force of order, I'm fine with it. Call it the shadow, and I'm sort of OK with it. Call it evil, and my brain goes dim.

But I think that Vonnegut was talking about Iago in two ways: both Iago as a certain type of character—not a villain necessarily but a catalyst, the part of this essay I'm the most comfortable with—and as evil in the way it's usually understood, as part of the very structure of the world. I think he was implying a kind of seriousness that he shares in fact with Debs and Dreiser, all three of whom end up saying something like what Vonnegut says in *Timequake:* "For God's sakes can't we just help as many people as possible get through this thing, whatever it is?" (And for this if nothing else, Terre Hauteans should be proud.)

I'm not going to talk about whether a writer has some sort of moral imperative or responsibility to name evil, though I'm certainly not averse to thinking about it. I am going to talk about how Iago creates dramatic tension and to say that there are aesthetic consequences of moral evasiveness or flinching away from evil in fiction—in addition to a lack of seriousness, a kind of muddiness, characters with a static sensitivity, a case of viral ennui that is never realized in dramatic action.

But I have to say that what probably interests me about the subject, honestly, has nothing at all to do with making fiction work and everything to do with the hope that it matters.

And, too, many writers have written and spoken about the question of the responsibility of the artist eloquently: Czeslaw Milosz, Toni Morrison, Wole Soyinka, Flannery O'Connor, Eli Wiesel, William Faulkner. I love their essays about literature and am haunted by them. I'm also haunted by a question/answer session I attended where a student was obviously deeply moved by Thomas Keneally's talk about the interviews he did with Holocaust survivors when writing *Schindler's List* and who asked what was the one thing he should do if he wanted to be an artist. And Keneally said, not at all glibly, that the student should try if at all possible to see the evil that no one sees and that will be, in fifty years, the thing that no one can believe we did nothing about. I've been haunted by that statement as well.

Although it is of course an incredibly dangerous thing to say to any human being, maybe in particular to a writer. There's the risk of projection, of intellectual arrogance, of blindness, of oversimplification or the possibility of falling unwittingly, like Oedipus, into an even greater evil. I think of myself, Keneally said earlier on the same day, when asked why he wrote, as a horrendous human being. Probably the best we can do is describe what we see and, when we're conscious of evil, to locate it in the characters with whom we most closely identify. Within ourselves. I'll come back to this.

My first thought is to think of Iago as a catalyst character. Iago slithers through the Garden of Eden because without him it's a dull, stagnant story; nothing would ever change. Human history *in time* begins with Iago. In fact, the first Iago begins the action all the way through the Old Testament. Evil or misfortune has a similar function in *the story* as it does in life. For the Gnostics and for the fiction writer evil is the source of all moral understanding; the function of evil, in the best of conditions, is tension and imbalance, the eventual creation, through suffering and misfortune, of wisdom. Suffering, misfortune, and, I should add, *honesty,* which is Job's (and Vonnegut's and any good fiction writer's) great attribute. "God damn the day I was born," Job says in Stephen Mitchell's translation, in the face of his neighbor's easy platitudes. With honesty and not one whit of patience. It's that honesty that allows him to hear, finally, the voice of God, a voice he wouldn't have heard if it weren't for Iago.

The "knowledge of good and evil," Martin Buber writes, "means an adequate awareness of the opposites latent in creation," the yes and the no. He said that the cause of all moral evil is *the lie,* the particularly human evil that creates illusion—inauthenticity is Sartre's word—in the liar and in those around him. We create illusion because we choose to maintain order. Often we create illusion because we need, as did Dr. Jekyll, at least the appearance of goodness. Over and over in the literature of evil the word *illusion* appears, not because it is an evil in itself but because it is the petri dish that allows evil to mutate and to grow. It was "illusion that ruled," Eli Wiesel says in his great Holocaust memoir, *Night,* "not the Germans."

Of course this assumes a world in which we can know what illusion is. It may be our particular evil, at times, to operate as though we can't hope to. I guess we'll find out.

But for now, let's think about Othello. His love for Desdemona and hers for him is a structure created out of opposites: passion and jealousy, trust and distrust (if Desdemona went against her father's wishes, might she go against his?) and illusion. The destabilizing half of each equation is repressed in favor of the half that tends toward order. Passion is foregrounded and jealousy repressed, etc. Othello was a braggart, in love with the heroic story of himself, and he loved Desdemona, he acknowledges to Iago, for loving that story. "She loved me," he says "for the dangers I had passed, / And I loved her that she did pity them."

Othello's happiness is constructed with a crack, but it is a happiness that could have gone on and on, as fairly uninteresting but nonetheless subtle tensions forever and ever Amen, the couple safely ensconced in Eden, blissfully unaware of how little they really knew one another, if it weren't for Iago. Iago brings Othello out of his illusion and into the real (and I'm thinking of the play as O'Connor might think of it, where the violence brings a form of cleansing grace, though not in enough time for poor Desdemona) and necessary for Shakespeare's play, where the latent or *potential* opposites are finally actualized in a scene because of Iago. It's Iago who makes the conflict real and therefore dramatic.

Iago's particular evil manifests itself as a conscious, Nietzschian will-to-freedom, though he rationalizes it plenty and, if pressed, would probably say he was a pretty good guy though misunderstood; he had his reasons. But he woke up one morning and realized that human freedom is limitless once you realize that what "seems to be" isn't true at all, that any ordered world is all a brave construction, a building of fragile material, a place enclosing light within darkness, and that this fragile building can be *re*constructed as he wishes it to be by someone like—himself. What power! Anyone can do it! Reinhold Niebuhr said, "Evil is always the assertion of some self-interest without regard to the whole," and Iago asserts his self-interest with a vengeance. He could consciously construct his identity as a mask and then set out to deconstruct other masks. He will *seem* to have Othello's best interests at heart. In that way, in part, he protects his own illusions:

> Heaven is my judge, not I for love and duty,
> But seeming so, for my peculiar end;
> For when my outward action doth demonstrate
> The native act and figure of my heart
> In compliment extern, 'tis not long after
> But I will wear my heart upon my sleeve
> For daws to peck at; I am not what I am.

Othello's ordered world is vulnerable to Iago because, within his world, chaos and order are separated by the most fragile of tissues. He's extraordinarily passionate, with opposites very close to the surface. The line that always seemed to me to be at the center of Othello's character is this one: "Perdition take my soul, / But I do love thee! and if I love thee not, / Chaos is come again." A character who says that is in a particularly vulnerable position. There's love or there's chaos, no in-between. (Though this is perhaps always true of love, which is a fulcrum balancing joy and despair, the yes and no, and it's this balancing, more than anything else, that places it at the center of so many of the world's stories.)

And here comes Iago: the deconstructor, the unsettler, the emperor of ice cream.

I think that Vonnegut is saying that Iago is inevitable because every human system contains the roots of its disorder, every order contains the seeds of its disintegration. Every last by-definition-contingent one. No exceptions. If it didn't, it would be perfect. If it didn't, it wouldn't be human.

There should be a law of thermodynamics, and perhaps there is, that says for every human structure there's a hairline crack, a fault line, and Iago is the character or force whose function in the plot is to *see* or at least to *sense* that fault line, to insert himself within it, flattened like a mouse under a door or, more accurately, to become like water finding a fissure in stone and settling in, causing the stone to crack.

And what happens as the rock is breaking, until the new order is restored as two rocks or as one or as unrecognizable rubble: that's where the story is located. Without Iago the wedge, there wouldn't be *this* story. There would only be the story that existed before the story began; there would only be the baseline story, which can go on and on interminably, all of its illusions intact, with its minor daily tensions and conflicts.

It's easy to begin a work of fiction with the sense that here's the way it is, it always was, will always be. That *always is* seems filled with so much conflict, day to day, isn't that the story? Isn't it enough? I've written six hundred pages. Isn't this it? Not until Iago finds the opposite lurking in what "always is." Something needs to cause those tensions to erupt into time. This day, this story.

Using this definition, Iago is a tool. When his work is done, he's silent, as much a victim, often, of his own evil as anyone. (Think of Sir Lancelot in Arthurian legends.) Shakespeare's Iago operates out of a self-delusion: he convinces himself that Othello has slept with his wife, that Othello has received honors that he himself should have received. The first illusion he creates is one of his own, the first recipient of his lies is himself. It's perhaps the self-delusion that causes the crack in Iago that allows evil to seep, smokelike, in. "Demand that demi-devil," Othello says, after he's killed poor Desdemona as the result of Iago's conscious lies, "Why he hath thus ensnared my soul and body?" And Iago says, "Demand me nothing. What you know, you know. / From this time forth I never will speak a word." The stone has broken in two, the illusion is exposed, and silence takes over. To live in the lie that was the world of the story at the beginning of *Othello* is to live nowhere at all: in nothingness. Like the Misfit in O'Connor's "A Good Man Is Hard to Find," Iago has been the tool of a kind of grace, and I'm using *grace* right now in a particular secular sense, as a knowledge of the real.

Martin Buber, in *Good and Evil,* explains that we experience evil when the lie exists so long that the "nothingness of the illusion has become reality," and lives are

> set in slippery places: so arranged as to slide into the knowledge of their own nothingness; and when this finally happens "in a moment" the great terror falls upon them and they are consumed with terror. Their life has been a shadow structure in a dream of God's. God awakes, shakes off the dream, and disdainfully watches the dissolving shadow image.

When I say six hundred pages, I don't say it lightly. Harriet Arnow in fact wrote six hundred pages of *The Dollmaker,* six hundred pages before she got to page one, six hundred beautifully crafted pages worth of sentences written early in the morning before she had to get the children up for school, to make the breakfasts and the lunches and find the homework accidentally kicked under the couch or thrown away and get the clean clothes in the dryer. These early pages described the family's rural Kentucky life, with its daily conflicts, each character locked in place. And she threw them away.

Because on page 601, the war, Iago, enters, and the father's restlessness and wanderlust and the mother's physical strength and love for her children and obedience to her husband reveal themselves as the hairline potentially destabilizing tensions they could have remained, and the family is thrown from the flawed but unchanging Eden of Kentucky to the wartime hell of Detroit. Iago is a force in this story: World War II. But it's primarily the mother's story, and, as the father is infected by the war, Iago very quickly takes on flesh and blood. The father becomes the unsettler, different from the first Iago in that he's not conscious of his role, which is to uncover the existential situation for the mother. Previous to this, in the long-running back story, her loyalty to her husband has been without choice, but it contained the seeds of its destruction. Her illusion was the hope that her husband shared, or would come to share, the same agrarian worldview, the one she's based her family's happiness on: self-reliance, a life within nature, the cycle of the seasons. When in fact her husband is restless. He wants technological solutions, loves machinery, loves cars, is a hunter not a farmer.

They could have gone on with these differences forever because they could live within the tension; there was no reason not to. But World War II gives the husband a release for the *authentic* not the *seeming* self: a patriotic move to Detroit with its burning steel mills and trains. Now the mother has to choose between loyalty to the family or the place, which has been up to this point only the potential conflict. By remaining obedient, she makes a choice that will affect her children and their lives and will result in the death of a child. The mother has now entered the world of her own illusion, her own lie. The world turns upside down, and the new status quo will only be accepted after the death of the daughter, that cleansing restoring violence, the end to this story. Of course from there we get a new status quo and a new crack, but for a while everyone holds on to the way things are, boxing themselves in with hastily built walls that were never really meant to last.

I'd like to give one more example of Iago both as a character and as a force, from Sudanese novelist Tayeb Salih's *A Season of Migration to the North*. This novel is divided into two distinct parts, and one of the interesting things about its structure is the way Salih consciously plays with the Othello/Iago narrative.

In the first part of the novel the narrator meets and then tells the story of Mustafa, a man who, like Othello, moves from Africa to England and not only murders one Desdemona but causes two others to commit suicide, though he insists that "I am not Othello. Othello is a lie."

In this astonishingly beautiful short novel there is more than one Iago, and Mustafa himself is an Iago who plays out the Othello role for one lover's Iago and then in turn functions once again as Iago. The novel seesaws back and forth between these poles: the community, the crack, the splitting apart, the new community, the new flaw, the new destruction. The crack that allows evil to enter this world (and I'm thinking of evil here in several ways—as negation, as violence, and as the force that leads to the destruction of a human community that has integrity, beauty, and history) occurs in part because of the illusory identities one culture creates for another. Mustafa is educated in "a language not my language" and leaves the Sudan for London, which is "emerging from the war and the oppressive atmosphere of the Victorian era." Like Iago, Mustafa has a mind "like a keen knife," and, like Iago, he becomes conscious of his ability to create alternative illusions, an ability made even easier because of his essential invisibility. Evil enters in, as Aron said and much of the world's literature suggests, through solipsism: one human being unable to see another human being as real.

In London, Mustafa becomes a master of seduction:
My store of hackneyed phrases [he says] is inexhaustible. I feel the

flow of conversation firmly in my hands, like the reins of an obedient mare: I pull at them and she stops, I shake them and she advances; I move them and she moves subject to my will, to left or to right.

All Mustafa has to say is that he grew up along the Nile, that he could reach outside his bedroom window as a child and dip in his hand, and the illusion of wildness and exoticism, of everything both glamorous and repressed, becomes an aid to seduction. Mustafa in his Iago-mode is conscious of the illusions in the women he seduces, and he inserts himself, so to speak, within that flaw.

"Poor Isabella Seymour," the narrator says of one of Mustafa's seductees, "She had eleven years of happy married life, regularly going to church every Sunday morning and participating in charitable organizations. Then she met him and discovered deep within herself dark areas that had previously been closed." Mustafa becomes an imperialist of love. Isabella's illusions, as is true of all of Mustafa's lovers, rest along essential fault lines in Victorian morality, hidden fault lines of repression and romanticism, that sex brings to the surface and which become intolerable. Two of Mustafa's lovers commit suicide. "You, my lady," Mustafa says, "have been infected with a deadly disease which has come from you know not where and which will bring about your destruction, be it sooner or later."

"I came as an invader into your very homes," Mustafa says, "a drop of the poison which you have injected into the veins of history, . . . the germ of the greatest European violence, as seen on the Somme and at Verdun, the like of which the world has never previously known."

All through the novel illusions lead to violence, and the first half of the book ends when Mustafa meets a woman, a passionate nihilist, whom he loves with the same either/or love/chaos intensity of Othello:

> She was my destiny [he says] and in her lay my destruction, yet for me the whole world was not worth a mustard seed in comparison. . . . The smell of smoke was in my nostrils as I said to her "I love you my darling," and the universe, with its past, present and future, was gathered together into a single point before and after which nothing existed.

This woman plays Iago to Mustafa's now Othello—since every system, including Iago's, contains a crack—and she manipulates him into murdering her, a history that he has to hide upon his return to Africa in the second half of the novel, where he brings the violence with him. In part because his past remains hidden, he functions as Iago once again for the Sudanese woman he marries and, finally, for the narrator. Evil is a virus in this novel, with its source in unreality, and it infects characters one by one.

When Mustafa returns to the village, the narrator is sometimes seized by the feeling, as he sees him,

> a drink in his hand, his body buried deep in his chair . . . abstractedly wandering towards the horizon deep within himself, and with darkness all around us outside [that] satanic forces were combining to strangle the lamplight. Occasionally the disturbing thought occurs to me that Mustafa Sa'eed never happened, that he was in fact a lie, a phantom, a dream or a nightmare that had come to the people of that village one suffocatingly dark night, and when they opened their eyes to the sunlight he was nowhere to be seen.

Because Mustafa is a lie, everything begins to seem like an illusion and mirage to the narrator. At the point where the narrator can act to save the woman he loves, he is overcome with the awareness of evil, which seems so large that it prevents action. "The darkness," he explains, "was thick, deep and basic—not a condition in which light was merely absent; the darkness was now constant, as though light had never existed and the stars in the sky were nothing but rents in an old and tattered garment." At his darkest point the *no* takes over, and he imagines that underneath everything is finally nothing at all, an empty room, and he participates in an impromptu boom-boxed "festival to nothingness in the heart of the desert." The only act that can break apart the illusion and sense of nothingness—without violence—is truth-telling, which has become impossible. Once again it's illusion that creates the fertile ground for evil to enter in, and Mustafa is both a victim and a perpetrator of illusion.

In part this novel's power comes from the catalyst characters. But part of its power lies in the fact that the novel has more seriousness and weight than many contemporaneous American novels, a weight that seems to come from the feeling that the story rests within something outside itself, a power with its own mysterious order. This is a novel in which tragedy is still possible.

The Iago story is often a story of the fall from innocence, and this novel is no exception. The fall is abrupt, and at the end the narrator almost drowns, both literally and metaphorically, in the *no*. He is conscious of the river's destructive forces "pulling me downwards . . . sooner or later the river's forces would pull me down into its depths." But in the end he chooses to fight against the current "because there are a few people I want to stay with for the longest possible time and because I have duties to discharge. It is not my concern whether or not life has meaning."

In the river Salih gives us evil with presence, the universe as a vast and brooding thing that threatens to overwhelm with the awareness of our condition in it, the condition we build these grand illusions in order to avoid.

So maybe Vonnegut wasn't talking about catalyst characters at all. When I think about the most beautiful and powerful novels I think of ones where the evil in the world itself is clearly drawn. It's easy to be blind to it. If we're in a position of power, it's easier to be blind to it. Anthropologist Lionel Tiger said that the industrial system itself provides "a uniquely efficient lubricant for moral evasiveness." Maybe what Vonnegut means is the acknowledgment of evil, the naming of it. That's what he finally discovers in *Slaughterhouse Five,* a kind of seriousness and honesty.

"The essential modern evasion," critic Andrew Delbanco writes in his book *The Death of Satan,* was the failure to acknowledge evil, name it, and accept its "irreducibility in the self."

> The repertoire of evil [he goes on] has never been richer. Yet never have our responses been so weak. . . . We certainly no longer have a conception of evil as a distributed entity with an ontological essence of its own. . . . Yet something that feels like this force still invades our experience, and we still discover in ourselves the capacity to inflict it on others.
>
> Since this is true, we have an inescapable problem: we feel something that our culture no longer gives us the vocabulary to express.

So "evil is returned as the blamable other, and we ourselves are seen as victim of it."

The power of *A Season of Migration to the North* rests in part in its recognition of the way imperialism requires both arrogance and illusion and so, *as a human system beginning in illusion,* is a medium for evil and, therefore, for violence.

I think that whatever evil we're living in the midst of we find particularly difficult to name. Of all our contemporary novelists Don DeLillo perhaps comes close to naming it, because his world is so unflinchingly and unsentimentally observed. "You're worried and scared," DeLillo writes in his novel *Underworld.* "The world somewhere took an unreal turn."

You find Iago in *Underworld,* not in a character but in a milieu: where cultural construction of identity is assumed, where our deepest wish is the flying carpet, the creation of an island floating in midair that will actually hold us, a perpetual motion machine disconnected from any source of power but its own, an eternity created entirely in culture, a world where Disneyland exists in order to give everything around it the illusion of the real. As critic Baudrilliard writes in his essay "Simulacra and Simulation," "All these people formed by language and climate and popular songs and breakfast foods and the jokes they tell and the car they drive have never had anything in common so much as this, that they are sitting in the furrows of destruction." DeLillo's characters experience a "moral wane," an ennui that needs the balance of an enemy. The characters' biggest problem, in fact their Iago, is the absence of Iago. They "need the leaders of both sides," DeLillo writes, "to keep the cold war going."

If evil slips in when illusion is created, as our literature suggests; or if evil is the elevation of self-interest over the whole; or if it is the inability to see anyone outside ourselves; or if human culture is only a system of signs referring to one another with nothing at the ground of things, not even an identity to mask, then we may be living in a particularly dangerous time. If signs are all there is, in DeLillo the signs are nothing but postapocalyptic waste, the accumulation of temporary stuff that we call home. Where's Iago? his characters seem to ask, over and over again. Out with the trash, gone with the wind; he's history.

Later the night of the winter solstice, everyone in Indianapolis leaves their houses. We've been told to turn on all our holiday lights at 6:14 and to go outside and wave at the dark sky. The spaceship *Mir* is passing over, with David Wolf inside. His mother lives in this city, which is, tonight, glittering with crayon-colored incandescent glass. He will have nine minutes to talk to her, and we will have nine minutes to light every light and wave our hands, which are, in the dark, invisible even to us.

We can hear radios through the night. We've been listening to radios communally every May of our lives. Though it's always been the whine of race cars, this sound of disembodied voices and technology is nothing new to us. We laugh as we listen to the radio and will wait to turn off the lights until he passes over.

Of course he will recognize his old neighborhood, this particular electricity pulsing through these particular wires, this brave sharp scattering of jewel-toned light.

And now David Wolf's mother, in the nine-minute window of communication open to her, speaks to the son spinning above her head exactly like you would speak to a son who had gone too high in the neighbor's tree: "You look good, David, but I'm not going to let you stay up there much longer," and the son says, "Too late, Mom, you already signed the permission slip," and then we hear some empty static, and we laugh and turn off the radios and lights after he passes over.

It's sweet, really, so human, but the night is cloudy, and we feel vaguely unsatisfied. A consciousness cast out beyond the campfire's light, some communication from all that brooding silence, but the night is cloudy, and the sound is bad, and we can't really see each other. Is he really there? We want a frisson, a chill, some recognition of the increasing distance between us.

This fog, these clouds, this dark night. What's beyond it? We've spent this entire year staring at the sky.

There were those pictures of galaxies colliding to form new stars, the swirling blood and amniotic fluid and coldness of it. One night the planets were aligned in such a way that they were strung in a row like science fair styrofoam models.

And in the summer, Mars was hanging right above the moon, the whole planet burning intense as cigarette ash, the pinkish orange of iodine.

Styrofoam, ash, and iodine: DeLillo's trash and drek.

In the summer there was that robot thing that walked around the surface of the red planet. We waited for it to confirm our fears: that at one time there were sentient beings living there, that Iago slithered through its texts, that it used to be a garden. But every message was contestable, filtered through something human made, with room for so much slippage between what seems to be and what is. In that slippage there is a great but illusory and temporary freedom. We need Iago. Because every story is a fall from innocence: from seeming grace into the hard truths of what is.

STEVEN SCHWARTZ

Finding a Voice in America

Eighteen years ago, when I was in a graduate program in creative writing, there was very little talk of voice. Mostly we spoke of the purpose of fiction—the story's intent. One of my class members couldn't appreciate anything so weak as intent. He always described a story's essence in hyphenated terms. "There's no you-got-to-have-it here," he would say, or "Where's the what's-at-stake?" Once I suggested a story lacked focus. "Focus?" he said, looking back and forth between me and the manuscript. His face flushed a tense shade of pink. "Don't you mean the-story-doesn't-take-any-chances?" I thought about this a moment then said, no, I meant focus. One of the other members of the workshop, a man who had recently joined a religious sect and wore a turban that kept unraveling and needed to be pushed back like wayward hair and whose stories had titles like "Fire of the Kundalini" and "Mantra in Majorca," informed us we were indulging in the deception of wordplay. Words could create binary or singular illusions, bifurcated or unified realities. Duality, he offered, remained the operative confusion.

We blinked at him then turned our attention to the other end of the table. Another class member who had sinus problems that produced a distinct whine said, "To tell the truth"—he wet his finger and hooked through the pages—"the problem is right here on page 3. There's a dog in this story. This is just another *dog story*."

I glanced at the author of the manuscript. She'd become white and motionless and looked like a victim left overnight in stocks. Our professor announced from the far end of the seminar table that perhaps we should consider voice. Does this story have a clear, convincing voice?

Someone ventured to ask what exactly is voice.

The oom-pah-pah-of-the-language, our hyphenatist volunteered.

No, our teacher corrected. In fact, voice had less to do with style than with content.

We drew closer at this idea. Voice wasn't style? Word arrangement? Syntax? Rhythm? Diction? Tone? Wasn't that all voice?

Yes, our teacher said, style was part of voice, but voice was more than

From the *AWP Chronicle* 24, no. 2 (October–November 1991).

style—something akin to the brain being part of the mind but the mind being greater than just the brain. Voice had inherent in it the immediacy to guide an author through early drafts, to infuse the writing with essentiality. Voice had to do as much with sensibility as with sound. Voice is what ultimately speaks to us in a story.

"It *transcends* style," the religious devotee announced.

The class member who had given his opinion about dog stories nasaled his protest. All this talk about voice, brains in mind, what did any of it have to do with writing a damn good story with lots of action that kept the reader turning pages? He was sure Jack London never worried about anything so effete as voice.

At this point the author of the manuscript under discussion stood up with quiet grace, gathered her belongings, and spoke for the first time. "Jack London would have fed you belly up to his dogs and not thought twice about it," she said and left the room.

After a moment of silence our teacher said, "That's voice."

Voice as a term provokes a perplexing range of definitions. Literary critics often speak of "presence" and "codes" and "intertextual discourse" when discussing voice, but writers can scarcely afford to be so theoretical or lofty in their approach. Voice is, to paraphrase Flannery O'Connor, the mud that we use to write. But ask any two writers what precisely makes up this mud, and you're likely to get very different if equally forceful answers. For Flannery O'Connor voice has as its unlikely ingredient manners, which form the basis of a Southern culture "rich in contradiction, rich in irony, rich in contrast, and particularly rich in speech." Margaret Atwood, in her introduction to *The Best American Short Stories 1989,* writes that "voice has become a catchall phrase; but by it I intend something very specific: a speaking voice, like the singing voice in music, that moves not across the page, but through time. Surely every written story is, in the final analysis, a score for voice." John Fowles has gone so far as to say that the entire evolution of fiction is tied up with "finding means to express the writer's voice—his humors, his private opinions, his nature—by means of word manipulation and print alone." Joyce Carol Oates, in possession of one of the more energetic and urgent of contemporary voices, sharply edged with interior menace and vulnerabilities, writes that "the storyteller experiences the ravishing phenomenon of stories being told through him and by way of him; his single voice generating any number of singular 'voices.'"

Where does this "single voice" come from, then? Even William Faulkner, surely one of the most phenomenal voices in literature for his skill in reproducing with astonishing pitch and resonance a whole region's history in sound, has accounted for his work by simply stating he liked to listen. "I don't go out with a notebook, but I like these people, that is, I like to listen to them, the way they talk or the things they talk about. . . . I would go around with [my uncle] and sit on the front galleries of country stores and listen to the talk."

The writer's expression of multitudinous voices seems largely an unconscious process, a compulsion to imitate others who in the act of being mimicked become agents of the self. The author's single voice hides in many smaller ones, cleverly so and repeatedly, as though a guest at a masked ball who through deft and surreptitious changes of costume manages to make himself reappear in many forms to the only other guest: the reader. Flaubert's famous claim, when asked who is Madame Bovary, "C'est moi," provides a truth about voice. The disguises may be elaborate and clever, appear not at all "autobiographical," yet authors always instill a trace of their own voices in their characters, much the way parents place their mark, subtly or blatantly, on their children.

For some writers voice is an organic compound born from the sparks of integrating an inner world that nurtures character with an outer one that inspires it. It is the struggle of birth, bringing from within to without; the full force of the writer's desire to be heard intersects the passionate will of the character's want of speech. In *One Writer's Beginnings* Eudora Welty explains her first successful story began spontaneously from a remark overheard by a neighbor on his travels: "He's gone to borry some fire." The words, which "carried such lyrical and mythological and dramatic overtones," awaken the fiction ahead, all of the story's vitality of character compressed in a single phrase that beguiles the writer, though the sentence itself may never appear in the writing.

But for other writers ideation and language play more of an influence in voice than character. The playwright Tom Stoppard admits he cares little for voice enforcing distinctions of character. "I'm only interested in the felicitous expression of ideas, and very often when I'm rewriting, it doesn't matter who says something—if I need those lines elsewhere I'll give them to a different character." Stoppard's comment suggests one of the essential rewards of writing, the experimentation and playfulness of inventing speech—the freedom to explore a voice fully, twist its components together like balloons to form an expanse of fused color and shape unrestrained by credible and precise characterization. It is an unorthodox idea, with challenging implications: character is subordinate to the author's voice, which engages attention for its own sake and imposes a ruling sensibility that unifies the work. Classical unities of emotion or action become irrelevant. Whatever sounds good fits. The attitude throws out on its ear a belief that characters act independently (and consistently) and at some point "take over" the telling of their stories, so that the author's job is only to let their voices come through him faithfully. Instead, voice—demanding ever greater amplification—creates and perpetuates itself.

Regardless of where voice comes from, there's no lack of comment about its forms. Annie Dillard in *Living by Fiction* speaks of the separate virtues of plain and fancy voices: "Fine writing has as its distinction a magnificent power to penetrate. It can penetrate precisely because, and only because, it lays no claim to precision. It sacrifices perfect control to ambition to mean." One has only to think of the memorable opening passage from Tillie Olson's classic story "Tell Me a Riddle" to understand the phrase *ambition to mean:*

> For forty-seven years they had been married. How deep back the stubborn, gnarled roots of the quarrel reached, no one could say—but only now, when tending to the needs of others no longer shackled them together, the roots swelled up visible, split the earth between them, and the tearing shook even to the children, long since grown.

There seems in this case, as in all mesmerizing voices, no other way for the fiction to speak to us of the essential humanity and sorrow of this couple. A simpler, more straightforward voice, one less aroused, would hush the story's meaning, so insistently spoken here through mythic tones, incantatory rhythms.

On the other hand, Annie Dillard describes the equal power of plain voices in an experience of listening to Wright Morris read to a large and crowded auditorium: "The father talks to his son. The son listens and watches his father eat soup." The two lines revere the familiar without sentiment, allowing the language to humbly serve its subject. Such writing has in it an extraordinary balance that can be observed but not easily explained and is quite frequently imitated with plodding falseness.

Writers often report having struggled with finding their voices before they chose to concentrate on what was always in front of their noses— what they may have eschewed as unworthy of literary expression or distanced themselves from because the mirror was too close. One of my students at Warren Wilson College had sent me a number of stories before I inquired why she never wrote about Asian Americans, since this was her background. She wrote back to me: "Although I might consider my narrator's Chineseness or half-Chineseness crucial–in some cases, the very reason for writing the story—this aspect of her character often seemed tacked on—as inessential, and easy to change as the clothes she wore."

She went on to say: "I suppose that in hedging my commitment I wanted the narrators of my stories to be universal. But trying to create a universal narrator is like trying, in realistic narrative fiction, to create a universal room. It can't be done. You have to put the armchair somewhere; the window must frame a specific view."

I responded to her letter with an admission of my own about being Jewish and growing up with anti-Semitism:

> Somewhere along the line I decided to claim that material, decided it was part of my background, and much to my surprise, given at what odds I was with it, found it informed many of my stories, if only subtly. I stopped avoiding the very material that represented all my deeper struggles with identity and that I'd spent so much energy disguising in my work, rather than transforming, a good thing in fiction. You might remember when I said that the writer's voice emerges at the place where her unique experience meets the larger culture. I believe that was true of me. It was necessary to locate that intersection where I directly met my background, claim that space rather than circle around it just because it caused me so much pain or intimidation or confusion.

Writers don't get very far in finding their voices until they are willing to face the intersection of their unique experience with that of the larger culture. The friction here from the self pushing against cultural forces produces a spark from which sound is born: often raw and untutored and shrill to begin with but eventually recognizable to the artistic ear that has been waiting to hear and will create meaning from potent noise.

Authors nevertheless spend untold hours worrying about whether they have any voice at all. This is not surprising given the pressure on writers today to distinguish themselves with special voices. Publishers regularly put out anthologies touting voices from distinct groups— Southern voices, Urban voices, Latin American voices, "Under Thirty" voices, and, yes, voices from the Writing Programs. Awards are given for the best "new voices." It is not unusual to get a letter from an editor that says, "Sorry, the voice didn't grab us." Peruse the dust jackets of contemporary fiction, and you'll be plied by cork-popping superlatives: An Original Astonishing Inspired Hilarious Unforgettable New Voice. Or in the case of the superannuated author's midlist book: A Wise Mature Voice.

Voice has taken precedence not only in the experimental, the avant-garde, the postmodern, areas, where language has never made a pretense of being anything but a self-contained and self-referential system, but also in traditional, mainstream fiction, where words still supposedly refer to objects and events outside themselves. Authors who would be better off sticking to the sureness of their grip and serving the narrative with plainer, less opaque language betray themselves and their work by insisting on present-tense, punchy imagistic sentences, turning away from exposition and reflection to fragmented, oblique observations, all in order to sound contemporary and be more marketable. Likewise, authors with fast and startling voices, crackling and nervy and clever, are led into believing that voice is enough. That voice, unlike vision, a once embraced, now faded literary term with its overtones more of purpose than technique, can obviate the question of meaning by breaking through the noise of the crowd, just by rising above the din and succeeding in being heard.

To discover a story under these conditions means to find the successful voice, the fresh and nimble sentence, the resonant line of dialogue culled from prosaic miles of weak writing. A kind of chiropractic intensity sets in, hands bearing down in search of symmetry and perfection, cracking the language in the hopes of alignment. Voice means a consistent signature. Voice means talent. Voice means knowing why you wrote the story. Voice means you've arrived. One's writing *is* one's voice.

Still, any writer knows voice is what remains. When the French ambassador drops out of the story (a main character, you thought) or the first hundred pages of the new novel become deceased or you must finally admit the narrative strategy of alternating chapters by the twin brothers separated at birth fails because of mind-numbing predictability, when any of the hundreds of changes are made that will significantly modify the final manuscript, what stays is always an element of voice; somewhere one finds that faint sound even in the earliest drafts. A first line perhaps, a casual remark in a minor scene, a final sentence written before you gave up in despair for the day—here one recognizes the note of triumph in the writing that has been there since the beginning and announces itself with clarion immodesty: I am the sound of truth. At least for this fiction.

So what does give voice significance? What makes us carry the sound around in our head, long after any trendiness has had a chance to wear off? What makes us wish for the same voice in the author's next work, yearning to rejoin this siren heard only in the private act of reading? What makes us read the words aloud, speak them to others with exuberance so that we feel as if we have found our own voice just in the repeating?

I know that these questions became more urgent to me when I woke up one day and absolutely could not write, the first real writer's block I'd ever suffered. I'd been stopped before but not like this. My fingers wouldn't budge. When I did squeeze out a word or two—the largesse of a sentence—I was irritated by the voice, *my* voice. What was lacking? What made voice worthwhile? What made it great—important? There was something I wasn't acknowledging and letting come out in the voice, a holding back that prevented any progress, some risk not taken.

I picked a few books off my shelf by writers of renowned voices. I looked at Salinger. Many authors could create sympathetic characters and do so with great skill, but Salinger made them hypnotic through voice alone. And Faulkner, with his stories of generational decay, what in the words here compelled? Other writers wrote with as much intensity, with as large a canvas, as great a vocabulary, but Faulkner could make us lasting witnesses to his intoned words. I looked too at Hemingway—the well-known detachment, the rituals of blood and sport, the nada who art in nada. Here was nihilism, brutality, despair, yet he had one of the most celebrated voices of the twentieth century. What drew us to these writers? More specifically, what did these writers, so different in their themes and styles and backgrounds, have in common through voice?

It had to do with praise, I thought. In Salinger there is a ubiquitous presence, honored through an idiom that speaks with precocity, with innocence, with imagination, with wonder—the child, a symbol of unconditional love, the unjudged self. In Faulkner there is a testament to the ties that bind, as strong an affirmation of the power of family relations as has ever been written. And in Hemingway one finds a combination of rhythmic naming, sensorial sweep, and sheer adjectival drive; modifiers pile into each other like crashed box cars resulting in language able to speak of nature felt in the blood, of forces mixed of violence and majesty.

But the essence of what these voices had in common didn't strike me until I was reading a story by Raymond Carver, "Cathedral," my favorite of his stories and one that despite the so-called minimalism has in every spare word the quality of a great voice. "Cathedral" is the story of a blind man who comes to stay with a married couple. The blind man, an old friend of the wife's, watches TV with the husband, the story's narrator, after the wife falls asleep next to them on the couch. A cathedral appears on the screen. Much to the narrator's surprise, the blind man has no idea what a cathedral looks like, so they both get down on the floor and draw one, the blind man's hand over the narrator's. When the narrator's wife awakens, the blind man offers this explanation of what they're doing.

We're drawing a cathedral. Me and him are working on it. Press hard, he said to me. That's right. That's good, he said. Sure. You got it, bub. I can tell. You didn't think you could. But you can, can't you? You're cooking with gas now. You know what I'm saying? We're going to really have us something here in a minute. How's the old arm? he said. Put some people in there now. What's a cathedral without people?

The passage is strange and funny and absurd, but it's also something else, between the lines where one hears the "intent" of the voice. "What's a cathedral without people?" It sounds like the first line to a bad joke, but the answer could be just an empty cathedral. A hollow, albeit architecturally interesting one. An empty voice. Voice must have more inside. Not optimism necessarily, not erudition, not simplicity or complexity alone, not even uniqueness by itself. Something else must be expressed through the voice. There is in great voices, regardless of whatever privation the authors might suffer, a generosity. It is a generosity of the human spirit that grants the writing its authority and the voice a means to survive.

CHUCK WACHTEL

Behind the Mask

Narrative Voice in Fiction

In the last years of their sixty-four-year marriage, my grandparents, who
spoke to each other in their native southern Italian dialect and to the rest
of America in English, spent their days in only two of the rooms, and
usually separately, of their five-room portion of the two-family house I
grew up in. My grandfather spent the afternoons and evenings in the living room, in his TV chair, whether the TV was on or not; my grandmother would sit in the kitchen, where she not only prepared their
meals but also read the *New York Daily News,* clipped coupons, played
solitaire, spoke to her nieces and sisters on the phone, said the rosary late
each afternoon, and soaked her feet in the electric swirl bath I'd given
her for her eightieth birthday. During these years—I'd long since been
living on my own and saw them only on visits—a strange phenomenon
began to emerge in their communication. My grandfather, in his living
room chair, would grunt, sometimes once or twice, but more often he'd
emit a series of linked grunts, and my grandmother would answer—in
English if I was in the kitchen with her, in Italian if I was elsewhere in
the house—*All right, already. In a minute.* The first time I observed this,
she cut up a pear, arranged the slices on a saucer, and handed it to me. I
brought it into the living room, set it on the snack tray beside my grandfather, and returned to the kitchen.

"You knew what he was saying?" I asked her.

She raised her arm, angrily toward the living room. "I always know
what *he's* saying."

They had, in the course of their long intimacy, transcended the limitations of words—two whole languages' worth—and come to co-
occupy a larger communicative vehicle: the one we call voice. A word
is a too-loose garment. Without the implications of context, the body it
clothes is barely recognizable; without the shaping force of the living
presence that has spoken it or written it, a word can have far less meaning than a monotone grunt. It is voice, heard aloud, absorbed from the
page, both, that ignites the latent meanings in language. In fiction it is
voice that transforms a series of sparse and diminutive symbols, combed

First published, in installments, in the August 1999–April 2000 issues of the *Writer's Edge*
(San Antonio, Tex.).

into narrative discourse, into a dynamic, ongoing reflection of experience. As a reader and writer of fiction, it is in this regard I wish to come to a better understanding of its employment and effect.

Webster's Ninth provides the word *voice* with a spectrum of definitions three inches long, from "a sound produced by vertebrates by means of lungs, larynx or syrinx" to "a medium or instrument of expression, as in, *The party became the voice of the people.*" These definitions, ranging from the physiological to the expressive, explain how the human voice operates when it is telling a story no better than they explain how my grandmother understood my grandfather's grunting or how he came to expect her to, yet I am certain the two are linked and that my comprehension of one will shed light on the other. This is where I start.

There are writers who seem to strip their fictions down to the bare essentials of voice, writers as unlike each other as Kafka, Gertrude Stein, Beckett, Robbe-Grillet. In their voices language is nearly the entire landscape and the first fictional reality. In contrast, there are Proust's overgrown garden of memory, the sensuously detailed impressionist novels of Maupassant, the densely populated regions of García Márquez and Faulkner. A voice can be soaking wet with the living persona of its speaker, as in the works of Grace Paley, Toni Morrison, or Henry Miller.

When we read, voice is the most immediate and authoritative presence. When we write, intentionally or not, we make it so. It precedes character and setting and the images and ideas that will form the conceived reality of a fictional narrative. As we travel deeper into the story, it seems to become a single element among the many. Or perhaps, it's just its *persona,* as first impression, that becomes one element among many—like a flat character or background music: We walk into a room, look around and take its measure, then, increasingly, relinquish our focus on the walls and furniture, as we enter upon the occupations—eating, talking, watching television, sleeping—that brought us there. What this tells me is that the voice's persona, often the beginning and end of most definitions, offers, in and of itself, an extremely limited representation of its function in stories and novels. I think that to comprehend a voice's identity as one might a character or a living person is to comprehend only this small portion of its complex role in fiction: that of providing the necessary degree of realness to relax our defenses against the unreal. Fiction excites and engages me in many more ways than I can comprehend. That is why I read it and why I work to write it. What I have arrived at, this far along in my thinking, is a more specific sense of the question I am trying to ask: How can voices whose identities I often lose track of transform lines of words hundreds of feet long into stories that can affect me so deeply?

Moses de Leon, the author of the *Zohar,* the main book of the *Caballa,* said that language has the quality of light, because it gathers light into itself. And that light is the only manifestation of God the living can perceive. Thus, he said that "to read the universe is to write the universe." That addresses, for me, one of the first functions, and first mysteries, of narrative voice in fiction. As I read, I often feel I am inventing the story as well as discovering something already there, one word at a time. In fact, I must be: since language can contain only the smallest fraction of what we perceive when reading, as the static canvas of a painted portrait is only the first idea in volumes that write themselves while we're looking at it and afterward.

Voice, as a phenomenon in human experience, is simultaneously real and metaphoric: as real as hamburger, as ethereal as song. You might say it is where mind and body meet—literally *and* figuratively.

In trying to understand the functions of voice in fiction, the first things that came to my mind were the issues of presence and immediacy I mentioned earlier. Voice is the first thing we most often encounter and usually—though not always—seems to decrease in presence as the characters and their conflict, the ideas and composition, begin to organize themselves into a purely conceived yet dynamic world. Add to those things that it is most often the voice of an absent speaker. Since fiction has replaced the tale, the voices that tell the story are most often read, not heard. Though there are many additional pleasures to hearing fiction read aloud, we usually experience it in private—it is most often written for that purpose—where we can control the rate of absorption, read over words and phrases and chapters and whole books as often as we want to or need to.

William H. Gass, from *Habitations of the Word:*

> Our oblivion has been seen to . . . and unless we write as though the ear were our only page; unless upon the slopes of some reader's understanding we send our thoughts to pasture like sheep let out to graze; unless we can jingle where we feed, sound ourselves and make our presence heard; unless. . . .
>
> So hear me read me see me begin.
>
> I begin . . . don't both of us begin? Yet as your eye sweeps over these lines—not like a wind, because not a limb bends or a letter trembles, but rather more simply—as you read do you find me here in your lap like a robe. And even if this was an oration, and we were

figures in front of one another . . . , holding up the same thought, it still would not be the first time I had uttered these sentences (though I seem to be making them up in the moment of speaking like fresh pies), for I was in another, distant, private . . . place when I initially constructed them, and then I whispered them above the rattle of my typing . . . ; I tried to hear them through the indifferent whirring of their manufacture as if my ear were yours, and held no such noise. . . . God knows what or where I am now—now as you read. Our oblivion has been seen to.

Gass has wonderfully articulated here so much of what constitutes the act of writing—of writing to be read at a distance, of both time and space. He notes that hearing fiction read aloud isn't that much different from reading the words on a page, in the sense that we only seem to be making up the sentences "in the moment of speaking, like fresh pies." In referring to the absence of the writer, he is also addressing *our* part, as readers, in the act of creation. We feel that we, too, are making up the sentences like fresh pies.

There is another sense of the voice touched upon here: the writer's, as opposed to, simply, the narrator's presence. Another thing I sense in voice, often, while reading, even in a first-person voice fully in costume, is the writer. She or he is never fully concealed. Perhaps, in the voice is the one thing that can cross the border between the real world and the world of art. Not like a puppeteer's strings (although they, too, can disappear as we get caught up in the drama); that seems too obvious. Something less probable comes to mind in my search for a comparison: the writer's presence is more like the air that passes invisibly through the green rubber hoses, disguised as underwater vines, that descend from the surface above, bringing oxygen to the underwater ballet dancers in the Weeki Wachee mermaid show in Florida. In this regard the voice contains those elements of style—more than subject, character, and plot—that often cause us to feel a sense of recognition when reading different works by the same author.

Sources

In a lecture he gave at New York University, E. L. Doctorow said that the best narrative voices we encounter *in* fiction come from *outside* fiction. As writers, he added, we must let them instruct us. He quoted Anna Biggs Heaney, a nineteenth-century Kansas frontierswoman, describing the life she and her family lived. (The man she refers to is her father. He has malaria, or ague as it was then called, and is suffering a bout of chills and fever.) "When Mr. Biggs was so with it that Mrs. Biggs had to cut the wood, she put the baby behind him on the corded bed-spread where his shiverings joggled the baby off to sleep."

This single sentence contains exposition and conflict in one graceful, economic bundle that speaks a novel's worth of words. No one has to explain how hard their life is nor how resourcefully Mrs. Biggs deals with the adversity. And that is the beginning, the way a good portrait is the beginning: life emanates from there.

I think of the moment that Rigoberta Menchu, as a seven-year-old child who had only known the harsh life lived by the Queche Indians in the mountains of Guatemala, riding in what she understood to be a truck with windows, entered Guatemala City for the first time.

When we reached the capital, I saw cars. . . . I thought they were animals just going along. It didn't occur to me they were cars. I asked my father: "What are they?" "They're the same as big lorries only smaller," he said. "And what we are traveling in now is what people go to the capital in, just to travel, not to work. And those little ones, they belong to rich people to use for themselves. They don't have things to carry." When I first saw them, I thought that the cars would all bump into each other, but they hardly did at all. When one stopped, they all had to stop.

As in the first case, our sense of who this person was, in relationship to the world she was discovering, is made absolutely, beautifully, clear. Neither Mrs. Biggs nor Rigoberta Menchu steps outside the moment and explains. In both cases the sensation of life contained in the persona of the voice, presented through actions, observations, thoughts thought within the moment, does all the work.

Now these two voices come from journals of lived and observed life. There are other kinds of sources. In a letter to Gershom Sholem, Walter Benjamin said that to truly understand Kafka is to realize that he wasn't so much influenced by literature and psychology as he was by the voice of modern science. To prove his point he quoted the early-twentieth-century physicist Arthur Stanley Eddington describing the physics of entering a room:

I must shove against an atmosphere pressing with a force of four-teen pounds on every square inch of my body. I must make sure of landing on a plank traveling at twenty miles a second around the sun. . . . I must do this while hanging from a round planet, head outward into space, and with a wind of aether blowing at no one knows how many miles a second through every interstice of my body.

These few quotes are meant to illustrate a point for which a much larger and varied herd of quotes is needed: that the voices that narrate fiction have their sources outside fiction. Interestingly, that doesn't necessarily mean life: their sources can be as far from the *oral,* and as far from the *real,* as the conceptual imagination of science.

Persona

The first source of the authority of a narrator's voice is probably the first thing we usually see: persona. A voice introduces itself to us at the onset of a story and deepens that self-introduction throughout. This is its persona as both an immediate and continuous source of meaning. This seems most often the case with first-person narrators and most often when they are telling their own stories—but not always. This must also, to some extent, be true across the spectrum of fictional narrators.

Here Sylvia, the narrator of Toni Cade Bambara's story "The Lesson," who has already introduced herself, the Harlem of the 1950s she has grown up in, and the characters who will inhabit the story with her, now takes us along on a wild downtown cab ride bringing her and her friends on their first visit—a kind of class trip organized by an adult neighbor interested in educating the children—to FAO Schwartz:

> Then she hustles half the crew in with her and hands me a five-dollar bill and tells me to calculate 10 percent for the driver. And we're off. Me and Sugar and Junebug and Flyboy hangin out the window and hollering to everybody, putting lipstick on each other cause Flyboy a faggot anyway, and making farts with our sweaty armpits. But I'm mostly trying to figure out how to spend this money. But they all fascinated by the meter ticking and Junebug starts laying bets as to how much it'll read when Flyboy can't hold his breath no more. Then Sugar lays bets as to how much it'll be when we get there. So I'm stuck. Don't nobody want to go for my plan, which is to jump out at the next light and run off to the first bar-b-que we can find. Then the driver tells us to get the hell out cause we there already. And the meter reads eighty-five cents. And I'm stalling to figure out the tip and Sugar say give him a dime. And I decide he don't need it bad as I do, so later for him. But then he tries to take off with Junebug foot still in the door so we talk about his Mama something ferocious. Then we check out that we on Fifth Avenue

and everybody dressed up in stockings. One lady in a fur coat, hot as it is. White folks crazy.

The world, as we see it, is invented by this angry, funny, graceful and obstinate voice. Perhaps the obstinacy is the first thing we perceive: Sylvia refuses to see the world as anything other than what she knows it to be. Since this is a retrospective voice, there is more to the persona than Sylvia as character, there is also Sylvia, somewhat older, elsewhere in life, as narrator. This latter Sylvia has an urgent reason for telling the story—all retrospective voices do—something that can't be conveyed any other way. Thus, we fill the space around Sylvia's words with our own common assumptions, search for what her life must inevitably teach her. To do that, we must relinquish doubt, suspend awareness that this isn't a life lived but one invented in words. And we do this not just because of the voice's grace, accuracy, anger, humor, poignancy, but because of its authority.

Rose Lieber, the main character of Grace Paley's "Goodbye and Good Luck," tells her story to her niece, during what seems a chance encounter. Rose, in late middle age, explains her adult life to this caring young listener, a member of a family that barely understands or accepts her. She recalls her interview for a job at a Yiddish theater:

> "Rosie Lieber, you surely got a build on you."
> "It takes all kinds, Mr. Krimberg."
> "Don't misunderstand me, little girl," he said. "I appreciate, I appreciate. A young lady lacking fore and aft, her blood is so busy warming the toes and the fingertips, it don't have time to circulate where it's most required."

Rose's niece, finally, has no more presence than a microphone that transmits the story to us. The reader, however, becomes her to an extent, as both the recipient of the affection in Rose's casual, funny, unsentimental voice and the ear into which the events of her life are spoken. Anyone else's dialogue, Krimberg's for example, never completely manifests its separateness nor do the words spoken by the more central characters. They are part of Rose, a filament of the thread of her own voice, a note in the rich chord Grace Paley has invented.

Writer as Narrator: A Seemingly Objective Authority

Here Edith Wharton, in her novel *The Age of Innocence,* introduces us to Mrs. Manson Mingott:

The immense accretion of flesh which had descended on her in middle life like a flood of lava on a doomed city had changed her from a plump active little woman with a neatly turned foot and ankle into something as vast and august as a natural phenomenon. She had accepted this submergence as philosophically as all her other trials, and now, in extreme old age, was rewarded by presenting to her mirror an almost unwrinkled expanse of firm pink and white flesh, in the centre of which the traces of a small face survived as if awaiting excavation. A flight of smooth double chins led down to the dizzy depths of a still-snowy bosom veiled in snowy muslins that were held in place by a miniature portrait of the late Mr. Mingott; and around and below, wave after wave of black silk surged away over the edges of a capacious armchair, with two tiny white hands poised like gulls on the surface of the billows.

What exactly are we told here? That Mrs. Manson Mingott has grown obese in the latter half of her life could indeed be the least of it. Though the narrator and the author are one, it is the nature of the document—a novel, not a tale—to hold up a thin curtain between. Mrs. Mingott is dehumanized, compared three times to something vast and geological, yet at the same time she remains quite real, and quite human, even possessed, to some extent, of a genuine grace, albeit an awkward and comical grace. We sense the presence of a more complex and personal agenda—perhaps the author's?—regarding fatness, grotesqueness: something beyond, and apart from, the critique of the young culture of affluence that existed in latter-nineteenth-century New York that characterizes this novel. Here is the kind of element carried inside the vine reaching down to Weeki Wachee's underwater mermaids: we can know nothing for sure, only absorb the inert gases along with the rest, consciously detect, or not, their effects on our breathing.

The voice in this excerpt is both unbenevolently funny and remarkably observant; it implies a knowledge of the world and is spoken from a place both near (yet outside of) and within the culture about which it speaks. Wharton freely lends elements of its arch humor, graceful articulation, its appreciation, or condescension, to the thoughts and words of her characters, combining these qualities with their own individuated humannesses, creating variations on the tone and identity, that remain within the gravitational field of the voice we first encounter—hers—at the outset of the novel.

Because Wharton speaks so directly to us and because of the authority of her voice, we later unite into a single remembered impression, the life of the story and its meaning, which, in actuality, she has presented in separate breaths.

Another novel bearing some relationship is Henry James's *The American*. Our author/narrator starts us off with three or four thousand words describing his main character, without having him act or think, without even telling us his name. There is no one, or thing, actually present yet, other than James's voice. One at least as ironic as Edith Wharton's and one that throughout the book—though it will give up some of its irony—will spend considerably more time expositing meaning, directly toward us, than telling the story. The character—his name is Christopher Newman: I have introduced him sooner than the author would—is seen casually, sitting in a divan at the Louvre, occupied with watching a young woman copy a Madonna painted by Murillo. He is lengthily described for two purposes: to represent American men of his age, race, and class and to introduce the voice (not his) itself:

> He had the flat jaw and sinewy neck which are frequent in the American type; but the traces of national origin are a matter of expression even more than feature, and it was in this respect that our friend's countenance was supremely eloquent. . . . It had that typical vagueness which is not vacuity, that blankness which is not simplicity, that look of being committed to nothing in particular, of standing in an attitude of general hospitality to the chances of life, of being very much at one's own disposal, so characteristic of many American faces.

We are well into the moment before James allows him to speak. The first words he utters, his first self-animated step into his own small independence from the voice, is to ask the young copyist, whom he is more interested in than the art, how much she would sell her painting for. It is an act entirely in keeping with the person so brilliantly described yet a step that, with surprising suddenness, brings us deeper into those qualities it has already revealed. It is as if the voice seems to step further back on the stage, but what it does—even a voice that speaks so directly to the reader as James's voice does in *The American*—is to widen its throat, allow the nouns and verbs to have more separate and dynamic lives, but always within the atmosphere of the larger voice. In discussing this aspect of voice, I find myself thinking of something the poet Gregory Corso (though later and in a very different cultural/historical context) would write: "O I would like to break my teeth / by means of expressing a radiator!"

The voices of both Wharton and James give meaning first, then cause

the story to reinforce and enlarge upon it. Fill the meaning with life—
the sensation of life—the kind of beauty that is particularly the possession of fiction.

We have crossed into the territory of structure. What I am finding is
that it is impossible to separate voice from the entire anatomy of a
fictional narrative. It is fiction's container of everything, and to discuss it
beyond the costume and makeup is to also talk about character, structure, dialogue, interaction, and the elements of composition. To talk
about it properly is to talk about all the things fiction writers do with
language.

Authority in the Most Deeply Subjective Voices

In both Wharton and James the narrator is a close approximation to the
author, though freer, in a sense, humaner, than a writer can be in most
other forms of discourse. It is in their presence, direct and active, that I
find their authority.

In a writer such as Kafka the narrator has a very different kind of presence: the voice comes from a place entirely within the story it tells. It
makes no reference to any other world.

And, whether third person or first, the narrator speaks from a deeper, far
more subjective consciousness than does Sylvia, in Toni Cade Bambara's
"The Lesson," or Rose Lieber, in Grace Paley's "Goodbye and Good
Luck." Both of these characters interact with the worlds they find themselves in, worlds objectively similar to ours, while Kafka's narrators have
created the world entirely inside themselves before presenting it to us.

It is nearly impossible to conceive the narrator, or the setting, of
Kafka's story "The Burrow" as real. Yet the voice that tells it, though it
doesn't at first appear so, has perhaps even greater authority than the
voices of *realer,* narrators. This is the case because it is even more in
control of meaning: its idiosyncratic and obstinate subjectivity exerts a
more powerful influence: it decides how it will allow us to conceive its
world.

But the most beautiful thing about my burrow is the stillness. Of
course, that is deceitful. At any moment it might be shattered and
then all will be over. For the time being, however, the silence is still
with me. For hours I can stroll through my passages and hear nothing
except the rustling of some little creature, which I immediately
reduce to silence between my jaws, or the pattering of soil, which
draws my attention to the need for repair; otherwise all is still.

In Kafka's voice the life of ideas and the life of character and event are not separated. (As readers, we are always, or never, spoken to directly.) They seem to have equal status on the screen of our perceptions. Characters *are* real—things *do* happen—but it is by a much narrower margin that they have a life separate from their role as metaphor (or symbol or allegorical figure or other less-than-real signifier). The familiar dramatic notions of setting or exposition—which also accompany the certainty we are being spoken directly to—are rarely present. As in dreams, few people or things exist until we come upon them. They arise as suddenly, as easily, as words, yet in the context of Kafka's voice, and within the conceived reality it establishes, they are possessed of a viable life.

The narrator of Merce Rodoreda's remarkable story "The Salamander" has been accused of being a witch and is burned at the stake:

> I felt fire in my kidneys and from time to time, a flame chewed at my knee. . . . My arms and legs started getting shorter like the horns on a snail I once touched with my finger, and under my head where my neck and shoulders met, I felt something stretching and piercing me. . . . I saw some of the people looking at me raise their arms, and others were running and bumping into the ones who hadn't moved. . . . It seemed like someone was saying, "She's a salamander." And I started walking over the burning coals, very slowly, because my tail was heavy.

We learn at this point that the story we have been reading—and will read through to its end—is being narrated by a woman who has been transformed into a salamander. It changes nothing, however. The life of the voice, in particular, its strange, accurate, lyrical beauty—the source of its authority—and its refusal to share in a single objective perception of its narrator's experience, holds us deeply inside its vehicle.

Silence

As my grandfather illustrated, the human voice uses much more than words. In most of its employments, lyrical and narrative, it must use, to an even greater extent, silence. Here is the opening of Raymond Carver's story, "What Is It?":

> Fact is the car needs to be sold off in a hurry, and Leo sends Toni out to do it. Toni is smart and has personality. She used to sell children's encyclopedias door to door. She signed him up, even though

he didn't have kids. Afterward, Leo asked her for a date, and the date led to this.

There is vast distance in time and space and event—in all the implications of life really lived—in the sequencing of these sentences. There's nothing but silence in the spaces between them, yet, as we read beyond this brief segment of narration and hold it in memory, it's as if each sentence began an entire page, that we, the readers, have written ourselves, containing more detailed impressions of the life that now attaches to it.

Another kind of silence arises in the disturbing, or briefly disorienting, spaces that can arise in a voice that frequently speaks in contradictions or non sequiturs. Here is a sentence by Gertrude Stein: "It looked like a garden but he had hurt himself by accident." Most disturbing about this sentence is that it contains a semi–non sequitur. There *could* be a relationship between it *appearing* to be a garden and also having the unlikely quality of being a place where one could hurt oneself by accident. In fact, the narrator implies that there is. It is up to us, however, to enter the silence that arises from the word *but* that links the two assumptions and discover how, or why, one follows the other. In that silence is the uneasy territory of how our thoughts pattern themselves into words. *That* is the reality of the voice; the garden is the reality of the story.

The retrospective narrator of Denis Johnson's collection of linked stories, *Jesus's Son,* will move from situation to memory to an entirely different situation to a vision to another situation to a dream, without a single transitional phrase. This, of course, is structure. But this, too, is the consciousness of a voice generated in the memory of an alcoholic and drug-addicted past self.

This voice also employs contradiction, frequently and naturally, in both direct and dramatic contexts. Here the silence is between what we say and *kind of* mean and what we deny, or try to, and actually, finally, communicate. It's a silence filled with humanness, with how little we can control what we present of ourselves to others. Here the narrator arrives at a bar:

A guy, a slit-eyed, black-eyed Nez Perce, nearly elbowed me off the stool as he leaned over ordering a glass of the least expensive port wine. I said, "Hey, wasn't I shooting pool in here with you yesterday?"

"No, I don't think so."

"And you said if I'd rack you'd get change in a minute and pay me back?"

"I wasn't here yesterday. I wasn't in town."

"And then you never paid me the quarter? You owe me a quarter, man."

"I gave you that quarter. I put the quarter right by your hand. Two dimes and a nickel."

William H. Gass, in his essay "Representation and the War for Reality," presents to us this single wonderful sentence wielding six semicolons:

A novel is a mind aware of a world, but if the novel is not performed; if it is not moved as it ought to be through the space of the spirit, the notation notes not; because our metaphors, our theories, our histories, do not merely fall upon their page like pictures sent in black pricks over a wire; they must be enacted, entered into; they must be rolled like drums; they must be marched in columns . . . ; they must be sometimes quietly hummed, or possible panted.

He creates a symbol—a dark square on the page. He calls it a "pant-point." It implies a large pause, more emphatic than a comma or period and meant to represent the area of silence, or absence of word, that occupies a single breath.

past moments—*pant-point*—old dreams back again—*pant-point*—or fresh like those that pass—*pant-point*—or things—*pant-point*—things always—*pant-point*—and memories—*pant-point*—I say them as I hear them—*pant-point*—murmur them in the mud.

If the novel is performed, it is the voice, even before character, that performs it. Silence is as much its instrument as words and their sounds. As writers, we manufacture silences with a deliberateness and add to those the silences we manufacture as unconsciously as our bodies add their physical grammar to our speech.

The Essential Reality: The Kind Prison

No art form asks its experiencer to conceive a more complex and specific world than fiction does. Yet it does so with what is seemingly the least help from its medium: there is no sound, color, texture, little music (usually), no screen, no stage, no sets, no one dancing or singing or enacting life before your eyes. The following two quotes, each from a different essay, will constitute my last reliance on William H. Gass for his wonderful articulation on fiction and language:

I have known many [characters] who have passed through their stories without noses, or heads to hold them; others have lacked bodies altogether, exercised no natural functions, possessed some thoughts but no psychologies, and apparently made love without the necessary organs.

The novelist, if he is good, will keep us kindly imprisoned in his language. There is literally nothing beyond.

At the same time, though the world of a fiction can be as vast and densely populated as Yoknapatwapha County, or Macondo, a writer cannot answer the questions that, when talking about real situations, inevitably arise and that do, actually, have answers: "How do I find the Interstate?" "Why was she eating something she knows she's allergic to?" "What was that squirrel doing in the bedroom?"

Many years ago a student at a college I was teaching at in the Bronx wrote a paper on James Clavell's popular epic novel *Shogun,* and in it he described a battle between the samurai soldiers of two warlords. In conference he told me about it: "It was great. Like forty, fifty guys died. I think it happened on a bridge."

I was struck by the last thing he'd said: "I *think* it happened on a bridge." Only in fiction (not just commercial fiction) can one enjoy a scene, get swept into its dramatic tension, draw from it its meaning, and not be sure *where* it happens. Assuming the novelist is good, we are *kindly imprisoned* in his or her words. Fiction doesn't answer questions; it prevents them from coming up.

I would like to make an assumption—correct or incorrect, I am not certain—about Rembrandt's portraits. When viewing one, you would immediately observe a subject that is clear and appears to be in relative perspective. You would then see the few, small areas on which a beautiful and unnaturally bright light fell: a cuff, the side of a forehead, a fold of cloth. These smaller areas you would see, without stepping closer, as if they were magnified: though still not larger than they should be, you would see their detail more closely. He chose these areas for a reason. There was something of essential importance in them—something more significant, more human, more indicative of what *he* saw, than there was in the other elements in the composition. You might say he magnified the essential and left the more ordinary in perspective. Over a century later Van Gogh wrote to his brother Theo that in his work he "exaggerated the essential and left the obvious vague." One look at his paintings, and this is explained.

As fiction writers, we conceive a world and its people, enter it, and make decisions as to what is essential and what is obvious. Of course, we do this deliberately, but also, and perhaps to an even greater extent, we do this as an automatic aspect of the process of narration, occurring within the natural sweep of our own voices.

In his lecture on "Lady with the Dog" Nabokov expresses his admiration for Chekhov's decision to use a single item—"on the table was an inkstand, grey with dust and adorned with a figure on horseback, with its hat in its hand and its head broken off"—to describe the sensation of being in a provincial Russian hotel of the late nineteenth century.

Decision is the keyword here. A conscious choice probably made after some deliberation. But that is the least of it. I don't have Nabokov's knowledge of provincial Russian hotels to test the accuracy. Much less, when I read this story, I didn't care. I was traveling within the life of the conflict, Gurov's sudden decision to travel to the city where the woman he could not get out of his mind lived with her husband. But, even more than that, I was happily contained, *kindly imprisoned,* in Chekhov's voice. It wasn't just in the conscious choices Chekhov made so brilliantly that he conferred reality on a fictional universe but in the graceful, living exhalation of his voice. Measured by mind as well as body, it controls the world, the meaning, it offers: it limits its periphery, and we accept, without questioning, the larger, unexpressed landscape of human time and space that surrounds it.

Eliminate the voice—strip Chekhov's music from the words—and we would envision nothing more than the inkstand: a broken, sadly insignificant, solitary, and contextless object.

The voice is the life-giving oxygen inhaled by the Weeki Wachee mermaids.

It is what expanded my grandfather's grunts into a whole literature of words:

I am hungry.
I am old.
I am angry.
We've shared a life for so long I can't remember a time before.
I've spoken nearly as many words to you as I've spoken to myself.
Why then, are you not here, inside me, as aware of my presence as I am?
As aware of my needs . . . my pain. . . .

If I imagine a narrator's voice stripped entirely of its persona, it becomes a purely structural thing: a vehicle that contains me, invents the world as it carries me through it, extends itself as it travels, like a train that adds cars as its means of forward movement—I can walk back to the last car for another look at the scenery I've already passed, and it will remain idling in its most recently achieved moment until I return to my seat. The world it simultaneously invents and gives me a tour of can satisfy all the needs my expectations have of a real world and more. There is little meaning out here where you and I are, in real time and space. We must see our lives from our own perspectives and through the universe's cold eyes at the same time.

Who's There?

When I began to think about the subject of voice, to speak of voice solely in terms of persona seemed as pointless to me as speaking of characters as if they were real. It seemed too simple. The *who* of voice, its most comprehensible aspect, its most consciously created aspect, seemed to begin and end all discussion: I wanted to go beyond. I wanted to depersonify narrative voice as anatomists depersonify the previous owners of the bodily organs they remove and examine. Voice can't be just its identity in the *Who's that?* sense. And since writers distend and make abstract the identity of a voice, as they do the identity of a character, why bother looking for the ways it resembles the living? Get hip. Get scientific. There's got to be more to it than that.

Yet now I look back over this rambling collection of thoughts and ask a new question. Is this all, finally, persona? Have I, in writing this, come to discover, for myself, all of what is implied in the term?

Perhaps I found that behind the mask is another mask or, better, discovered that the part of the mask that can be removed is only its first layer, and what lies beneath is more substantial and mysterious than I'd imagined, in that voice in fiction, and its source—a writer's self encountering the world—are so interpenetrated one cannot be detached from the other. In drama a mask expresses an identity in opposition to other identities that somehow reflects the conflict of needs and personalities that exist in the real world. Thus, it must first inform us of how that character will perceive the world. If so, we are talking about voice in its operative, structural aspects as well. A voice, whatever the person or tense, can present itself to us in a form we conceive as a personality. Yet it most often is, or quickly becomes, a skin of clear glass through which we see a mind, not a brain, and one that is more complex yet simple, more omniscient yet narrow-minded, than implied in our initial sense of its identity: one so pervasively present it seems absent.

A voice, in its persona, represents the limited scope of all human perception and its own subjective territory at the same time. A mortal chorus, made up of writer, narrator, reader, and a human history of common assumptions and shared sensations: this is what shapes the vehicle, the *kind prison,* we are contained in.

I have not so much proven myself wrong as, perhaps, made the point irrelevant. The question seems to drop away, and I do not arrive at the destination I set out for. In fact, I haven't yet arrived anywhere. What I know with certainty, however, is that the voice that narrates fiction can transform the world it invents and, thus, transform the real world it is a reflection of. It is the measure of, the nature of, and the life force that animates the least substantial of worlds, in that it is not real, and the greatest of worlds, since it is without limits. Cynthia Ozick, in her brief essay on the word *Chekhovian,* addressed the energetic presence of the human voice in narrative literature at its very best. She spoke, perhaps, not just of Chekhov but of those voices so important, so essentially human, we've been listening to them for centuries, or will be, as part of the fabric of our collective voice—even independently of the stories they first told. She said that this term, derived from Chekhov's name, refers to the "new voice his genius breathed into the world." And that each story written in this voice, "however allusive or broken off, is nevertheless exhaustive—like the curve of a shard that implies not simply the form of the entire pitcher, but also the thirsts of its shattered civilization."

WORKS CITED

Bambara, Toni Cade. "The Lesson." *Gorilla, My Love.* New York: Random House, 1979.
Carver, Raymond. "What Is It?" *What We Talk about When We Talk about Love.* New York: Knopf, 1970.
Corso, Gregory. "Discord." *The Happy Birthday of Death.* New York: New Directions, 1960.
Eddington, Arthur Stanley. *The Nature of the Physical World.* Cambridge: Cambridge University Press, 1933.
Gass, William H. *Fiction and the Figures of Life.* New York: Knopf, 1970.
———. *Habitations of the Word.* New York: Simon and Schuster, 1985. Including "Emerson and the Essay" and "Representation and the War for Reality."
James, Henry. *The American.* Boston: Houghton Mifflin, 1965.
Johnson, Denis. *Jesus's Son.* New York: HarperCollins, 1993.
Kafka, Franz. "The Burrow." *The Selected Stories of Franz Kafka.* Trans. Willa and Edmund Muir. New York: Modern Library, 1952.
Menchu, Rigoberta. "First Visit to Guatemala City." *I, Rigoberta Menchu.* London: Verso, 1984.
Ozick, Cynthia. "A Short Note on 'Chekhovian.'" *Metaphor and Memory.* New York: Vintage Books, 1981.

Paley, Grace. "Goodbye and Good Luck." *Little Disturbances in Man*. New York: Doubleday, 1959.

Rodoreda, Merce. "The Salamander." *My Christina and Other Stories*. Trans. David H. Rosenthal. Port Townsend, Wash.: Graywolf Books, 1984.

Sholem, Gershom, ed. *The Correspondence of Walter Benjamin and Gershom Sholem*. Trans. Gary Smith and Andre Lefevere. New York: Shocken Books, 1989.

Stratton, Joanna L., ed. *Pioneer Women: Voices from the Kansas Frontier*. New York: Simon and Schuster, 1981.

Wharton, Edith. *The Age of Innocence*. New York: Collier Books, 1993.

JOAN SILBER

Weight in Fiction

At times when I've had to read large batches of fiction all at once, trying to be fair while judging acres of pages for a program or a contest, I've come through it complaining that the trouble with all this work is that it's too small. Too light, too slight, too trivial. Too lacking in *weight*. It is one of those inarticulate generalizations a person makes in the onslaught of any experience, a tourist's eagerness to find a pattern in the rush of unsorted sights.

Friends who hear me make this complaint are apt to ask what I mean, and I'm always hard-pressed to explain. Do I mean too limited an emotional range, everything too fluffy and safe, not enough hard-core trouble and misery? Do I mean too unambitious in its themes, too unwilling to venture into deep philosophical waters? Too banal in its subject matter, too familiar in its march of events?

And why am I, of all people, complaining? For much of my early years as a writer I was very much a defender of dramas in miniature, a believer in anybody's right to see eternity in a grain of sand, and I am still, although my tolerance for how this can be done has changed. I've mostly thought the hard part was not choosing material but shaping it, giving it form. When anyone raised questions about whether to chronicle the ostensibly ordinary or the small-scale, I've thought: hasn't that battle been fought long since? It is a century and a half since Flaubert had to go around making pronouncements like "Yvetot donc vaut Constantinople"—a cruddy little podunk town in Normandy is worth as much as any Constantinople.

As it happens, public taste of late has been changing (is always changing) about what seems most suitable for fictional treatment. The domestic realm of family novels and the hard-edged close focus of minimalism have, in turn, ceded ground to showier effects—magical elements, historical layering, and fiction that calls attention to its own artifices. Students don't talk about Carver or Beattie or Cheever; they talk about Ondaatje or Rushdie or Winterson. All of this is fine with me; how could it be otherwise?

But in its weaker forms the showier and more inventive fiction, it turns out, is just as likely to strike a weary reader as too light or slight. If the problem isn't subject matter or texture or mode, what is it?

To ask this question is, for me, to think of Jane Austen. We like her now—the huge crop of major motion pictures from her novels has been a genuine success—but she has not always been so generally liked. There was a time when a woman writer was apt to be asked whether she really thought Austen's *Emma* was as great as, say, Melville's *Moby-Dick*, whether a drawing room could ever yield the same literary depth as a whaling ship. It's not a completely stupid question, although it was often asked stupidly. Jane Austen knew enough to worry about this herself. In a famous letter she referred to her fiction as "the little bit (two inches wide) of Ivory on which I work with so fine a brush, as produces little effect after much labor" (letter to J. Edward Austen 52). Her novels remain great examples of work that is miniature but not slight. How does she do it?

It may be useful to look at Austen's well-known opening sentences:

It is a truth universally acknowledged, that a single man in possession of a good fortune, must be in want of a wife. (*Pride and Prejudice*)

Emma Woodhouse, handsome, clever, and rich, with a comfortable home and a happy disposition, seemed to unite some of the best blessings of existence, and had lived nearly twenty-one years in the world with very little to distress or vex her. (*Emma*)

Sir Walter Elliot, of Kellynch Hall, in Somersetshire, was a man who, for his own amusement, never took up any book but the Baronetage; there he found occupation for an idle hour, and consolation in a distressed one; there his faculties were roused into admiration and respect, by contemplating the limited remnant of the earliest patents; there any unwelcome sensations, arising from domestic affairs, changed naturally into pity and contempt. As he turned over the almost endless creations of the last century—and there, if every other leaf were powerless, he could read his own history with an interest which never failed—this was the page at which the favorite volume always opened:
"ELLIOT OF KELLYNCH HALL." (*Persuasion*)

Compare these sentences of Austen to the openings of any contemporary novels lying around your house, and Austen will not, on the surface of it, seem to be weightier or more ambitious. In content she is placing the fiction in a distinctly limited sphere—what is most striking (comparisons will show) is that she is the writer who *knows* this. She is not a writer blinded by parochial glamour.

In *Pride and Prejudice* the joke of the first sentence is: *that's* a universal truth? A bit of commonplace venality is mocked by its elevation to rubric. And in *Emma* everything we hear about the heroine makes us wait eagerly for the other shoe to drop, for the arrival of events that will distress and vex her; we know what she doesn't, that trouble will find her as it finds us all. Austen is most trenchant about narrowness in *Persuasion,* her last book, written when her patience seems to have been severely worn. Sir Walter, contemplating his lineage, is laughable (and later hideous); his title is not the same wonder to Austen that it is to him.

Austen has the stylistic advantage—in her hands it is an advantage—of a prose in which authorial "telling" is not taboo; she can openly go outside a character's consciousness. Right from the opening of *Emma,* the reader has no excuse for being under the same illusions as Emma herself. Austen's point-of-view conventions are not ours, but generations of writing students have been taught the subtleties of using first or third person to imply more than a character knows; any narration, skillfully used, can be deeper than the character it's attached to. This is one way great books are written about frivolous and short-sighted people. *Madame Bovary,* with somewhat different methods, is another majestic example of this.

Clearly, one way to use a narrow range of event is to be critical of it. In nineteenth-century novels—particularly those written by women—we feel the frustration of social confinement. Austen gets considerable humor out of this, but her annoyance gets sharper and more like outrage as the books go on. In the works of Charlotte Brontë or George Eliot this frustration darkens the prospects of female characters who are walking around with a capacity for great feeling and nothing to attach it to—Jane Eyre or Maggie Tulliver in *Mill on the Floss* or Dorothea Brooke in *Middlemarch.*

Austen's own experience was severely limited, according to our notions of what experience is. She never married, I think it is safe to say she never had sex, she never traveled beyond a small radius, and she spent most of her adult life as a working aunt and daughter. She may well have had unrequited yearnings, but she was not, like the Brontës, of an openly passionate temperament. She did have, in addition to a fond family life, a fairly public social life with ample opportunities for observing.

The tension in any Austen plot is over whether the fools will win—whether the spiteful, vain, and ridiculous will be able to ruin the futures of the fine and sound and deserving. Austen's heroines, whether high-spirited and overconfident or meek and put-upon, are in the most crucial and delicate phase of their lives—their marriageable years—and the fools' triumph can cost them greatly.

Austen is always astute about reckoning the *consequences* of what happens in her plots. If she is known for keeping her eye on a low level of action (one tiny bit of rudeness to a powerless old maid turns the plot in *Emma*), it is because these closely watched characters are making ineradicable decisions. Their marital ties are their fates. To lose is to pay for a lifetime.

However, nobody dies of a broken heart in Austen. In Austen's fiction even Marianne, the sister who represents emotional susceptibility in *Sense and Sensibility,* recovers in due course of time, as she should, in Austen's view. There is, I believe, an implicit awareness in Austen about what spot her characters occupy on the spectrum of human suffering. This is why we find her perspective "bracing," a favorite description of her effects.

Perspective is one of the things we go to fiction for. We emerge from a good novel seeing more clearly what counts and what doesn't. It is why we think good books help make life bearable. A person who has perspective is not a fool.

If small matters are essential to fiction—even the most abstract work has to contain mundane textures (think of Kafka)—the job of fiction is to sort through these textures, to accord them their ranks. Chekhov said, in a letter, "My business is merely to be talented, i.e., to know how to distinguish important statements from unimportant, to throw light on the characters and to speak their language" (letter to A. S. Souvorin 270).

As it happens, Chekhov has a story that is directly about the issue of perspective. "Strong Impressions" takes place in a Moscow circuit court, where a group of jurymen, left in court for the night, fall into a conversation inspired by a witness's testimony about going gray after one terrible moment. The jurymen decide that each will tell *his* most terrible moment. One man says he was nearly drowned, another tells of almost poisoning his son by mistake, a third talks about suicide attempts. The fourth tells a story about his courtship. He took up a dare from a lawyer friend (who claimed to be able to argue anyone out of anything) that he could be convinced to give up his beloved fiancée, Natasha. And the lawyer, bit by bit, succeeded in getting him to doubt the woman and to write a note breaking off the engagement. Once the note was mailed, the lawyer argued the other side, and the man was smitten with regret and anguish—only to be told to his great relief that the envelope was misaddressed after all. The fifth juryman is about to tell his tale when the clock strikes:

> "Twelve . . ." one of the jurymen counted. "And into which class, gentlemen, would you put the emotions that are being experienced

by the man we are trying? He, that murderer, is spending the night in a convict cell here in the court, sitting or lying down and of course not sleeping, and throughout the whole sleepless night listening to that chime. What is he thinking of? What visions are haunting him?"

And the jurymen all suddenly forgot about strong impressions; what their companion who had once written a letter to Natasha had suffered seemed unimportant, even not amusing; and no one said anything more; they began quietly and in silence lying down to sleep. (133–34)

What Chekhov does so beautifully at the end of the story is, of course, to switch the scale of event; we are ambushed by the last-minute arrival of "weight." Until then, the Natasha tale has "amused" us as well as the jurors—how could we have guessed we were going to be in another kind of story altogether? We are suitably instructed. When I was thinking about this story, it struck me that the shift from the idly chatting jurors to the accused murderer is akin to what Alice Munro does in the leaps across time in her stories: events we thought we understood become quite different seen in the light of other events.

In, for instance, Munro's "The Albanian Virgin" an exotic saga about a single foreign woman living with an Albanian tribe in the 1920s becomes a commentary on the more ordinary narrator's roles as a married and unmarried woman. In "Royal Beatings" a child's punishments and the family's rituals of compromising comfort afterward are set against the town's murderous beating of a neighbor and the normalization of the event. Munro's shifts in perspective force us to connect elements across a wide field.

It is stretching a point only slightly to say that these shifts bear some kinship to what Austen does when a voice we know as the author's rises up in a landscape of tinkling conversation. Virginia Woolf says, in her essay on Jane Austen in *The Common Reader,* that Austen lets a character like the untrustworthy Mary in *Mansfield Park*

rattle on . . . but now and then she [Austen] strikes one note of her own, very quietly, but in perfect tune, and at once all Mary Crawford's chatter, though it continues to amuse, rings flat. . . . From such contrasts there comes a beauty, a solemnity even which are not only as remarkable as her wit, but an inseparable part of it. (145)

So it is contrasts we are talking about here, and I suppose it is a simple enough notion that things are weighed in comparison to each other. But perhaps something should also be said about beauty, about the leaping and connecting that are the basis of form. No rules of proportion can be laid down for all fiction, but an intuition that proportion is somehow there gives pleasure. "Intuition" and "somehow there" beg the question, but to talk about weight is to be always begging the question of what's "important" and to admit that the aesthetic and the moral are necessarily conflated. Within the closed system of a story the contrasts tell us what counts and how much the lack of what counts may cost any character in suffering.

WORKS CITED

Austen, Jane. *Emma*. New York: Bantam, 1984.
———. Letter to J. Edward Austen, 16 December 1816, qtd. in "Austen, Jane." *The Oxford Companion to English Literature*. 5th ed. New York: Oxford University Press, 1985.
———. *Persuasion*. New York: Bantam, 1984.
———. *Pride and Prejudice*. New York: Bantam, 1984.
Chekhov, Anton. Letter to A. S. Suvorin, 30 May 1888. "Selections from Chekhov's Letters." *Anton Chekhov's Short Stories*. Selected and edited by Ralph Maitlaw. New York: W. W. Norton, 1979.
———. "Strong Impressions." *The Schoolmaster and Other Stories*. Trans. Constance Garnett. New York: Ecco, 1986.
Munro, Alice. "Royal Beatings." *The Beggar Maid: Stories of Flo and Rose*. New York: Penguin, 1984.
———. "The Albanian Virgin." *Open Secrets*. New York: Vintage, 1995.
Woolf, Virginia. "Jane Austen." *The Common Reader*. New York: Harcourt Brace Jovanovich, 1984.

EHUD HAVAZELET

Chekhov and Form

To begin, two favorite quotes: The first is spoken by Mischa Auer to Una Merkel in *Destry Rides Again*. Auer is a Russian immigrant, a ne'er-do-well, and after losing his clothes to Marlene Dietrich in a card game he tells his wife, "All I want is to be a cowboy and wear my own pants," which seems to me about what any of us could reasonably hope to want.

The second is from Flannery O'Connor, who, in a letter to a young writer known to us only as "A," says: "You don't dream up a form and put the truth in it. The truth creates its own form. Form is necessity in a work of art."

It's that last sentence—"Form is necessity in a work of art"—I'd like to look at. What interests me is the word *necessity*. Not, as might have been expected, *necessary,* as in "Form is *necessary* in a work of art," for almost no one would dispute that some form of form is necessary.

But *necessity?* This is taking a large further step, from component to cause. O'Connor seems to be saying that form is not just the best, most appropriate packaging for story but is much more, is involved somehow in the ontogeny of story, in its discovery. Bernard Malamud, in the introduction to his collected stories, put it nearly the same way (O'Connor read and admired Malamud's early stories; I'm not certain if he ever read her): "form as ultimate necessity is the basis of literature." *Necessity* again. What notion of form could they be talking about?

First, what do we mean by form? For writers form is the alchemy of craft as it is applied to the base metal of event. We mean point of view, setting, voice, narrative irony, the arc of scene and dramatic line. Often we begin by distinguishing form from content. I hear writers suggest to each other, "try it in third person" or "what if it was told by a retrospective narrator?" and this is valuable advice, to a point—valuable as an aid to exploration, valueless when it seems to suggest that form is adornment, packaging, or mere style choice, me telling myself if I went omniscient and extended my sentences I'd be Jane Austen, not Tom Clancy.

Webster's, among forty-two definitions of both the noun and verb (and it seems worth mentioning that *form* comes just after *forlorn hope* and right before *formaldehyde*) puts it like this: "The shape and structure of anything as distinguished from the material of which it is composed; particular or distinctive disposition or arrangement of matter; figure."

The first sense seems straightforward enough, "the shape and structure of anything as distinguished from the material of which it is composed"—form, again, as separate from content, though shaping and structuring begin to complicate things. The second, "particular or distinctive disposition or arrangement of matter" seems closer to what we do, suggesting it is the ordering, the "disposition" and "arrangement," that give the matter its particularity or distinction.

Then we come to the last sense, "figure." *Webster's* offers these among twenty-three definitions of the verb *figure:* "to make an image of, imagine"; "to portray, as by description or enactment"; "to represent or express by a metaphor, to symbolize"; "to embellish with designs, to adorn with figures."

Notice we have now moved from the abstract to the sensory, from "disposition and arrangement of matter" to "image," "enactment," "metaphor," "design." Form, in this truest sense, is about the way in which matter—read story—is perceived: "To make an image," "to portray," "to represent," "to embellish," and "to adorn." In this conception of the verb *figure,* without form there can be no content, not one that is perceivable or at least persuasively so.

Form, I'd like to suggest, is not versus content, as we've often been told; it *is* content. Without it there is no story, as once the defining figuration, pants, are removed from miserable Mischa, there is no cowboy.

Form, then, is desirable, is unavoidable, is . . . necessary. Still, *necessity?*

Joseph Conrad says, in the preface to *The Nigger of the Narcissus:* "Art itself may be defined as a single-minded attempt to render the highest kind of justice to the visible universe." Art is to *render the visible,* to do it *justice.* An odd and lovely and surprising sentiment. But doesn't he have it backwards? Isn't art about *using* the visible universe to render the highest kind of justice to my stories? Isn't what I have to say more important than the suit I dress it up in, certainly more important than the world it imperfectly reflects? Are not form and all its components there to help me process and deliver my message?

Or is something else at work here? Is Conrad suggesting what may be more important than message, than the news I have to tell? Is he suggesting that only by observing then picturing humanity in its troubles with the greatest accuracy and the greatest sympathy can we finally hope to involve, perhaps move, the reader?

Later in the same preface Conrad says, "My task . . . is by the power of the written word to make you hear, to make you feel—it is above all, to make you see. That—and no more, and it is everything." Notice

Conrad does not talk about representation as a means to convey content, an adjunct applied *post facto*—representation is all. Once again, no pants, no cowboy.

Why is this? Why can't I just come up with my imperishable stories about third-generation died-again Jews and let form follow dysfunction?

Three more quotes, from the letters of Flannery O'Connor and Anton Chekhov, may provide a clue.

When you present a pathetic situation you have to let it speak entirely for itself. I mean you have to present it and let it alone. You have to let the things in the story do the talking . . . to learn to paint with words. . . . Let the old man go through his motions without any comment from you as author and let the things he sees make the pathetic effects. Do you know Joyce's story "The Dead?" See how he makes the snow work in that story. Chekhov makes everything work—the air, the light, the cold, the dirt, etc. Show these things and you don't have to say them. (O'Connor)

In nature descriptions you must go after tiny details, grouping them in such a way that once you've read them you can close your eyes and see a picture. . . . In the domain of psychology, more details. . . . It's best to avoid describing the characters' psychic states, which should be clear from their actions. (Chekhov)

When you portray the unfortunate and the down and out and wish to move the reader to pity, try to be colder. It will give a kind of backdrop to their grief, make it stand out more. All your heroes weep, and you sigh with them. (Chekhov)

These are, of course, sound advice, first of all, good craft tutelage and canny insight into psychology. But see how they rely again on form—detail, description, painting with words—rather than message, the adenoidal despair of the old man and his wheezy cohorts. Form is emotion made plastic; it is the part of story that works most deeply on readers. For us to be moved, Chekhov and O'Connor seem to be saying, for us to be involved in the inner emotional lives of characters, we need their external trappings portrayed, we need to be enthralled not by the pain and turmoil they are feeling but by the way that pain and turmoil are rendered, through perception, alive in each of us. Remember Conrad: we need to feel, and to feel we need to hear, above all to see.

To be brought to a proper consideration—of Kurtz on his deathbed; Anna Karenina on the station platform; Gurov and Anna Sergeyevna, an inch from salvation, moving instead into a life of misery and devotion; Mr. Head taking in the look on Nelson's face as he turns from the lady on the sidewalk into a new world; Pinye Salzman, under revolving violins, watching his daughter rise from the dead to greet her lover—we need a good story. We need good drama and interesting characters and a narrator whose voice is pleasant and beguiling—all these are part of it. But what we need most is form to work unnoticed on the reader so that, again from Conrad in the preface, "the light of magic suggestiveness may be brought to play for an evanescent instant over the commonplace surface of words: of the old, old words, worn thin, defaced by ages of careless usage."

What we're finally talking about is seduction. And we need to be seduced, because we see all the messages coming. We're awash in messages, deafened and nearly drowned. Anyone with six weeks of prime-time television under his belt has seen them all, all the messages and sermons and feel-good-about-yourself-because-Goddammit-you're-an-American home truths. Readers resist—perhaps I mean "readers should resist"—rhetoric; they resent being told how to feel, why to feel it, and why their feeling it that way is good for them. Readers revel in the illusion of freedom, the illusion that they experience fiction first-hand and decide for themselves what it means. They don't, of course; nothing could be farther from true. But the illusion is necessary, this illusion, conveyed by form, that the fiction is a live experience happening in the reader's head and gut, and in making the fiction live this way in the reader. Is not form very close to necessity?

When O'Connor says Chekhov "makes everything work," she is talking about form, about how, in the best stories, the masterpieces we learn from, all a writer's formal tools–point of view, voice, narrative irony, theme, etc.—are brought into play. In the stories that most closely approach perfection—and the two I'd like to discuss are fine candidates—to tease out the thread of a single formal device is to risk losing sight of, if not dismantling, the whole garment. Still, one can learn about how a story is put together, can gain access to a fuller appreciation of form, by approaching via one device. I would like to do this, using setting as a portal through which we can enter two stories by Anton Chekhov, "A Journey by Cart" and "In Exile."

"A Journey by Cart" tells the story of Marya Vasilyevna, a schoolteacher of thirty years, making the trip to town to collect her salary, as she has done so many times "it would be impossible for her to count the number." We meet her and her driver, Semyon, on the return leg of the trip—this matters: we are already seeing Chekhov's formal choices—and along the way they meet Khanov, a man of forty, an estate owner, of whom "it was said . . . that he never did anything at home but walk about and whistle, or else play chess with his old manservant." Khanov greets the travelers, rides along with them awhile, then turns off the road.

Marya finds Khanov handsome but a reprobate. Watching him beside old Semyon, she thinks him gallant and tall but notices "an almost imperceptible something about his walk that betrayed a being already rotten at the core, weak, and nearing his downfall." The next sentence tells us, surprisingly, "And the air in the woods suddenly seemed to carry an odor of wine." This observation is tied to Khanov, whose papers, when he examined her students a year earlier, smelled of scent and wine. Is his fragrance so strong it permeates the woods? Is this a projection of Marya's infatuation? Or is his dissolution so advanced she can actually smell it? Marya doesn't tell us. She is a character who is very reticent about the meaning of things.

Marya idly daydreams of love—no, not quite; the distinction is the point. Here is the text:

> Marya Vasilyevna's thoughts turned to her scholars, and the coming examinations, and the watchman [who has been beating the children], and the school board, until a gust of wind from the right bringing her the rumbling of the departed carriage, other reveries mingled with these thoughts, and she *longed* [my emphasis] to dream of handsome eyes and love and the happiness that would never be hers.

Keep this sentence and the verb *longed* in mind.

They stop at an inn, where she is first ignored then greeted with respect by some peasants, and they resume their journey. Water has been on the side of the road the entire story; it is flood season. "Torrents of water were rushing down on either side of the track," we're told, "and seemed to have eaten away the road bed." But Marya is nearly out of it: "Only a few miles to go, and then they would cross the river, and then the railway track, and then they would be at home."

They see Khanov above them, crossing the river on a bridge, but Semyon thinks he's found a shorter way. They plunge into the river, and Marya feels "a sharp wave of cold water lap her feet." Her precious provisions are ruined by the water, the cart is nearly toppled, and Marya is soaked. Finally, they near the village. She sees the church with its cross blazing in the sunset and a cloud of rosy steam rising from a train loading at the station. As they wait for the train to leave, we get, oddly enough—shouldn't this have come earlier, at a more dramatic moment?—our first real glimpse into Marya's loneliness and need. She remembers her family (all we've seen of them earlier is a photograph of her mother, so faded all the features have disappeared except the eyebrows and hair). Now, from the story's last page:

> For the first time in all these thirty years Marya Vasilyevna saw in imagination her mother, her father, and her brother in their apartment in Moscow, saw everything down to the least detail, even to the globe of goldfish in the sitting room. She heard the strains of a piano, and the sound of her father's voice, and saw herself young and pretty and gaily dressed, in a warm, brightly lighted room with her family about her. Great joy and happiness suddenly welled up in her heart and she pressed her hands to her temples in rapture, crying softly with a note of deep entreaty in her voice:
> "Mother!"
> Then she wept and could not have said why.

Khanov appears again, and for the briefest moment Marya imagines them as sweethearts (somehow the only appropriate word). Her life, she briefly muses, would not have been long and trying, full of disappointment and loss. "All that," she thinks, "had been a long, strange, painful dream, and now she was awake." Then Semyon tells her to sit down or she'll fall, she sits, they arrive, and he announces that the journey, and the story, are over.

So we have what appears to be a straightforward, not to say sentimental, portrait of a spinster schoolteacher, a day in the life of an old maid. Except for some beautiful writing, there might seem to be nothing of great note in here. Depending on your predilections, you weep for Marya, or you cringe at her stereotypic and done-to-death misery.

But something else is going on here. I've given two examples of what Chekhov does several times throughout the story. The first was in the sentence "she *longed* to dream of handsome eyes and love and the happiness that would never be hers," the keyword being *longed*. The second was in the lengthy quote, from the last page, where, shivering with cold— and Chekhov, in a lovely sleight-of-eye, describes Marya's shivering, making the whole scene before her seem to shiver—she remembers her family, in colorful, lively detail, for the first time in thirty years. Marya's sole emotional outburst follows, "Mother!" then her reveries break through—life is a painful dream from which she has finally awoken, somehow she and Khanov will be brought together, all will be well.

Wouldn't most writers have given us this reverie earlier, given us the depth of Marya's loneliness and need earlier, so we could understand exactly what the dashing Khanov means to her? Couldn't we then "sigh along" with her? By waiting until now, until the journey is over, until the waters have reached her, Chekhov is showing Marya as not simply a sad and pathetic creature, this just one of her barren days; Chekhov is showing us a woman reluctant to dream, afraid, for to dream is to want, and she puts it off as long as she can, on this day, which may be the turning toward the rest of her life.

The first encounter with Khanov shows this fear in her refusal to respond to him directly, in her seeing him only as a wastrel—she does not dream; she *longs* to dream. But we see—through that miracle of narrative technology, irony—where her imagination takes her, a world scented with wine. During the inn scene she turns from conversation with a foul-mouthed but lively peasant, and throughout she is dismissive of Semyon's imaginative gossip about local officials. At the very start we get a beautiful description of the countryside, "the listless, misty woods flushed with the first heat of spring . . . the flocks of crows flying far away across the wide, flooded meadows . . . the marvelous, unfathomable sky into which one felt one could sail away with such infinite pleasure." But Chekhov tells us there was nothing "new or attractive" for Marya in all this: "It mattered not to her whether the season were spring, as now, or winter, or autumn with darkness and rain; she invariably longed for one thing and one thing only: a speedy end to her journey."

Seasons, rebirth, even the procreative, sexual imagery of the first flush of spring, mean nothing to her. In a brilliant use of narrative irony Chekhov shows us all these beautiful things, only to tell us Marya, the point-of-view character, does not see them. She turns away from them, from life. We have here a woman not only trapped by circumstance but collusive with fate—she turns from life as she has seen life turn from her. To dream is to want is to realize you will never have—much better, then, the wan pathos of an unfulfilled existence.

So that's the irony—she is not just victim but oppressor, oppressor of herself. She turns from nature, from conversation, from Khanov, even from memory. She is chilled to her soul, has chosen a living death out of fear and lack of will. Our portrait of Marya is not sentimental but ironic; we are meant not to sigh but to sneer.

But Chekhov is after bigger, and fresher, fish. In the long paragraph I quoted earlier we see, we who may have been judging her harshly, the exact cost of Marya allowing herself to dream, of allowing her imagination rein over what she has lost, what she most deeply desires. In that one word, *Mother!* and in the brief, rending moment she allows herself to imagine her entire life as a dream, we see the pain she has been turning from in sudden, vivid detail, all she has left behind, all she will never have. This changes everything. She would rather we didn't see this side of her. Everything about Marya, her stoicism, her whiny but upright demeanor, her asking for little, expecting less, all are meant to hide, from herself as well as from us, this woman so alone she cannot even bear the comfort of memory. All she can do is hide, and Chekhov won't allow it. Her previous denial of life becomes, in this light, in its small, circumscribed way, heroic—not prim but desperate.

How does setting deepen this reading of the story?

What we first notice is the title. "A Journey by Cart" seems innocuous enough as to be dismissible, more a reminder of plot than evocative of something more. But when we look at it from the perspective of allegory we see, clearly, the journey as her life, its monotonous round made so often she can't even bear to remember it. We see the cart as both her entrapment and the fragile bark that sustains her over life's rising waters. Her turning from spring and landscape is the setting of her turning away from all of life, its fecundity and unseemliness and gossip and desire. We meet her halfway through the journey, again pointing out its monotony—why bother with the details of town, the shops, since she in all likelihood didn't even see them—but suggesting also we are nearing journey's end; this is not, as Marya believes, simply the latest in an innumerable and featureless aggregate of journeys made before. It evokes a more famous journeyer who also began his trek midway through life. And it suggests, too—in its bland invocation of the commonplace—all that is submerged, unnoted, all that is repressed by Marya, her whole life, until the end, when she can keep it down no longer.

The journey, then, is life's journey, the round, life's, and the cart and the willful turning from all deviation Marya's sole protection. On both sides of the road are the rising waters, ahead of her is the river, still rising, and all she wants to do is get home. Enter Khanov. Only he can ride on or off the road at will. He tells Semyon, when asked why he would go driving on a day like this, "It is tiresome staying at home, Daddy. I don't like it." He reappears, dramatically, as they enter the river but above it, dry on the bridge, and then again, at the story's climax, both catalyzing and abandoning Marya to her moment of rapture and defeat.

Marya is sticking to life's worn groove, afraid to venture out. But life—the slow rising water; time, as evoked by the seasons; and Khanov, representing the risk and unpredictability of living your life—all are closing in. We may blame Marya for being too weak hearted to get wet, to jump out of the cart and follow life's boisterous, confusing call, but then doesn't she, in her own way, after all? She opens herself, finally, to life, to desire. We see her at story's end, soaked, collapsed back into the cart, finally shocked into awareness (as perhaps we have been wanting her to be), fully alive to her unending isolation and loss.

"In Exile" is a nearly plotless story about a young Tatar whose name we are not given. He has been exiled to Siberia for crimes his brothers and uncle committed and has found work during the flood season assisting an old ferryman, Semyon, nicknamed "Preacher." The Tatar misses his wife, his home province of Simbirsk, where "even the stars were quite different, and so was the sky." He is an open-hearted boy, looking for some small comfort, from the fire, from the natural world, perhaps from old Semyon, a veteran of this life. Certainly from the latter he will not find any. Semyon is preacher of a most cynical faith, telling the young Tatar to forget his wife, Simbirsk, anything of his former existence; to abandon any dreams of change or salvation, for even to hope, Semyon says, is "mere foolishness . . . the devil confounding you."

The bulk of the story is taken up with another story, recounted by Semyon. We all recognize the framing device, "a story within a story," and should bear in mind that this formal structure calls to our notice at least two things: that the real story is most likely not in either the frame or the picture but in dialogue between the two and that the nature of the telling itself—the form of the story—will be worth attending.

The inner story is of Vassily Sergeyich, a nobleman exiled to Siberia fifteen years ago, who has refused to give up hope. He first checked the post constantly for money and messages from home. He convinced his wife, young and beautiful, to join him in exile, and, even after she ran off with an official and left him with a child to raise, he persevered, raised a beautiful young woman, doted on her. His credo, which he made the mistake of repeating to Semyon, is "Even in Siberia people can live!" Now his daughter has taken ill with tuberculosis, and Vassily is obsessed, as any father would be, with finding a cure. He travels constantly to far-off villages to seek medical assistance, all of which brands him, in Semyon's eyes, a fool, a dreamer, confounded by the devil. She will die in any case, Semyon assures us, and Vassily will hang himself or run off, only to be caught and thrown in prison.

The Tatar breaks into Preacher's narrative here to say "Good! Good!" his broken speech a nearly strangled affirmation of everything moral in the face of Semyon's cold, eloquent cynicism. Semyon asks him what is good, and the Tatar says:

His wife, his daughter. . . . What of prison and what of sorrow!—anyway, he did see his wife and his daughter. . . . You say, want nothing.

But "nothing" is bad. His wife lived with him three years—that was a gift from God. "Nothing" is bad, but three years is good.

The Tatar tells Semyon of his wife, her own promise, like Vassily Sergeyich's wife before her, to join him and ease his exile. Semyon, having finished the vodka he was drinking, goes off to sleep, and the Tatar thinks of home, wonders how he will care for his wife, should she actually come, and then, in a turn reminiscent of Marya in the previous story, nods off and dreams that this life is just a dream from which he need only rouse himself to be returned to Simbirsk and his old, his true, existence.

What rouses him, instead, is shots from the far side of the river—Vassily Sergeyich on yet another journey to find a doctor for his dying daughter. As they ferry Vassily back across, Semyon mocks him. The father gone, the Tatar launches another tirade at old Semyon, saying Vassily "is good, but you are bad. God created man to be alive, and to have joy and grief and sorrow; but you want nothing so you are not alive, you are stone, clay! . . . God does not love you but he loves the Gentleman!"

Everyone laughs; all but the Tatar head for the hut and sleep. From inside they hear the Tatar crying. Semyon has the last word, saying, "he'll soon get used to it," and then they fall asleep, too lazy or cold to rise and close the door.

On first reading, this, too, might seem a straightforward, even simple story, a tale of morality and cleaving to life versus a dark and life-denying cynicism. Certainly the Tatar, open-hearted, emotionally responsive, is more attractive to us than old Semyon, who has remained outside the hut just so he won't be forced to share any of his vodka, who laughs at the devotion of the father to his sick child, who espouses no creed beyond an arrogant and dark fatalism. The Tatar invokes life as it should be, and Semyon, in rejecting this view, seems beyond the scope of what we would call reasonable human behavior.

But if we look a little deeper we see Chekhov countering, having activated, our reasonable, not to say romantic, notions of life. Once the Tatar, near the end of the story, actually begins to think on his wife's arrival in Siberia he himself realizes almost immediately that he would have no way to keep her, that life here, barely enough to sustain him, would be fatal to her. While his plea that even a moment of his wife's company would make all the loneliness after it bearable is, again, soundly human and attractive, we have the living example of Vassily Sergeyich, who amiably rises from the inner story to demonstrate to us, a page later, how wrong the Tatar is: Vassily had his wife three years, his daughter ever since, and has found no such contemplative satisfaction. And last, while Semyon's habit of mocking others' misery is not endearing, one can't, on the face of it, much dispute his claims. Prisoners under the czars, as later under the Soviets, were not sent to Siberia to be rehabilitated in preparation for a return to life but to be eliminated, forgotten, erased. To hold onto beliefs that life will improve, seems, on the evidence, to be foolhardy indeed, even mad, and perhaps it *is* only the devil's prompting that makes men continue.

So who is right? Our moral leanings favor the boy and the long-suffering Vassily, but practical considerations of reality seem to favor Semyon. We want to know. Are the old moralities upheld? Is life, after all, good? Or a cruel, sustained joke? Our (My?) Hollywood-impregnated minds want clear answers, the balm of resolution. Is it to be John Wayne strutting his certainties across a landscape of lesser men and ideals; is it to be Hepburn?—feisty and talented and smart but finally meeting her fate, and salvation and comeuppance, Tracy reining her in as wife nonetheless? Or is the whole old outmoded, complacent system junk, and we thumb it in the eye, simpering along with James Dean, barely able to enunciate our contempt, like Brando? Which side is Chekhov taking?

Neither.

While I think it fair to assume Chekhov would like to side with the Tatar, would like to be writing of a world where the simple, old verities abide, he knows this is not the case. This story, like many from this period in his writing, arises from a year-long trip Chekhov made to the prison island of Sakhalin, where he gathered information about the conditions of the prisoners, their treatment, their medical problems. While we, and even Chekhov, might have earlier felt that nothing could shake our certainties about family, loyalty, faith in God and man, he saw a different world in the east. This, from the book he published about his journey, is Chekhov's description of the lashing of a prisoner:

The torturer stood to one side and struck the victim in such a way that the lash hit the body diagonally. After each five lashes he slowly moved to the other side, allowing the victim a thirty second respite. The victim's hair soon stuck to his forehead. After only five or ten blows his flesh, covered with weals from former beatings, turned crimson and deep blue; his skin peeled with each blow. "Your worship!" we heard through the screams and tears, "your worship! Spare me, your worship." After twenty or thirty blows he started lamenting, as if drunk or delirious, "I'm an unfortunate man, a broken man. . . .Why are they punishing me?" Suddenly his neck stretched out unnaturally, and we heard vomiting. . . . He did not say another word, only moaned and wheezed.

The world Chekhov writes about is the world where man's intentions are pitted against his failures, where the will to live is tested by life's crushing lessons. Semyon, in his vitality, in his finding a path to some manner of living, has, I believe, some of Chekhov's approval. And so does the Tatar, with his battered sensitivity, his clinging, along with Vassily, to a life become illusory, a form of imaginative self-torment. But Semyon is damned to his darkness, he is Charon ferrying the dead like himself endlessly across the night river, while the Tatar lives: he will be disappointed, his faith is naive, foolish, no doubt evanescent, but it is worth noting.

The quality I believe Chekhov admires most is striving. Marya and Semyon bear his gentle and sympathetic censure because they have heeded life's lessons and turned from it in fear (Marya) or contempt (Semyon). He may not admire, finally, their choices, but he understands them. The parallel notions of accomplishment and idealism are both abstract to Chekhov, who takes man's measure not by what he claims to have done or believed but by the minute-to-minute life he has lived. In his long story "My Life" he puts is this way: "Alas, the thoughts and doings of living creatures are not nearly so significant as their sufferings."

How does setting play into this reading of "In Exile"?

Let me suggest, again, that Chekhov activates, indeed counts on, our reading this story as a simple battle between good and evil, assuming most of us will side with the good, the life-affirming. Then he pits these chubby complacencies against quite irrefutable arguments, to show not that these other, darker truths are vindicated but that neither can be, that life is an endless shuttling between the dark and light, the hope filled and the despairing, and it is the shuttling itself that matters. These characters, then, are stuck, suspended between realities, and the method Chekhov uses to fix them is inversion, a tipping over of our expectations.

Let's begin again with the title. "In Exile" syntactically suggests a location, a place to be "in," but contradicts itself, for, while exile has become idiomatic of a place outside, it is actually a nonplace, a constant negation, defined by what it is not. The characters, from the start, then, are in a nonplace, are nowhere. Consider our hero, the Tatar, a man with no name, imprisoned for a crime he did not commit, sent to a place that is a negation of place.

The landscape Chekhov gives us is nearly a negation as well. It is night, and cold. There is a hut on a dark river, a small fire; lights can be seen in the distance. That's all. He brilliantly dramatizes a landscape of near insubstantiality using the dark and the cold, the bumps of the ferry and the murmurings of the river.

The main physical attribute of the story is the river. Rivers, throughout history and literature, evoke a specific imagery. They are borders, crossed to begin or to end journeys. They are demarcations between old lives and new, old lands and new. And here, on the surface, the river seems to be functioning in the same way. Semyon ferries people across, presumably to continue their journeys. But an odd thing happens on this river—no one leaves. The only character to cross the river is Vassily, who is defined by his endless futile crossings and recrossings. Charon and the River Styx seem appropriate analogies: no one crosses this river to leave, they are permanent crossers, there is no world beyond the dim fire and the cold-battered hut. The river does not demarcate a larger world; it has become the world.

These inversions set up the inversions that follow in Semyon's logic. To have faith is to listen to the devil. To pray is to blaspheme; to hope is to despair. The tag line he applies to Vassily, "one can li-i-ve," in its mockery suggests that life itself is a joke. In this world loyalty, hope, fatherhood, family, are all illusion. The life the Tatar hopes to regain is as effaced as if it never had existed, and once the flood season is over he will disappear himself into Siberia, leaving no trace. All that is left is the river: "The dark, cold river . . . floating ten paces away; it grumbled, lapped against the hollow clay banks and raced on swiftly to the faraway sea" this boy will never reach.

Still, life goes on, in the boy's longings, in Vassily's futile travels, in the motion of the ferry and the river and the seasons' unpausing cycle. Chekhov shows us, through the setting of this piece, that the world will upturn our pieties, our assumptions, our dearest, most closely held beliefs. Neither one creed nor the other prevails here, simply the dialectic, the tension between the two. And fittingly we end on a note of ambiguity, as the door to the hut remains open, physically, allowing in both the cold and the living cries of the boy near the fire, and formally, suggesting there is no certainty, no closure, no end to this story.

In a letter Chekhov wrote, "When I am finished with my characters I like to return them to life," and it is life, not the Good Life or the Bad Life, not the proclamation of a triumphant creed either over or through his characters but the characters themselves, their vital, their "significant," sufferings, that Chekhov shows us in his small, miraculous stories.

There is much more in these stories, much that could be said about characterization, dramatic line, point of view, other matters of form. It has been my intention to demonstrate how one formal device—setting—can help illuminate part of the subtle, mysterious machinery of Chekhov's art. These two stories, leeched of their setting—the cart and flood, the river and ferry—become something else entirely, something perhaps more tenable and unambiguous, solid, moral tales, but become so much less: inert, hortatory, check marks on one or the other side of those lists of Virtue and Vice now being compiled and admired, where message is all.

CHARLES BAXTER

"You're Really Something"
Inflection and the Breath of Life

Give me the daggers. . . .
  —Lady Macbeth

He'd kill us if he had the chance.
  —Francis Ford Coppola, *The Conversation*

Before Spielberg, and before *Jurassic Park,* and before *The Lost World* was found and filmed and sold to millions, and before there was tie-in merchandising of Jurassic Park lunch boxes and T-shirts and video games, before special effects and multimillion dollar box-office receipts, before all this, there was, and still is, along Highway 12 in southern Michigan close to the Ohio border, a humble tourist trap, Dinosaur World. Dinosaur World is a little roadside attraction in Michigan's so-called Irish Hills. It shares the neighborhood with a Mystery Spot, where the laws of gravity are violated and where, the billboards claim, scientists are baffled; a fireworks outlet called The Boom Box; the Dwight D. Eisenhower Presidential railroad car set up next to a chocolate fudge stand; Chilly Willy's putt-putt golf course; and other odds and ends of local tourist interest, including a water slide and a go-cart track. Most of the businesses could use a few coats of paint. The place has seen better times. Like Norman Bates's motel, the area has suffered neglect ever since, to use the local phrase, "they moved the highway," meaning the freeway, which is now fifteen miles north.

When our son was seven years old, my wife and I decided to make a day of it and take him to Dinosaur World. We figured he was ready for the terrors of prehistoric killer raptors and reptiles. He thought so, too.

Outside Dinosaur World a fountain of sorts spouts water tinted dark blue, thanks to heavy doses of blue dye. You pay the entry fee and are loaded onto a train of what seem to be about eight rusting golf carts, Cushman Cars, linked together. There are no rails. These carts are on kid-sized rubber wheels. While you wait for the guide, you watch the

An earlier version of this essay appeared in *Creating Fiction,* edited by Julie Checkoway (Cincinnati: Story Press, 1999).

Triceratops, the one dinosaur available for free viewing. He is constructed out of chicken wire and some sort of painted plaster. His mouth opens and shuts every five seconds, like an elf in a department store Christmas window display, and the sound of reptilian indigestion emerges from a hidden loudspeaker in the bushes.

At last our guide arrived. He was a high school kid. This was his summer job. It was August, and you could tell from the expression on his face that he had just about had it with Dinosaur World. He was exasperated and bored but was playing it cool. He looked at us, his customers and fellow adventurers, with ferociously undisguised teenaged indifference. "Welcome to Dinosaur World," he said in a flat monotone. "We are about to go into a land that existed before time began." He had said the line so often that it had turned, almost Germanically, into one word. "Weareabouttogointoalandthatexistedbeforetimebegan." He plunked himself down into the driver's seat of the head golf cart and began speaking into a microphone. "Fasten your seat belts," he said, unnecessarily. His voice came out in that distinctly distorted tin foil PA system bus tour manner. "Lemmeknowifthereareanyquestions."

The hapless train, moving backward in time in several respects, followed the asphalt road around the displays of chicken wire and painted plaster. The multinational technology of Disney World was far, far, *far* away. Every once or so often the guide would stop to explain a prehistoric wonder that was before our eyes, reciting his memorized script with incremental boredom. At the climax of the tour he said, mumbling into a microphone close by an eight-foot-high killer dinosaur, "This is the fearsome Tyrannosaurus Rex." He yawned, and the three of us, my wife and son and I, burst out laughing. The guide looked slightly taken aback. "What'ssa matter?" he asked. "You're not scared?"

I can't remember what my wife and son did, but I shrugged. I had loved his use of the word *fearsome,* however, and I resolved to remember it and use it someday in a story.

Feeling slightly defeated, however, we rode back to the gift shop, where Dinosaur World salt-and-pepper shakers and postcards were for sale. There we bailed out. I could imagine how the tour guide would sound when he was behind closed doors, talking to a fellow guide. "So they're, like, *sitting* there, and I'm like, doing the tour? and man, these *ass*holes, begin to, y'know, *laugh?* and, jeez, it just totally fucking freaks me *out.* I tell you, man, Dinosaur World is *the* job from hell. You know what I'm sayin'? This place is the fucking armpit of the universe. Man, I cannot *wait* until football practice starts." All the inflection missing from his tour would have found its way into his inventory of complaints.

Coleridge's "willing suspension of disbelief" is a curious category. What makes it curious is not the "suspension" but the "willing." None of us at Dinosaur World expected to believe what we were seeing. We expected to be invited to a little party where the host acted as if *he* believed, or at least was interested in what he was seeing, and was inviting us into that *as if*. The tour guide had an actor's job, and he had to perform a role and play a part. His job was to encourage us, to invite us, to will our suspension of disbelief. That was his task, his summer vocation. His role was to pretend, within limits, that he was inside a moment of time and that we could join him there. He was supposed to hypnotize us a little. This is the technical problem of narratives concerning fantasy materials. He was supposed to pretend to be interested, and he had to be the first person to believe. He had to perform his belief. All his information about dinosaurs was secondary. He didn't perform magic, and we didn't really expect him to. There was no true magic to be had, and we knew that. No: *He was supposed to act as if there was magic.* As Orson Welles once said, there are no magicians; there are only actors who are playing magicians. A great magician is a great actor. And great actors perform hypnosis on a small scale. They make us fall asleep into another world.

You get involved in a story when, among other reasons, you get attached to a set of narrated events, or when the tone of the narrative has so many signs of emphasis that it rouses itself to life and disbelief is suspended. The story starts to believe in itself, and it often does so through inflection. You also acquire the sensation that somebody has believed this story. That's called conviction, and it may be pleasant or unpleasant. "Once a bitch always a bitch, what I say. I says you're lucky if her playing out of school is all that worries you" (Faulkner, *The Sound and the Fury*).

Inflection, the tone in which something is said, particularly when applied to extreme events or circumstances, can be relentlessly important to writers of fiction. It signals belief. It is not emotion recollected in tranquillity; it is emotion reenacted before your eyes. The story is singing or groaning itself awake. And belief creates a feeling of being inside a moment and re-creating it. Inflection is the sign of spoken intensity; it is the sign that somebody cares about what's being said.

Writers of fiction not only stage events but often must suggest how those events and statements are to be inflected, that is, how they are to be acted, how they should be pitched, how they should be voiced. As fiction writers, we are both the creators and the directors. My dictionary defines *inflection* as an alteration in tone or pitch of the voice. This might seem to be a small matter, but an alteration in tone or pitch can be the difference between being inside a moment and literally being out of it, or between fighting words and a statement of love, using the identical phrase, such as "You're really something." Say it one way, it's a caress. Say it another, and it's a slap. Say it flatly, and you're thrown out of the story.

Inflection, then, is two things: an indication of life-in-the-moment and an indication of how a phrase is to be understood. How a phrase is to be understood, or is understood, is often more important than what is literally said. It is the life of the story and its subtext. It is the difference between a tone of uninvolvement with one's own story and a sense that the story is alive, that it is going on *right now,* in front of us. A shift in tone constitutes a shift in meaning, from sincerity to irony or exasperation to incredulity, and it is a shift that has the strange capacity to bring a scene to life, to suspend disbelief.

But here, as writers, we have a large-scale problem. The trouble is that every page is silent. Every writer sooner or later runs up against the silence of the page, where tone and pitch are only implied. Sooner or later, the reader's imagination must take over. Indications of inflection encourage the reader to become active.

In real life you start to inflect statements when you don't quite believe that the words alone will carry the emotional meanings of what you need to convey. "So, they're *sitting* there, and I'm, like, doing *the tour?*" It's like saying: I can't believe what I'm telling you. Inflection is often a substitute for eloquence for the inarticulate—it can convey feeling despite a screen of poor or approximate word choices, because the words that it *does* employ are being subjected to so many tonal shadings. Multiple inflection typically gives the sense of the speaker's great involvement in what he or she is saying. It puts stress on the words, it weights them, it *enthusiastifies* them. And it is particularly necessary to those who don't have access to official language and official eloquence— to teenagers, and the dispossessed, to minority groups, and those who are baffled and broken, the hopeless and downcast, the obsessed and the fantasists, outsiders of every kind and stripe, and those who are feeling two contradictory emotions at the same time. Inflection is the home of fugitive feelings and of layered or compounded emotion. It is the eloquent music of colloquial language. It is the homing device of effective liars, magicians, outcasts, and hypnotists.

Is it possible that some fiction may be underacted? This is not a criticism we usually hear. After all, stories can be told without being brought entirely to life, and one of the signs of this semi-lifelessness, this zombie condition, this Dinosaur World narration, is that the whole story seems uninflected, as if the writer had not quite believed his own story, or was an agnostic about it, or didn't want to get involved in it, or was bored, or wanted to keep a safe distance from it or from the audience. Sometimes writers want to tell a story without being committed to it. How odd that is! It's as if the cooking temperature of the story has been set too low.

I am on an Amtrak train in Oregon. Right behind me there is a little girl commenting on the trip, town by town, mile by mile. When we cross a river, and the bridge under the tracks is not visible underneath us, the girl says to her mother, "I'm frightened! We'll all fall into the river. We will be *destiny*." I immediately write down the sentence and am simultaneously plunged into despair about how to convey on a page the way the girl sang out the word *destiny*.

Inflection in fiction writing can probably be understood to include the writer's use of indicators about how a line of dialogue was spoken or emphasized or repeated or how it might be heard or misheard or misunderstood. Inflection can be built in to the dialogue itself. After you've written the line, you sometimes have to decide how you want it to sound or to be acted. This is the art of acting as applied to the art of writing. Inflection provides a context for a line, so that we know how the words, "You're really something," are to be understood. When a statement is operatively vague, like "You're really something," inflection or its context fill in what the vagueness leaves out. Sometimes we know how to hear it by noticing how other characters re-act to it. And good acting often gives us an unexpected inflection, a reversal of what's expected, that makes a scene with dialogue come to life.

Often beginning writers are warned against telling the reader by means of adverbs how a person said something. When I was a kid, these writerly dialogue adverb tags were called Tom Swifties, in honor of those Tom Swift young-adult books for boys. A Tom Swifty is an adverb tag that stupidly points up what is obviously there already. "'I won't do it!' said Tom, stubbornly."

But most of the time we are saying what we are saying in a manner that isn't obvious. And we are accompanying these statements with a large inventory of pauses, facial gestures, body movements that can intensify or contradict the apparent meaning of what we're saying. You can say, "I love you," while at the same time your body's actions can disprove it. A conversation can go on entirely by means of body language, with no words at all. In dialogue we emphasize some words over others, thereby giving a special meaning to the sentence. In act 2, scene 2, of *Macbeth*, for example, the woman who plays Lady Macbeth has to decide how to deliver the simple line: "Give me the daggers" (she means the bloody knives that Macbeth has used to murder Duncan). If she says, "*Give* me the daggers," she's exasperated; if she says, "Give *me* the daggers," she's mocking Macbeth's weakness and emphasizing her own strength and ability to get the job done; if she says, "Give me the *daggers*," then she's triumphant and bloodthirsty.

The plot of Francis Ford Coppola's remarkable movie *The Conversation* hinges entirely on how a single line of dialogue spoken by two young people is inflected and how the movie's protagonist, Harry Caul, hears it or mishears it. The line is "He'd kill us if he had the chance." If the inflection, the emphasis, is on *kill*, then the two people who are overheard in the conversation are frightened for their own safety ("He'd *kill* us if he had the chance"). If the emphasis is on *us*, then they are plotting a murder themselves ("He'd kill *us*, if he had the chance"). In the second reading, by the way, it helps to have a pause, a comma, after *us*. What happens, in that reading of the line, is that inflection flips the statement's apparent meaning.

Notice this flip in tone. Actors sometimes describe a "flip" as an unexpected reading of a line that wakes you up. The actor switches or flips the emotion so that the tone you had expected isn't there. Instead, the line is delivered, altered, with a tonal shading you hadn't expected but which was buried in the line nevertheless and makes the line more immediate. Christopher Walken has described seeing Laurence Olivier playing Dr. Astrov in Chekhov's *Uncle Vanya* and flipping the tone in Astrov's first long speech. In this speech, near the beginning of act 1, Dr. Astrov comes on the stage and describes losing a patient, a railroad worker, who has died on the operating table under chloroform. Most actors, playing this role, deliver this speech using a commonsensical tone of slightly depressive anxiety and unhappiness, reflecting Dr. Astrov's despair over his inability to do much good for anyone.

But that was *not* the inflection that Olivier used, according to Walken. What Olivier did was to laugh during this speech, but not a laugh of relaxed good humor. Far from it. Olivier's laughter was exhausted and giddy, arising from the sort of spiritual fatigue that is so intense that it has gone a little crazy, laughter that's soul-sick. Walken says that watching Olivier laugh like that on stage was mesmerizing. It was, he said, hypnotic.

One of the filmed versions of Vanya, *Vanya on 42nd Street*, is full of moments like this, and I would recommend it to any fiction writer as an example of what can be done with unexpected tone shifts. In the middle of act 2, for example, where Sonya, among other things, asks her stepmother, Yelena, if she's happy, and Yelena simply says, "No," both Julianne Moore and Brooke Smith flip the tone. They play the scene with barely suppressed expectancy and giggles, as if they had finally been able to get to the big questions they had always wanted to ask each other. They are *not* solemn about these solemn questions. The effort to get to that place has apparently made them feel like adolescent girls, trading secrets back and forth while the men are out of the room, and they can't quite shed the feeling of girlish coconspirators. In this way, avoiding male self-importance and solemnity, they are able to admit the most devastating emotional truths in a way that provides distance and comfort to each other in a manner that binds them together. By upsetting the seriousness of the moment, they relieve the pressure on each other by, almost literally, being flip.

Similarly, Wally Shawn, playing Vanya, never lets you forget that Vanya feels despair about his own life but that, in addition, *he finds his own despair comic.* Vanya is a master of combining emotions, layering them. He is a desperate comedian, handling his despair through clowning. Wally Shawn delivers the comedy lines with a woebegone mournfulness and the lines of resignation with a strange, heady exhilaration, as if he were a brave heroic explorer, a sort of Scott-of-the-Antarctic, in the poorly mapped continent of patient despair.

Sometimes a slight shift in tone or pitch can be marked simply by a pause. Think for a moment of the last scene of Eugene O'Neill's *Long Day's Journey into Night.* The aging Mary Tyrone comes on stage, completely stoned on morphine, and in her last speech, in front of her husband and two grown sons, drifting in a free-floating reverie, she remembers how, years ago, she met her husband. This last statement consists of four sentences.

> *That was the winter of senior year. Then in the spring something happened to me. Yes, I remember. I fell in love with James Tyrone and was so happy for a time.*

Now, on almost every occasion when I have seen this play, the actor playing Mary Tyrone is careful to insert a little pause between *happy* and *for.* That little pause is an expressive air pocket of dead silence, during which reality, for that one microsecond, floods back into the mind of a woman lost in a fog of drugs and nostalgia.

Yes, I remember. I fell in love with James Tyrone and was so happy [split-second pause] *for a time.*

She doesn't say that she was so happy, period. She turns it around at the last split-second. She was so happy *for a time.* Those three words signal the difference between the working methods of kitsch and a masterpiece.

Now let's look at the way that inflection can be signaled in a work of literary fiction. In Katherine Anne Porter's story "The Leaning Tower," set in Berlin in 1931, Charles, an American, has been staying at a hotel and then finds an apartment house where he would rather reside. His ability to speak German isn't as good as he would like it to be, so, like most foreigners, he has to study facial expressions and body language to make sure that he has understood what he thinks he has heard.

In signing a lease for the apartment, Charles accidentally knocks over a little plaster Leaning Tower of Pisa in the landlady's parlor. The landlady tells him, "It cannot be replaced," and then the author adds that the line has been said with "severe, stricken dignity." Note the compounded emotion here. This is a sign that Charles is paying attention to her intonation, but it is also an small indication of how she is reinforcing her distress, dramatizing it, theatricalizing it, with visual cues. We can see her physically stiffening. A few moments later the landlady adds, "It is not your fault, but mine. I should not have left it here for—" She doesn't finish the sentence. The text tells us, "She stopped short, and walked away carrying the paper in her two cupped hands. For barbarians, for outlandish crude persons who have no respect for precious things, her face and voice said all too clearly."

What Katherine Anne Porter signals here is that conversations are *not* over when people stop speaking. Conversations continue for several moments in the silence that follows, often by means of facial expressions and body language. The largest, most emphatic point in the sentence may arrive not with the last word but with a refusal to say a word, allowing the silence to be suspended in the air. After all, which is worse or more effective in a quarrel? To say, "You're such a creep and a liar," or "You're such a—"? You can argue with option A, but you can't argue with option B.

Anyway, in the following scene Charles goes back to his Berlin hotel to move his belongings and to check out. Here he must deal with the "sallow wornout looking hotel proprietress" and her "middle-aged, podgy partner." Charles had previously agreed to stay in the hotel for a month, but now, after eight days, he is leaving. What follows is a masterful scene of telegraphed malevolence and dramatized malice, indicated by both words and physical indicators.

"Our charges here are most reasonable," the proprietress says, "her dry mouth working over her long teeth." Why does Katherine Anne Porter insert this detail of the mouth and the teeth? Partly, perhaps, to slow down the scene. To convey the woman's anxiety and suppressed rage. But also to put those "long teeth" into our mind's eye, so that we don't take her as a purely comic figure.

"You will find you cannot change your mind for nothing," she continues, in what we are told is a "severe, lecturing tone." We would probably figure out this tone for ourselves, but the statement of it intensifies the feeling and adds a slight aura of danger, a sense of the woman's horror of flexibility and her pedantic vehemence. This sense is increased when the narrator illustrates the woman's facial change. "She glanced up and over his shoulder, and Charles saw her face change again to a hard boldness, she raised her voice sharply and said with insolence, 'You will pay your bill as I present it or I shall call the police.'"

Enter the proprietress's podgy partner, who, hands in pockets, smiles "with a peculiarly malignant smile on his wide lipless mouth." The author here is not only writing the words of the scene, she is directing them for us, showing us how they are to be played. Charles pays the proprietress all the money she has demanded, to the last pfennig, and then, the podgy man, whose "pale little eyes behind their puffy lids were piggy with malice," asks to see Charles's identification papers. I should stop here again and point out that now, in the late twentieth century, many writers are reluctant to characterize a character so judgementally and so maliciously as Katherine Anne Porter does the podgy partner. Contemporary writers don't like to use phrases like "piggy with malice," maybe because we've grown sentimental about pigs and because judging characters that quickly is regarded as bad taste and mean-spirited. But it's an extreme situation, and it's important to note that the author's details are not purely malicious but are instead both malicious and carefully observed. This makes them a considerable pleasure to read.

Insisting on seeing the papers, the podgy man is then observed with a series of what we might now call close-up details. "He seemed struggling with some hidden excitement. His neck swelled and flushed, he closed his mouth until it was a mere slit across his face, and rocked slightly on his toes." After Charles has shown him the papers, the man says, "'You may go now,' with the insulting condescension of a petty official dismissing a subordinate." In the next sentence we learn that "they continued to look at him in a hateful silence, with their faces almost comically distorted in an effort to convey the full depths of their malice." Notice how, again, a silence is being drawn out and how this silence is not peaceful but hateful. It is a hateful silence. Notate your silences if you can. Fully expressive silences are by no means easy to create in fictional narrative. Finally, after Charles has left the hotel under their "fixed stare," he hears, "as the door closed behind him," the two of them laughing "together like a pair of hyenas, with deliberate loudness, to make certain he should hear them."

The cruelty here, and the malice, is very great indeed, and it's marked by all its small details of gesture, speech, and gratuitous meanness. But cruelty, as Henry James and Katherine Anne Porter knew, is increased and intensified by shades of detail. Cruelty often lives off small signs and hints, closed rather than open doors. Cruelty is not increased by brutality but is *diminished* by it. Cruelty and brutality are two different things. One is gestural, and the other one isn't. Brutality makes everything easy—easy to respond to, easy to judge. Subtle cruelty, by contrast, as we all know, is a web meant to catch you in a couple of different directions and to keep you hanging as you are punished by small but incremental wounds. Brutality is rather common, and true cruelty is rather uncommon. You might say that Katherine Anne Porter's scene demonstrates the effective malice of indirection, of cruelty slowly turning *into* brutality. She shows you, as clearly as she can, exactly how these people are signaling what they feel. The scene is intensely alive on all counts. Despite its great literary qualities, it feels immediate. No Dinosaur World zombie effect here.

Another means of combating the zombie effect appears in Eudora Welty's "A Visit of Charity." The ground situation in this story is quite straightforward: Marian, a junior high Campfire Girl, has been assigned to take a flower to a retirement home for old ladies and to sit there and chat for a while. This visit of charity is part of the procedure for Marian's earning of a merit badge. Simple enough.

I think I should stop here and say that this ground situation is not particularly promising, and in our own time old ladies and old men have become objects of commonplace writerly pathos. There is no place like a retirement home or a hospital to turn up the needle on the pathos meter. Running into a scene in an old-folks home is like meeting a bully at the end of an alley. It preprograms your responses. And I should know; I've used such places myself for those purposes. But it's hard to get *real* feelings, as opposed to preprogrammed ones, out of those settings now, in a work of fiction. If you locate a scene in a retirement home or a hospital without flipping it or defamiliarizing it in some way, every reader knows that his or her assignment is to feel sad and to weep dutifully. But when you know your assignment, you tend to resist it.

But what Eudora Welty does in this story is to upset the expected tone of the story so that pathos is a minor element. Instead, there is a kind of dry wit at work, not pitiless but in the service of genuine but very dark compassion and understanding, and this dry comedy moves the proceedings in the direction of what I will call, for the sake of brevity, the abyss. Suddenly, the mystery of existence opens up in front of Marian and the reader. Eudora Welty does all this by carefully inflecting every moment of the scene. After a few pages Marian's old ladies stop being pitiful creatures, old Southern ladies down on their luck, and seem more like Samuel Beckett's tramps, Vladimir and Estragon, in *Waiting for Godot,* struggling with time itself.

The reader is given, moment by moment, very careful and close direction and detailing of the scene. Notice that this *is* a scene and is *not* summarized. Marian has walked into the room with her gift of the potted plant. There are two old ladies in the room, one lying down and one standing up. The one who is standing up has a "terrible square smile stamped on her bony face." Think of that: a *terrible* square smile. We're not told what makes it terrible. Nor are we told exactly how to visualize it. It seems contradictory. Her hand, "quick as a bird claw," grabs at Marian's cap. The room is dark and dank, and Marian starts to think of the old ladies as robbers and the room as the robbers' cave: "'Did you come to be our little girl for a while?' the first robber asked." The plant is snatched out of Marian's hand.

"Flowers!" screamed the old woman. She stood holding the pot in an undecided way. "Pretty flowers," she added.

Then the old woman in bed cleared her throat and spoke. "They are not pretty," she said, still without looking around, but very distinctly.

After the first old woman repeats that the flowers are pretty, the old woman who is lying down says in return, batting the ball back, that the flowers are "stinkweed." So much for nice old ladies. Somewhat disarmingly, the old woman in bed is described as having a bunchy white forehead and red eyes like a sheep. When she asks Marian, "Who are you?" the line is interrupted by dashes to indicate slowness of speech, and the author tells us that the words rise like fog in her throat and that the words are "bleated." In the direction of a line of dialogue, you can't get more specific than this.

We learn that the woman in bed is named "Addie." Addie and her unnamed old companion then commence to have an argument about a previous visitor and whether they had enjoyed that visit. Triangulated by the two ladies, Marian, the Campfire Girl, begins, very mildly, to hallucinate, to go off into the hallucinations of ordinary life created by the scene before her. At this point Addie and the other old lady have a surrealistic discussion about who is sick and who is not and who did what as a child. The standing woman speaks in an "intimate, menacing" voice, another unusual combination. This is interrupted by Addie's first long speech. It is directed, interestingly, toward both her roommate and, I think, obliquely to Marian. Notice how the author gets out of the way here and lets the speech speak for itself.

"Hush!" said the sick woman. "You never went to school. You never came and you never went. You never were anything—only here. You never were born! You don't know anything. Your head is empty, your heart and hands and your old black purse are all empty, even that little old box that you brought with you you brought empty—you showed it to me. And yet you talk, talk, talk, talk, talk all the time until I think I'm losing my mind! Who are you? You're a stranger—a perfect stranger! Don't you know that you're a stranger? Is it possible that they have actually done a thing like this to anyone— sent them a stranger to talk, and rock, and tell away her whole long rigmarole? Do they seriously suppose that I'll be able to keep it up, day out, night in, night out, living in the same room with a terrible old woman—forever?"

At the end of this speech the author notes that Addie turns her eyes toward Marian, eyes that have gone bright. "This old woman," the author notes, "was looking at her with despair and calculation in her face." We then get an image of her false teeth and tan gums. "Come here, I want to tell you something," she whispered. "Come here." Marian is frightened, we're told, and her heart nearly stops beating for a moment. Then Addie's companion says, "Now, now, Addie. That's not polite."

This scene, I would argue, is packed, completely layered, with seemingly contradictory emotions: Marian's fascination and terror, Addie's despair and calculation, her companion's fake sentimentality and cynicism—the scene is a mixture of despairing comedy, pathos, terror, and metaphysical giddiness. These elements are built into Addie's speech through the use of repetition of words like *empty, talk* and *stranger* and the use of carefully deployed dashes and pauses. And they are then cemented by the brilliant inflection tag following the speech, noting that Addie is now turning toward Marian with despair *and* calculation on her face. Please note this. Addie is not feeling one thing. She is feeling several emotions at once. One of them makes her pitiable, the other makes her dangerous. We then learn that today happens to be Addie's birthday.

As if this weren't enough, when Marian leaves, the nameless woman (the other half of this terrible octogenarian vaudeville team) who has been playing the straight woman to Addie's riffs of calculation and despair, this nameless woman then goes into a riff of her own. "In an affected, high-pitched whine she cried, 'Oh, little girl, have you a penny to spare for a poor old woman that's not got anything of her own? We don't have a thing in the world—not a penny for candy—not a thing! Little girl, just a nickel—a penny—.'"

The "affected, high-pitched whine" notation tells us that this woman may have fallen into a moment of senile dementia. Or, more likely, she may be playing a role for her own amusement to scare and disconcert Marian, maybe even to get some money out of her. You simply can't tell. And that's the way the author seems to want it—your uncertainty parallels the uncertainty that Marian must feel. You can see clearly and distinctly what you see, but *you simply can't be sure of what you're looking at.*

This transcendently wonderful scene worries me. It worries me because I think it's true, moving, beautiful, and funny. And yet it worries me because I think that if it were brought into a writing workshop, someone or other might accuse it of being "unfair" to old women or "mean-spirited" or, even worse, "ageist." Why? Because it doesn't reinforce an orthodoxy: it doesn't reinforce what we are *supposed* to feel about the old, namely, that we are expected to pity them and to love or admire them more than we usually do. Nor does Eudora Welty's scene mock them, which would also be easy and shallow. In some sense the scene has no *social* purpose at all. It has another purpose altogether in mind. It presents these women, as Samuel Beckett presents his tramps, with all the complexity of art, of realism flying off into the metaphysical and then flying back, flipping and inflecting the scene until it's so layered that you cannot describe the scene's feeling tone in one word. You can't do that. It's impossible. What's going on with the two old ladies, triangulated by Marian, is too complicated for that.

There is much to be said for the uses to which the opposite—an uninflected voice—may be put. There may well be certain justifications for what might be called zombie voicings in literature, a deliberate tonal blank-out. Certainly it's notable in Kathryn Harrison's recent memoir, *The Kiss,* and in virtually all the work of the novelists Craig Nova and

Rudy Wurlitzer. And this tone of blank uninflected death-in-life is put to interesting use in Tim O'Brien's recent novel *In the Lake of the Woods,* though just in the main body of that text, not in the footnotes. There is a certain Dinosaur World narration effect all the way through O'Brien's novel, and I think, oddly enough, that it often works, given the subject of that book, which happens to be posttraumatic stress disorder. There is something about uninflectedness that suits trauma very well.

What can be bothersome about uninflectedness from the last two decades generally, however, is that it can seem like a decadent form of hipsterism, a retro form of cool, of being removed, which can harden into a posture. Against middle-class fake sincerity, fake patriotism, and fake fervor of every sort, uninflectedness and ironic withdrawal, at least since World War II, have been deployed massively and effectively in every form of postmodern art. It is, however, now completely mainstream. The trouble with uninflectedness is that, because it is an attitude, it has a tendency to be inflexible. And this, it strikes me, is what has happened to some otherwise interesting contemporary writers who shall go nameless here, whose work sometimes seems to be trapped in the effort to turn attitude into subject matter (a fault, I might add, of a certain percentage of Ernest Hemingway's work).

The guide at Dinosaur World was at pains to demonstrate that he was above what he was saying, detached from it, *better* than it. And so he was. But as triumphs go, this is a very minor one and, in its way, is as much a miscalculation as overacting would be.

In his recent memoir, *Crabcakes,* James Alan McPherson describes a moment during which he listens to two African Americans flirting with each other. Then he remarks:

> The kindly flirtation between the two of them reminds me of something familiar that I have almost forgotten. It seems to be something shadowy, about language being secondary to the way it is used. The forgotten thing is about the nuances of sounds that only employ words as ballast for the flight of pitch and intonation. It is the pitch, and the intonation, that carries *meaning*. I had forgotten this.

Nabokov once said that the price of being a writer was sleepless nights. But, Nabokov added slyly, if the writer doesn't have sleepless nights, how can he hope to cause sleepless nights in anyone else? If the writer doesn't indicate interest in the story through inflection, how can she expect the reader to be interested and willingly suspend disbelief? To close the book or finish the poem and to say, "You're really *something*"?

Exercises

1. Write two scenes in which the same sentence is inflected differently, so that it means one thing in the first scene and has the opposite meaning in the second scene.

2. Write a scene with dialogue in which emphasis and repetition substitute for eloquence.

3. Write a scene in which crucial moments of dialogue are "flipped," that is, given an inflection that seems to go against the way they would customarily be said or spoken.

DEBRA SPARK

Getting In and Getting Out
First Words on First (and Last) Words

First memories, last words. When my sister was dying, we all told each other our first memories. Who knows why? I was the one who instigated it. I made everyone in the hospital room tell their story. I offered my sister's—since I happened to know it, and she had already spoken her last words. Her memory was of throwing a pair of maracas on the floor and being surprised to see beans spill out. So *that* was what made the sound. The memory that most startled me—perhaps because it replicated my current situation, beginning and ending in the same moment, the family crowded around the bed of the dying—was my grandmother's. Her first memory was of trying to stick her head between the many adult legs that surrounded her younger sister's crib, of reaching up to pull a toy from the blankets. But she was scolded away, for the baby was dead. I hadn't known, till that moment, that my grandmother had had a younger sister.

Of course we are alive before our first memories, and we survive, often enough, for a while past our last words, but, even for the nonliterary type, these markers seem like life's bookends, undeniably significant.

And as it is with life, so it is with fiction. We expect a lot from our openings and closings, more than from the rest of the lines we write. One might ask why. Why should firsts and lasts matter more than everything in the middle? Of course, this is an easier question to answer for fiction than for life. The opening is what entices a reader into a work. It doesn't matter how great the middle and end are if the reader never gets there, and the end is what the reader is left with, an impression of the whole that, ideally, resonates long after the book is closed.

A writer friend tells me that she once read that closings stick in a reader's short-term memory and openings in a reader's long-term memory. I'm not sure what this means for the overall experience of a story, but invert the wisdom, and I'm reminded that all *my* real lessons about writing came from my elders and were about cocktail parties. Rule number one: It's always nice to make a good first impression, to handle

From the *AWP Chronicle* 29, no. 6 (May 1997).

yourself well for the short-term of the evening. Rule number two: It's always nice to depart before you make an ass of yourself, to leave a favorable long-term impression.

And even these rules chafe. What rules don't when it comes to writing? We're all more or less mystics about what works and what doesn't and how to do what it is we do. That said, there are some generalizations one can make about openings and closings, a few eminently breakable rules that—when considered in light of specific examples—might serve as inspiration to those struggling to start or finish their work.

But, first, a story about something that helped me in my own thinking about beginnings and writing:

When I was in graduate school, I had a friend, Michelle, whose job it was to screen manuscripts for the Iowa Short Fiction Prize. At the time, I had a job ghostwriting health textbooks for junior high school students. While I was busily typing up paragraphs on the dangers of smoking, she was lying on her bed and reading book after book of stories. Of course, I was jealous. I thought reading stories and getting paid for it was just my kind of job . . . and yet it was hers. When I was with Michelle, I liked to tell her how lucky she was to be snuggling up to all that fiction.

"No, no, no," she told me, on more than one occasion. "It's not what you think it is, Debra. If I have to read one more story that begins, 'The alarm clock rang,' I'll shoot myself."

"Oh, come on," I said. Michelle was given to hyperbole.

"No, seriously," she insisted. Half the stories she read started this way.

I don't know that I would have thought of this conversation again if not for the fact that I finally got a job I wanted. In my second year of graduate school I taught a fiction writing class. One evening, early in the semester, I went home, all eager, to read my first batch of student papers. I turned to the first story, and, sure enough, there, at the top of the page, were the words "The alarm clock rang."

Of course, I laughed.

Just as I laughed the other day when I asked Don Lee, the editor of *Ploughshares,* if he had any advice about openings to stories. "Oh, you know," he said, somewhat tiredly. "No sunlight through the window. No alarm clocks. No transit stories about meeting stupid people on the bus. No hangovers."

Apparently, not much has changed in the fiction world since I was a graduate student. Back then, though, when I was a novice teacher, I wanted to understand why the alarm clock opening was so ubiquitous. Why would so many people start a story with this particular cliché? The answer was fairly obvious. If you don't know when your story begins, you simply start at the beginning of the day of the story. Better, of course, to start with the story itself. I wrote a note to my student, something to this effect, and turned to the next paper.

But later I thought about some of the stories I've most loved and realized that many don't start when the story begins, anymore than they start at daybreak. Instead, they begin in the middle, once a great deal of action has already taken place.

I asked my friend, the writer Steve Stern, if he had anything smart to say about how a story opens, and he sighed, presumably at the paucity of his knowledge, and said, "Well, only that old bromide. You know, how the story has to be in motion when you start and then you can sneak around to the back door and fill in with whatever expository material you need."

Now, plenty of good stories *don't* start in the middle of things, but ever since Horace this "begin in the middle" advice has been a mainstay of writerly wisdom. Alice Munro adheres to it when she opens "Miles City, Montana" with the line "My father came across the field carrying the body of the boy who had been drowned." Clearly, this is an in media res opening, since, before the story even starts, a boy has been drowned, and the narrator's father has gone to retrieve the body and has started back. Part of our expectation of a good story has to do with how much has already happened—there's so much to be explained; we're interested in all that expository material that is going to be introduced through the back door. But we're interested in the future as well. If this much has already happened, if we already have a drowned boy and a father trying to save that boy, what could possibly be next?

As storytellers, we imagine the best question we can be asked is "And then what? What happened next?" In this way we're all closet Scheherazades. But we're also all would-be analysts and nosy ones at that. We want to know what happened before, what in the past explains what is before us in the present. Consider the opening of Cynthia Ozick's "Rosa": "Rosa Lublin, a madwoman and a scavenger, gave up her store—she smashed it up herself—and moved to Miami."

Madwoman, scavenger. What's happened that Rosa is characterized this way? And *smashed it up herself.* What's that all about? The in media res opening appeals to our gossipy selves. It makes us ask snooping questions, and it promises answers . . . if we'll only read on.

But what makes Ozick's opening effective is more than its in media res status. The authority of the writing, the intensity of the information, and the very queerness of the details intrigue.

And, of course, one of the bad things about "the alarm clock rang" opening is that it's boring, overly familiar. No surprise, then, that many openings succeed by opting for the unfamiliar, if only for a moment.

The writer Eberle Umbach has a story that starts, "The flesh opened in pink folds." She's describing the carving of a ham, but at first you don't know that. You jump at the image then check the cover of your high-minded literary magazine. A metamorphosis? When did it turn into *Playboy?*

The writer Elizabeth Searle notes that a lot of fine openings have the virtue of the carving-a-ham line; they make you think, "Wait. That can't be right." They offer a moment of confusion that is interesting rather than discouraging.

Stuart Dybek opens "Hot Ice" by writing, "The saint, a virgin, was incorrupted. She had been frozen in a block of ice many years ago." And Louise Erdrich begins "Saint Marie" by saying, "So when I went there, I knew the dark fish must rise." Your second reaction to these lines may be, "Oh, intriguing image," but your first, your immediate, reaction is probably, "Huh?"

Certainly, the first words of Robert Olen Butler's "A Strange Scent from a Good Mountain" are a puzzle: "Ho Chi Minh came to me again last night, his hands covered with confectioners' sugar."

How can you *not* love that? The wild image of the famed leader with sugar on his hands, so ordinary a detail, is almost magical in this context. And what a strange sentence. He "came to me." Well, who are you? And what do you mean that he "came" to you? And then there's that small word *again*. This, too, is a "middle of things" story, for apparently Ho Chi Minh has been visiting regularly. This story has a history with . . . well . . . History. And finally there are the words *last night*. That's the kind of small phrase that orients the reader, economically and effectively. The "now" of the story is "this morning," the morning after "last night," and the speaker is ready to tell us all about it.

Often enough, slightly curious sentences deliver an image or line so fantastic that we feel the promise of a good story ahead. That same sense of promise can be given in a line that isn't initially confusing, can be given because a character is so startling or insistent or passionately presented that we can't help but want to stay with him or her. Consider Mona Simpson's short story "Lawns." The story begins with two easy-to-understand words: *I steal.*

"My God," says the writer Jessica Treadway of this opening sentence, "who *wouldn't* want to read on?" What could be next? And what can we expect of the kind of a person who would say something like this about herself?

And what can we expect of the self-conscious narrator of James Alan McPherson's "The Story of a Scar"?

Since Dr. Wayland was late and there were no recent newsmagazines in the waiting room, I turned to the other patient and said: "As a concerned person, and as your brother, I ask you, without meaning to offend, how did you get that scar on the side of your face?"

The woman seemed insulted. Her brown eyes, which before had been wandering vacuously around the room, narrowed suddenly and sparked humbling reprimands at me.

With the McPherson opening, the very energy of the telling is as much a goad to further reading as the prickly relationship established in the second paragraph and the sense that there's an interesting story about the characters' respective injuries.

And here we're back to my cocktail party theory of writing, which is that the pretzels can be stale, the wine can be Mad Dog, but you've still got a good gathering if the energy is right. Honest, unforced emotion of any stripe is always interesting, and immediate emotion, as much as anything else, plunges us into a story.

Joel [Margaret Atwood writes at the opening of her story "Uglypuss"] hates November. As far as he's concerned they could drop it down the chute and he wouldn't complain. Drizzle and chill, everyone depressed, and then the winter to go through afterwards. The landlord had turned down the heat again, which means Joel has to either let his buns solidify and break off or use the electric heater, which means more money, because the electricity's extra. The landlord does this to spite him, Joel, personally. Just for that, Joel refuses to move.

Already Joel sounds like an Uglypuss himself, but we don't need to like Joel to be engaged in his thoughts. Indeed, we may feel, right away, that he's going to teach us something about the inner life of a crank like him, and the way in which the narrator, à la Joyce, adopts the manner of speech of Joel—"drop it down the chute," "let his buns solidify and break off"—makes the story feel as "in your face" as we must imagine Joel is.

Beyond this advice about beginning in the middle, intriguing with momentary confusion and aiming for passion, what else can we say about openings? We can observe that sometimes the world really does bead itself in a drop of dew, that the germ of the whole story may be in the initial part.

Rust Hills, the fiction editor of *Esquire* and the author of *Writing in General and the Short Story in Particular,* claims, "What the beginning of a short story *should* do, what the beginnings of most successful modern short stories usually do, is begin to state the theme of the story right from the very first line."

Now to judge how well a beginning does this, you'd have to read the whole story, but I think you can get an *idea* of theme from the first line of a story like David Quammen's "Walking Out": "As the train rocked dead at Livingston he saw the man, in a worn khaki shirt with button flaps buttoned, arms crossed."

What you can guess here about "theme" is that there's something significant about the tight way this man is holding himself, that the phrase *rocked dead* has some import and that it makes a difference that this is a train coming in, since we know the title of the story is "Walking Out."

You can also get an idea of theme from the first line of Bernard Malamud's "The Last Mohican": "Fidelman, a self-confessed failure as a painter, came to Italy to prepare a critical study of Giotto, the opening chapter of which he had carried across the ocean in a new pigskin-leather briefcase, now gripped in his perspiring hand."

The ironies here are a clue to what the writer is eventually going to touch on. We can presume that Fidelman is the name of a Jew, so what's he doing with a "pigskin-leather briefcase"? That's hardly kosher. Clearly, his relationship to his own tradition is a bit shaky. Or really more than a bit shaky because his chosen subject of study is Giotto, the great Christian painter, a subject with which (presumably) he doesn't have a pure relationship, an honest feeling. And what do we make of the fact that Fidelman is that academic cliché, the failed artist who becomes a critic? The story ends, indeed, with a poor Jew quoting Tolstoy and asking, "Why is art?" The answer, the revelation that Fidelman has in the final moments of the story, is that art, as Tolstoy says, is the means of transferring feeling from one man's heart to another, and, for the first time, Fidelman understands why his Giotto project is so very misguided.

Theme in Malamud is clearly stated from the very first line, but I don't think that you should, therefore, use Hills's advice as a rule but as a potential source of inspiration. Theme, as Flannery O'Connor has said, isn't something you can simply "add" to your story, like calcium to orange juice, to make it better. But a first line can, as the writer Elizabeth Searle says, be like a seed, a whole story can come out of it. Sometimes, once you have found the right first line, you've found your story.

The title story of Searle's collection *My Body to You* starts with the line, "Above me, a boy is trying to guess my sex." The scene she is describing takes place in the subway. The speaker is seated, "the boy" hanging on a pole by her. Now there's definitely something off in that line. It does seem to be the opening to a story that's starting in the middle of things. What Elizabeth says about the sentence is that it helped her discover what her story was about. From the start she had the line "A boy is trying to guess my sex," but things didn't take off till she added the words *above me.* And even then she spent a lot of time shifting things around, trying to figure out where to put that new phrase.

A boy above me is trying to guess my sex.
OK, but the first half of the sentence seems less strong than the second half.

A boy is trying to guess my sex above me.
Not grammatical. What's that *above me* supposed to modify?

Above me, a boy is trying to guess my sex.

All that time spent shifting the phrase around helped Searle figure out that the story she was writing was about her female narrator and the position of that woman's body in relation to others. So, in the end, her first line helped her discover her story, discover its theme and some of its content. Which is a lot of good work for one sentence.

For many writers closings are harder to do than openings. The difference between potential and realized potential. At the start of life saying "Da-da" and "Ma-ma" is an accomplishment, and simply to have a first memory is valuable; we don't expect ourselves to have a significant first memory. But we do expect something out of last words, something that will make the life that is lapsing, as well as Life in general, less of a mystery. We want, in short, our ends to have meaning, or, if that sounds too grand, we want our endings to make some sense of what has come before. The convention is that a closing will tie together the body of the story by offering an image or thought or final piece of information that gives one last, perspective-enhancing look on what has just happened.

In his letters Anton Chekhov wrote, "My instinct tells me that at the end of a story or a novel, I must artfully concentrate for the reader an impression of the entire work, and therefore must casually mention something about those whom I have already presented. Perhaps I am in error."

Now this modest statement comes from a man who holds that fiction needn't answer questions, only pose them, from a man who gave his characters, as Grace Paley might say, "the open destiny of life." Indeed, Nabokov noted that a Chekhov story "does not really end, for as long as people are alive, there is no possible and definite conclusion to their troubles or hopes or dreams."

All this would seem to make closure less of a problem. The story needs only an "impression," not an unnatural resolution, not a gravity-defying epiphany. What's more, the end doesn't need to be The End.

But it's more complicated than that, for Chekhov specified that the impression is to be "of the entire work." Rust Hills, in *Writing in General and the Short Story in Particular,* insists that one of the two requirements for short fiction is that the whole fit to the part and that the part fit to the whole. Till you get to the end of a story, the jury is essentially out on whether the piece has satisfied this requirement—which puts a fair amount of pressure on the end to do what (conceivably) the story itself has yet to do. As a less compressed form, novels aren't under as much pressure when it comes to the close, though I'm not quite sure I'd go as far as the writer Josip Novakavich, who contends, "With novels, while it's essential to resolve the conflicts you raise, frequently the last page does not matter much—it is a kind of exit two-step jig."

I thought I'd make the point about the pressures that are on an ending, particularly the pressures to answer for the body of the story, by describing an accomplished story that I don't like: T. Coraghessan Boyle's "Killing Babies," which appeared in the 2 December 1996 issue of the *New Yorker.* I always struggle when I think about Boyle's work, because he is an undeniable talent: a dazzling wordsmith, a fine satirist, an engaging, playful storyteller. Yet his work, though it entertains me in the beginning and middle, often irritates me in the end. "Killing Babies" is a perfect example of this; it's a reconfigured Cain and Abel story. The bad brother is Rick, recently out of rehab and staying with his "good" brother, Philip, a physician who lives with his wife and two children outside of Detroit. Both men veer toward clichés: Rick is the misbehaving addict whose ease at dismissing things doesn't mean he has a better idea about how to live his life, and Philip is your classic, uptight suburbanite. His face—we are told—is "trenched with anal retentive misery." Only Philip happens to work at an abortion clinic—perhaps the good doctor is not so conventional, after all?

Early in his stay with Philip, Rick learns that Philip's clinic and home are targets for right-wing anti-abortion protesters. When Philip takes his addict brother with him to work, Rick is enraged, but also clearly excited, by the fatuousness he sees in the protesters and by the nobility he imagines he sees in Sally, a young woman who forces herself through the crowd, presumably for an abortion.

As the story proceeds, Rick's anger at the protesters and his interest in

Sally, whom he has only glimpsed once, grow out of control. Rick says of the young woman that her look was "so poignant and so everlastingly sad I knew I'd never have another moment's rest till I took hold of it." Finally, Rick—high on whatever drugs he's been able to steal from his brother's supply closet—steps out of the clinic's front door and into a crowd of protesters, a group of fanatics draped over the building's entrance. Rick concludes:

> The light was burning in my head, and it was all I needed. I reached into my pants and pulled out the gun. I could have anointed any one of them, but the woman was first. I bent to her where she lay on the unyielding concrete of the steps and touched that snub-nose to her ear as tenderly as any man of healing. The noise of it shut down Jesus, shut him down cold. Into the silence, and it was the hardware man next. Then I swung round on Mr. Beard.
> It was easy. It was nothing. Just like killing babies.

And so the story ends with a twist on the right-wing view of things: abortion isn't murder, but murder is "merely" abortion. What is shooting people but killing babies? Adults, after all, are only babies with some years on them.

In Boyle's story, at the moment when, as a reader, you expect revelation or truth or something transcendent, you get just the opposite: no revelation, no truth. Instead, the story closes with a descendental, anti-ethical moment—which may be precisely T. C. Boyle's strategy; he's a postmodernist, resisting the modernist demand for meaning, but it is precisely why for all his prodigious talent, his stylistic skill, I find his stories so very frustrating. In the end it feels he has nothing to say and believes there is nothing to say. Irony is an end in itself. That's the favorable reading of Boyle. The unfavorable one is that he doesn't know how to pull it off, that he doesn't know how to end his story—to resolve the intriguing complication of Sally, to finish the tale of the brothers—that if he could figure out something equal to all the great balls he's thrown up in the air, he'd catch them. Which is, I think, a clue to why endings are so hard for us. We don't know what to make of our own great material.

An unrelated example: years ago I was in an undergraduate writing workshop. A man in the class handed in the first half of a story. No one had ever done this before—submitted an incomplete work—but we forgave him for we were quite taken with the fragment we got. It was about a photographer, long unemployed, presumably because of a dark depression, who spends nights listening to the police radio. One night a fire is reported, and the man pulls himself out of his slump to go photograph it. When he develops his film, he discovers that every other shot on the contact sheet is Ansel Adams's famous photograph "Moonrise over Hernandez."

"Cool," we all said to him. How would it turn out? We professed ourselves uniformly eager for the next installment. Which never came. The student writer slipped into his own malaise, writing nothing for the rest of the semester and, as far as I know, for the rest of his life. The student's curious idea about the contact sheet had done him in. He'd painted himself into a corner with his very skill. This is, I suppose, my criticism of Boyle's end. That he paints himself into a corner and then tries to jump over all that wet paint with a bit of outrageousness that shocks but doesn't satisfy.

All this means, what? That we should paint in the other direction, to the easy escape route, the door? That we should be less wild and ambitious with our material? But this hardly seems like good advice. Perhaps endings simply require more patience than the other parts of the story. In speaking about endings, Elizabeth Searle says, "The end has to hit you." She means, the end is a matter of inspiration. It has to come to you. You can't fake it. It's like a title in that way; it is, more than other parts of the story, something that is less worked for than received. But, she adds, once you've been hit, you can write toward the end.

Steve Stern echoes this piece of advice when he speaks of his own writing process: "I get the image that resolves a story before I get the story itself. Everything else is a retroactive process, a story that culminates in that image." He goes on to explain how this worked in his short story "Aaron Makes a Match." He had the idea, he says, of

a boy whose aunt was dying and her soul was trying to escape from her body, and her body was hanging on, and I knew this kid would help the soul escape. That would be his gift to his aunt, but I didn't know why any of this was happening and what there was between the boy and his aunt that would make this gesture resolve whatever dynamic there was between them.

To list strategies for ending a story may be less helpful than it is for openings, since a list of strategies begs the larger question of inspiration, of how to understand your own story, how to discover what you mean to say. That said, in general, when we think of effective closings, we think of a resonant final image or a powerful thought or a "killer" line. Or we think of some combination of these three.

John Cheever's "The Country Husband" ends in a suburban yard with this paragraph:

"Here, pussy, here, poor pussy!" But the cat gives her a skeptical look and stumbles away in its skirts. The last to come is Jupiter. He prances through the tomato vines, holding in his generous mouth the remains of an evening slipper. Then it is dark; it is a night where kings in golden suits ride elephants over the mountains.

Who knows what that final image means? I sure don't, but I love it, love how suddenly porous my skin feels when I read it, love the sense that the world—this very world with its scavenging cats and workaday vegetation—opens, and opens readily, easily, to contain this mysterious image.

A less puzzling, but equally impressive, final image comes from Amy Hempel's "In the Garden Where Al Jolson Is Buried." The narrator of this story goes to the hospital to visit her best friend. As close as the friends have been, the narrator has not come before, for she is unable to cope with her friend's terminal illness. What's more, during her single visit, the narrator tries to deflect emotion with humor and trivia. But this suits her friend just fine. Indeed, the story opens with the ill friend saying, "Tell me things I won't mind forgetting. Make it useless stuff or skip it."

So the narrator responds, "Did you know when they taught the first chimp to talk, it lied? When they asked her who did it on the desk, she signed back Max, the janitor."

The ill friend laughs but declines to hear more, since the narrator says the rest of the story "will break your heart."

Later, much later, at the story's conclusion, when the friend has died, the narrator finishes off the chimp story. First, though, the narrator confesses that, in her state of extreme grief, she can't think clearly. She remembers nothing—or she only remembers trivia, "things that she won't mind forgetting." Otherwise, nothing, nothing true, reaches her until she thinks of the chimp with talking hands. And then Hempel concludes with this combination of image and thought:

> In the course of the experiment, the chimp had a baby. Imagine how her trainers must have been thrilled when the mother, without prompting, began to sign to the newborn. Baby, drink milk. Baby, play ball. And when the baby died, the mother stood over the body, her wrinkled hands moving with animal grace, forming again and again the words, Baby, come hug, Baby, come hug, fluent now in the language of grief.

What the narrator had earlier promised is true; the chimp story does break our hearts. The conclusion ties the piece together. Till the end, everything in the story has been either a metaphor for injury or a bit of trivia, but the final bit of trivia embraces the very thing that the narrator cannot: her own terrible emotions. And as sad as the end is, it has, I think, some of the same largeness as the Cheever close. There's the same sense of the story opening up, in its final moments, to how enormous things are, in this case, how enormously painful.

Robert Olen Butler's "A Good Scent from a Strange Mountain" uses a resonant line and something like an olfactory image to achieve a similar effect. When "A Good Scent" opens, the story's Buddhist narrator is at the end of a long life and is being visited nightly by Ho Chi Minh's ghost. Years earlier the narrator worked in a pastry kitchen with Ho Chi Minh. Now Ho Chi Minh's ghost is unable to rest, because he cannot remember how to make a glaze, a recipe he learned in that pastry kitchen. Much else happens in this wonderful story—it's criminal for me to reduce it this way—but the piece finishes up with these words from the narrator:

> I know now what it is that he [Ho Chi Minh] has forgotten. He has used confectioners' sugar for his glaze fondant and he should be using granulated sugar. I was only a washer of dishes but I did listen carefully when Monsieur Escoffier spoke. I wanted to understand everything. His kitchen was full of such smells that you knew you had to understand everything or you would be incomplete forever.

Perhaps the reason I so love this line is it says the opposite of what the T. C. Boyle "Killing Babies" close seems to say: "It all counts. Everything makes a difference. It's all important."

For this affirmation the Butler story is, I think, as political as it is spiritual. The critic Jan Clausen says that political fiction is not fiction that elaborates, necessarily, on what's going on in Bosnia and the like but fiction that reminds us that what happens to humans matters and matters desperately. Even endings that show people going on with their lives, virtually dismissing the story's main character, do this. When Kafka closes "The Metamorphosis," Gregor isn't even in the picture. And here is the end of V. S. Naipaul's *A House for Mr. Biswas*, the lengthy depiction of a life in which Mr. Biswas's desire for a home becomes symbolic of his desire for an independent identity:

> The cremation, one of the few permitted by the Health Department, was conducted on the banks of a muddy stream and attracted spectators of various races. Afterwards the sisters returned to their respective homes and Shama and the children went back in the Prefect to the empty house.

Both Kafka and Naipaul's final lines seem to declare the superfluity of the characters we've been engaged with. It's as if, with the endings, the narrator has said, as Carol Shields does say in the final line of her novel *The Stone Diaries,* "Ah, well." But it's a dismissive expression we don't, as readers, share in, and that's part of its strength. We don't forget the ignored or forgotten. The large cockroach, mad Mr. Biswas—they stay with us. They make themselves matter and make us, as a result, matter too.

"Bring stones," Harriet Doerr writes when she closes her novel *Stones for Ibarra,* and the command is directed toward memory. Don't forget. This meant something. This all meant something.

And it doesn't matter that we can't quite articulate what that something is, for the best endings seem to be barely contained by the words in which they are expressed. They feel bigger than mere words; they practically transcend themselves on the page. And the words' ability to slip out of their own skins may have to do with accumulated meaning rather than beauty of expression. For example, Roddy Doyle's novel *Paddy Clarke Ha Ha Ha* ends with a relatively simple passage. Paddy Clarke's father—his da—has left his mother but returned for a holiday visit. The concluding scene takes place at the door to the house:

> He saw me.
> —Patrick, he said.
> He moved the parcels he had with him under one arm and put his hand out.
> —How are you? he said.
> He put his hand out for me to shake it.
> —How are you?
> His hand felt cold and big, dry and hard.
> —Very well, thank you.

I cried at that final line, and there's no accounting for my fat tears, unless you've read the whole book and seen what a masterful portrayal of boyhood it is and seen how Paddy—a sharp, funny, curious, cruel but wonderfully observant and sensitive boy—has for himself only one wish: not to care about what happens around him, not to care about the fights between his ma and da, not to feel everything so profoundly. And it seems, horribly, with that formal final line to his father, that line that is such a lie, that Paddy has, in fact, been granted his desire. He's becoming hardened to the world. The story ends not with a revelation, exactly, but a transformation, a shift the reader can't welcome, even if it feels inevitable.

And we see these transformations at the end of the best fiction. One variant of this transformation often appears at the close of coming of age stories, like James Joyce's "Araby," Frank O'Connor's "The Guests of the Nation," and John Updike's "A&P." In all these stories the concluding transformation is violent and wrenching, and there is a frank acknowledgment of it as the story ends. "And anything that ever happened to me after," says Frank O'Connor's young Irish soldier-narrator, "I never felt the same about again."

The "largeness" of so many final transformations is often accompanied by a startling intimacy, as if, just before the illusion ends, the writer wants to remind readers that, by sheer virtue of being human, they participate in the conclusion. Certainly, this is what seems to happen in the famous final paragraph of James Joyce's "The Dead":

> A few light taps upon the pane made him turn to the window. It had begun to snow again. He watched sleepily the flakes, silver and dark, falling obliquely toward the lamplight. The time had come for him to set out on his journey westward. Yes, the newspapers were right; snow was general all over Ireland. It was falling on every part of the dark central plain, on the treeless hills, falling upon the Bog of Allen and, farther westward, softly falling into the dark mutinous Shannon waves. It was falling, too, upon every part of the lonely churchyard on the hill where Michael Furey lay buried. It lay thickly drifted on the crooked crosses and headstones, on the spears of the little gate, on the barren thorns. His soul swooned slowly as he heard the snow falling faintly through the universe and faintly falling, like the descent of their last end, upon all the living and the dead.

In her essay about "The Dead" Mary Gordon analyzes the images in this final paragraph and notes how everything is distinctly separate but still subject to the general snow, then she concludes her thoughts with praise for Joyce's final line. "Consider," she writes,

> the daring of Joyce's final repetitions and reversals: "falling faintly, faintly falling"—a pure triumph of pure sound, of language as music. No one has ever equaled it; it makes those who have come after him pause for a minute, in awed gratitude, in discouragement. How can any of us come up to it? Only, perhaps, humbly, indifferently, in its honor and its name, to try.

And he did it all when he was twenty-five. The bastard.

A funny close for an essay, I think. And a wise one, for who would chide Mary Gordon for her professional jealousy? After all, it's unsettling to see someone getting the ending so right so early in a career.

And as it is with fiction, so it is with life. We want our beginnings and endings separated. We want—don't we?—the middle to have its chance.

PART TWO   *Maps and Legends*

KAREN BRENNAN

Dream, Memory, Story, and the Recovery of Narrative

I want to begin with a dream I had last summer in Mexico. Because it was a dream with two parts to it, I entitled it: Dead Girl in Two Parts. What follows is a direct transcription from my journal. Part 1: A girl in a school uniform falls from a ledge, from between the arches of a wrought-iron railing, to her death. I am sitting on the ledge and my daughter Rachel may be there as well. The girl falls, I realize, because she is smaller than the arches, and (I think at the time) the wind blows her off. She is simply swept through the railing. When I look down I see her little pile of school clothes—it seems to be all that's left of her. I feel regretful but not horrified.

In the second part of this dream we—me, Rachel, and the little girl—are at the seashore, sitting on the beach, close to where the waves lap up. Suddenly a large wave washes over the little girl and kills her. Rachel and I look at her face staring up at us from beneath the water. It is a distinctive image, the face of the girl, eyes closed, under the shallow water, which moves softly over her. I feel more than regret now; I feel guilt. I feel that one of us (Rachel) should have been more attentive. There is a sense that Rachel had been in charge of this girl. I am therefore a little annoyed with Rachel's irresponsibility, but this isn't a major annoyance. It's more like the resigned feeling I get in real life when someone's done something wrong (as if, for example, Rachel wrecks the car I give her), and I realize, while it's futile to make a big deal over it, I'm nonetheless pissed.

Approximately a month after I transcribed this dream in my journal I received a phone call in my Mexico flat at 6 A.M. informing me that my twenty-five-year-old daughter Rachel had been in a motorcycle accident and that she was presently in a deep coma in Denver General Hospital's intensive care unit. Her friend, the driver, was fine, but Rachel's CAT scan, the informant, a neurosurgeon, told me, was very very ugly.

By 11 that morning I was on a first-class flight from Leon to Denver,

From *The Business of Memory: The Art of Remembering in an Age of Forgetting,* ed. Charles Baxter (St. Paul, Minn.: Graywolf Press, 1999).

sitting next to a woman who owned a travel agency in Guanajuato. She had been pretty, I remember, dark-haired, dressed in cream-colored slacks and a white blouse. She wore a tiny silver watch on her wrist, which, because I had misplaced my own somehow, I had recourse to consult now and again. She was on her way to Dallas for a romantic weekend with her husband. We had, what seems to me in retrospect, a pleasant conversation. I told her about Rachel's accident; she consoled me. I did not cry. I spoke reasonably, I thought at the time, having all the while that bizarre sensation that I was speaking someone else's words about someone else's daughter. I suppose I must have been in shock. I refused the first-class meal.

I remember that as we conversed my mind seemed to race along another track, somewhat at odds with our conversation. I imagined Rachel, even at that moment, woozily coming too, rubbing her eyes, her (perhaps) sore shoulders. I envisioned seeing her fully awake, out of the intensive care unit by the time I would arrive, and I planned her homecoming, her few weeks of rest. I even went so far as to imagine my sudden memory of this time—on the first-class flight to Denver next to the woman in the cream-colored slacks, when I was terrified out of my mind. How amusing it would be in retrospect! How unfounded this terror, this unreasonable refusal of first-class food!

As it turned out, what was unfounded were these wishful thoughts. And in the months that have followed that 18 August day I have come to have a terrible familiarity with the way the mind—my mind—makes up comforting stories, this narrative propensity akin to the instinct for survival and just as precarious.

Rachel continued in her coma for two months, more or less. I say more or less because, as it was explained to me, her injury was diffuse— literally, a diffuse axonal injury—and so her wake-up would be diffuse.

But when I arrived in Denver that first evening I knew nothing of brain injuries, of axons, of intercranial pressures, of ventilation or tracheotomies, of motor strips, frontal lobes, aphasic disorders, or unilateral neglects. I knew nothing of comas. What I knew was what I witnessed in the ICU unit, like a particularly grisly episode from "ER": bodies being whirled by on stretchers or corpselike in beds, hooked up to monitors, a nurse with a clipboard positioned at the end of each.

Rachel was one of these bodies. She had a tube running down one nostril (nagogastric) for feeding, another in her mouth (intubation) for breathing. A little semicircle of her hair had been shaved, above the forehead on the left side, from which protruded a three-inch metal bolt. This was to measure her intercranial pressure. All the monitors flashed above the head of her bed on a large green screen: heart, respiration, blood oxygen, blood pressure, and intercranial pressure.

Rachel's eyes were closed. She had a small scrape on her cheek. The toes of her right foot were badly burned and grotesquely blistered. Occasionally, she moved, but these movements were not reassuring; rather, they were the unnatural movements of one who has severe brain damage called, in med-speak, posturing. At this stage Rachel's postures were the most severe variety—decerebrate—indicating damage at a deep level of the cortex. They consisted of Rachel flexing her body and limbs rigidly into an extended position, her hands and feet turned inward in a bizarre way. Every time she postured, her intercranial pressures rose, meaning that the fluid in her brain was increasing to a dangerous level. Eventually, another half-moon of hair would be shaved on the other side of her brow and a drainage tube inserted to draw off the excess fluid and blood.

But that evening, the evening I first saw her in her intensive care cubicle with the tubes and drains and breathing steadily through the ventilator, her intercranial pressures were holding their own. I held her hand for a long while, and then I went outside to smoke a cigarette.

Denver General Hospital is called, not so jokingly, the Gun and Knife Club. Some of its members—gangsters with cryptic faces and oversized jeans—smoked cigarettes nearby. In the orange lights I spotted and fixated on a little crop of dying zinnias. They seemed to be an important, if obvious, metaphor. Some had lost their petals; their color was drained in the artificial light. They were in concrete beds. A litter of cigarette butts surrounded their stalks. My thoughts were disorganized, I realized at the time—I had no story to tell myself, no future I could conceive of without horror. At which point a wheezing woman rolling an oxygen tank bummed a smoke from me. She was homeless, she explained; she had been evicted from her apartment. Now she was almost out of oxygen. I gave her a cigarette and twenty bucks. I sat in the grass.

My thoughts were disorganized, and so I needed an idea. I recalled the Buddhist wisdom, that impermanence is the true nature of things, the Hindu adage that everything is maya, illusion, that those who are enlightened can pass their hands through the fabric of the world. It was then that it occurred to me that Rachel would be OK. I had been looking at the sky, at a particular formation of gray cloud, and at the moon, which was clear rimmed and precise—and it came to me. She'll be fine. It will go on, and it will change, and it will be fine. She will. I stubbed my cigarette and went back to the ICU unit. Around the bed next to hers, a group of doctors were "harvesting" a body—one of the Gun and

Knife Club. The monitors were flat above the head of that bed, but Rachel's were beeping along—pulse 82, blood pressure 118 over 70, ICUs about 12. I held her hand. I kissed her. I began to talk to her as if she could hear, to call her back from wherever she was.

After the journal account of my dream of last summer—Dead Girl Dream in Two Parts—I had appended a few notes. I noted that this was an important dream, having been recalled with that special lucidity one attributes to dreams of significance. I wondered about the two parts, the two scenes of the dream, wondered which came first in the actual dream and wondered why two parts. Were the two parts of my title, for example, a simple reference to the two parts of the dream, or were they, in a Freudian ambiguity, literally two parts of the girl—physical or mental?

Accompanying my dream account and dream notes were a series of sketches. I sketched the arches of the railing through which the girl fell to her death, and I sketched the girl herself standing under an arch, a stick figure with a skirt. Then I sketched the relative positions of Rachel and myself on the ledge, behind the railing, looking down on the little pile of school clothes, which I also sketched. After my account of part 2 of my dream, I made only one sketch, which I labeled "dead girl's face under a wave." The girl's eyes were closed, her hair snaked around her head, the wave replicated in a series of quivering lines, not unlike the surreal bars of some prison. Interesting, I noted, that in both dream scenes there was some reference to prison, both in the wrought-iron railing and in the lines I drew to suggest the wave over the dead girl's face. I wrote: Why a rooftop? Why a ledge? Why a threesome? Why two scenes? Why Rachel? Why guilty? Why pissed?

According to my notes, I had apparently figured that the dream had to do with me foisting off some little girl part of myself, that I had been neglecting some self-care, that I was shirking some responsibility. But I was not satisfied with this glib reading—I had written, "but the dream seems more complex than this."

Coming upon this account of my dream after Rachel's accident, of course, I read it in a new light. Now the dream seemed, absolutely, to be a portent of some sort. Indeed, the sketch of the dead girl's face under the wave struck me as bearing an uncanny resemblance to Rachel's face in her coma, a coma that lasted, by the way, for a grueling two months. And weren't the lines of water moving across her face, in fact, a brilliant figure for the hazy boundary that separated us at this time, she in her world, me in mine? Such an interpretation defied all that was reasonable and yet, oddly, was the most "reasonable" of any I could come up with: that is to say, it was able to connect most of the disparate elements into something that cohered. On the other hand, it was an entirely "unreasonable" account. What Aristotle would call the probable impossible, more the material of fiction than "reality."

For in Freud's schematics of dream interpretation, doesn't the dreamer participate in the dream interpretation precisely to discover the latent content of her unconscious? Certainly, a portent would refute all that. The significance of a portent exists outside the dreamer, in both space and time. A portent conflates time and space, conflates, in Yeats's formulation, the dreamer and the dreamed.

Still, as I sat at Rachel's bedside, looking at her perhaps dreaming face, the monitors measuring the steady waves of her vital functions, I recalled my dream of the dead girl in two parts and wondered which part was me and which part Rachel. Since that first evening I continued to speak to her as if she could hear me. I told her her life's story over and over. What I couldn't remember, I invented. I felt that it was more important to deliver a coherent narrative than to be faithful to a disjunctive truth. Even though I value fragmentation, in all its forms, I felt that had I been lying there in some kind of netherworld, I would want a story that made sense, whose points *a* and *b* and *c* were nicely connected.

But whose story was it? I became, more than occasionally, confused. Parts of my own life mingled weirdly with my story of hers just as, during that time, the outside world seemed to take on the sensual attributes of this inside, hospital one. I spent, on the average, eight hours a day by—or more usually in—her bed, and so I suppose it was reasonable that during my infrequent ventures to that other world expresso machines would sound like the suctioning apparatus for her trach, that someone's beeper would send a rush of alarm through me.

Finally, she began to really awaken, her left eye cracked open to reveal a tiny, beautiful chink of blue iris now roving back and forth, to sounds, to light; and she began to move her left thumb over the knuckles of my hand in an actual caress, a response; and on one joyous afternoon she reached and pushed a strand of my hair behind my ear, taking the initiative (a higher brain function) in an activity that I had neglected as a matter of course. Finally and suddenly, when all these things and more happened with a rapidity that stunned me, having become accustomed to the tabula rasa of her sleeping, motionless face, our merging, far from loosening, seemed to intensify, at least in the mind of this dreamer. At home, in front of my medicine cabinet mirror, for example, my hand through my hair felt oddly like her hand, and in my own bed before sleep I felt my body assuming her positions, right arm locked upward against my cheek, fingers rigid and clenched.

And when she began to speak—her first sentence on 15 November was, gratifyingly, "I want my Mom"—you'd think that hearing her voice would deliver me to myself, but it didn't. She spoke in breathy whispers at first, and so did I. We spoke endearments and bodily discomforts, having to pee and having to move the covers over our shoulders. Around this time I felt lightheaded as I walked through the hospital corridors; it seemed to me the ground was shifting under my feet. Rachel's head lolled to one side; at that point she was unable to hold it erect.

*   *   *

I might say: I love my mama. She is the one. Next to her everyone pales. That's the truth of it. But I'm too old for these feelings. I tell her this. She says, Oh who cares? Or I think she does. She is wearing a green sweater covered with white vines that are of the same fabric of the sweater, which is wool. In the rectangle of the door, which is blue and rough, there is a toilet. There is a white towel on a floor of many small tiles of many hues of blue. The grouting is not clean. She is standing in her bare feet in front of the medicine cabinet mirror, and it is a sorrow to me that I cannot see her reflection, only her right-side-up face, which is to me quite beautiful. She says, Oh I'm a vain old woman. Vain perhaps, Mama, I say.

Sometimes she asks, How are you doing? How are you doing, Lou? Are you feeling good? I say, Totally good, Madre. I call her all names for mother or, that is, as many as I can get a hold of. I remember words, this is true, language is my strongest point.

Matcha, I say, Why does everyone have to watch me pee? No one does, she says, see? I'm not watching. I'm brushing my teeth, I'm watching the brushing of my teeth. It's OK, Matcha, I say, you can watch me pee. You can give me a shower. You can snuggle with me at night when we hear the floor creak and someone who may be opening the door, only you say no.

*   *   *

As of this writing Rachel, after five and a half months of hospitalization, has been home for two months. Her language is completely intact; indeed, it is eloquent. Her sense of humor is as sharp as ever. She is attentive; she is perceptive; she is occasionally philosophical and frequently wise. Her most severe deficit—aside from some paralysis that affects the right side of her body and keeps her confined, for the moment, to a wheelchair—is her short-term memory. Although memory deficit is common in traumatic brain injuries (TBIs), Rachel's seems especially severe. There have been some small improvements, but she frequently cannot remember from one five-minute segment to the next. If, for example, I ask her fifteen minutes after dinner what she ate, she'll shrug and say in her wry fashion, "Who can remember?"

★   ★   ★

14 March 1996: "Dear Sweet Diary: I feel as though I'm waking up from a bad dream because I mean I don't know the difference between right or left. I mean I do, but I'm trying to simplify everything. Today I have been learning about myself. That is to say I'm learning about the details of my accident. So granted I may never ever walk again. My memory sucks. But I'm beginning to understand what happened to me and such. Except I have very little to do with, well what will I do in the future? Perhaps I will become a famous shoe tyer. But maybe not; maybe I will be quite ambitious. Maybe I will become a teacher like my madre. So I hope I'm well enough to conquer the world again."

★   ★   ★

Memory, according to Bergson, occupies the space between mind and body. It conveys mind to body and body to mind. It gives us our quality of life—makes possible, in other words, the narratives that keep our lives going forward to the next thing. If the thing is not *next* it loses its richness—isolated and unlinked to a history, it becomes meaningless, even ridiculous. Biologically and neurologically, we are creatures of context, of narrative.

Consider, for example, the activity of the neurons or brain cells. Unlike the body's cells, which divide and multiply, microcosmically illustrating the propagation of the species, neurons are systems of communication. Their most salient features are a clutch of dendrites, which branch out to receive information across the synapses between cells, and a single, long axon, which reaches to the synapse—literally the space between neurons—through which chemical and electrical information are conveyed to the next cell.

By nature, then, the activity of the neuron is narrative, metonymic, associative. The information conveyed by each neuron accumulates along a complex circuitry of neurons and produces a thought, a corresponding action in the mind-body. If the information that passes from neuron to neuron is somehow tampered with—if the transmitters or receptors are artificially altered by drugs or disease, for example—memory, at its very biological foundation, will be altered or even incapacitated.

★ ★ ★

Her feet are covered with blue veins. Blue veins on a blue tiled floor. So many blues. Which kind of vein are you? I ask her. She is brushing her hair, which is brown; which flies up into the brush like TV static.

I keep having the same dream. I do not remember details. Try to remember, she says. Was there a wave? Was there wind? I think, I say. Was there a girl? Perhaps, I say. Everything is skewed a little to the left: the table, the chair with its black-and-white pictures of parasols and ladies, the overhead fan with its wide white wings. All to the left. Where am I? I say.

You are here, she says. She leans over and puts her mouth to my ear. Here. Her breath is hot, like a mirror glare. Like a glint on tin. I say, If not her, then what? and this makes me worry. But she says, don't worry, just enjoy everything for the time being. Just look at that little fly on the kitchen table having a sip of orange juice or listen to the car roll by outside or brush your hair, here Lou, brush your hair.

She both understands everything and doesn't understand a thing. She goes on as if all were normal. She hands me the brush. Then she puts on lipstick. Next she will put lipstick on me. Why would I want lipstick? I am thinking, but I love my mama.

★ ★ ★

Memory is always configured on a gap—to *re-member* suggests the forgetfulness, the loss upon which it is founded. This forgetfulness, too, has its biological equivalents in the neurological activity of the brain. Indeed, in this most complicated of operations, the electrical impulses received by each neuron are converted to chemicals—packets of neurotransmitters—which are able to diffuse across the synaptic gap and activate the electrical signal in the next neuron. The process of conversion itself, as well as the infinite number of variables in each neuron, point to what has vanished as well as to what can be retrieved, point to the loss of the Real (in the absolute, psychoanalytic sense) and the construction of a representation.

Narrative has been the business of my life for many years now, both as a teacher and writer of fiction, but it was not until Rachel's brain injury that I realized these biological correlatives. We are hard-wired into narrative; it is, I would go so far to say, the purpose and not merely the effect of memory. The account of my dream of the dead girl, for example, is presumably based on my memory of it—but this memory is, at best, a shaky representation of a neurochemical process whose sparks and ebbings are irretrievable (if not nonsensical). What is important, we've learned from Freud, is the representation itself, assembled from whatever fragments, into a story that is the very material that divulges, if we are attentive, unconscious wishes.

Even our interpretation of dreams reveals a wish to make sense of the fragmentary, to weave into story, into history, an event that, unconnected to the life, may be troubling. Why else would I suspend my disbelief in portents than that I yearn for narrative continuity, even in retrospect, something to explain, however mystically, the strange and terrible turn of my daughter's and my life? The narrative inclination takes precedent, in this example, over reason itself, over what we know to be sensible and "true" about human experience. Which inclines me to believe that these fictions we call narrative and memory are at the foundation of our beings.

★　★　★

The days are a daze. I like that sentence because it is so truthful. I say it's the one true thing I am feeling. This feeling, which is the urge to push away some part of the air from in front of my face. It would be risky, I know. Because behind that part of air, there are things I actually want to forget. Now that I've said it and the minute I say it I think, no that's not true. Because why? Because it isn't.

Most of the time I just float in. I laugh quite a bit. Things strike me funny, and I can feel my lips go way up over my teeth in a manner that is not very attractive. The photo of my great-grandfather hanging on the wall in a brown frame is really quite funny to me, for example, though I couldn't tell you why exactly. He is very faded, and maybe it's the fadedness of him that is so like my own idea of things these days. That we all exist in a vault. That inside the vault are scraps with no meaning—torn photographs, letters from people we don't know, receipts, single words, like jewelry.

★　★　★

You *are* my memory, Rachel tells me, and it's true. I remember the actual as well as I can, and what I don't remember I shamelessly invent. You got up, you brushed your teeth, your therapists came over, and you stood up; you walked with your walker; you made everyone laugh when you asked for a big-assed cup of coffee. You admired my outfit and said, "You've got it going on, girlfriend."

What will we do tomorrow? she worries. She has less tolerance for the uncertainty of the future than the rest of us. What do I have to do? she says. We make lists of questions and answers; we record her voice and her day's activities as they occur into a palm-sized device called a voice organizer; we plan. We talk. Together we assemble an imperfect representation, a narrative we can rely on nonetheless, one that compels us forward to the next thing.

In brain injury literature there are several pathological behaviors associated with short-term memory loss, and these behaviors, I was stunned to discover, correspond to narrative pitfalls and graces, that is to say, to the way in which we all make narrative texts. Perseveration is the inclination of the brain-injured patient to get stuck obsessively on one track and to thus repeat over and over this one-tracked concern. Perseveration—a word I find especially illuminating, to persevere too much, as I take it—reflects a rigidity on the part of the perseverator. A failure of imagination, a failure of metonymy, of association, free or otherwise. The perseverator can only repeat, sometimes in different words—Rachel, for example, is quite eloquent in her perseverations—and this repetition, while in some cases may reinforce a narrative, cannot of itself deliver a narrative. The perseverator suffers from too much focus and a surfeit of schemes. He is the student of writing who can't seem to move beyond his one good idea, the student of fiction who gets stuck in a scene with a character who doesn't move or change. We all know these authors, these dull and doomed texts.

And while perseveration is this rigidity, this refusal or inability to change tracks, confabulation is exactly the opposite. To confabulate—literally to replace fact with fantasy in memory—is to wildly trope. The confabulator suffers from an unruly, unstoppable imagination, an inability to focus and develop a theme. The brain-injured confabulator concocts wild tales to compensate for his lack of memory—he fills in the gaps. Back when Rachel was confabulating, she thrilled (as well as alarmed) me with her imaginative richness, which seemed, for all its craziness, to make odd and accurate tropes for her situation. Cinderella smashed all the windows, she announced one day, sadly. On another occasion she confided that she *knew* we were on a plane over Vietnam and that she had been shot. Then there was the time, during a particularly arduous session of stretching her spastic arm, that she joyfully proclaimed to her occupational therapist that she was giving birth to a baby. The confabulator is compelled by the absence of specific space/time representations. There is no focus to her story, no organizing principle, and, perhaps in extreme cases, a failure of mimesis.

Having made these links to all-too-common narrative pathologies, it occurs to me that without the compulsive activities of confabulation and perserveration a written narrative (much less a fiction) of any interest at all could not be made. The memoir I am at such pains to deliver, woven among bits of speculation not unrelated to my situation and your situation, perseverates in its relentless return to several subjects, not to say several perseverating rhetorical strategies. I suppose I confabulate. Had there really been decaying zinnias in a concrete bed in the Denver General smoking area? Had the moon really been as I described it, clear rimmed and precise? And my companion on flight 331 from Leon, Mexico, to Denver, Colorado, had she actually worn cream-colored slacks and not, say, a brown twill skirt? Had it been, in fact, flight 331? Or have I forgotten in the blur of anxiety and sorrow the details of my own experience? I confabulate to fill in the gaps. I perseverate to bide time. Both activities rely on, are compelled by, my forgetfulness; indeed, my narrative, I believe, benefits from this forgetfulness. I believe it brings me mysteriously closer to the truth.

★   ★   ★

I think I am going somewhere. I think I must have been in an accident. I was not driving. I do not remember it.

There was a piece of light that evaded me, then I was doomed.She wears red lipstick, as do I.

When I woke up I was in a cloud, so really I have not woken up. You could say that. On the other hand, a building has a reality, and so does a banana. All things exist, therefore I do.

Only I am looking at her string of pearls. Very pearly white. I finger them with my fingers and blow a bubble into my milk. Outside the world is covered up and cold.

★   ★   ★

Yet there is something in us—in me—that yearns for the seamless life, for a resolution (termination? thanatos?) of the chaotic or unbearable. Conventionally speaking, a memoir promises to deliver the kind of product that will pacify my anxieties. In its seamlessness—its artful seamlessness, I should say—the memoir seeks to fulfill a certain kind of desire for narrative "truth." It is nothing, I realize nervously, if not credible. Because a fiction is not concerned with credibility in the same way, it's able to represent the disjunctiveness of what's real. Stylistically, it can indulge and even parody its own compulsive operations. Consider this perseverative bit from Donald Barthelme's "The Falling Dog": "A dog jumped on me out of a high window. I think it was the third floor, or the fourth floor. Or the third floor." Or this confabulation from *Ulysses:* "Walk on roseleaves. Imagine trying to eat tripe and cowheel. Where was that chap I saw in that picture somewhere? Ah, in the dead sea, floating on his back, reading a book with a parasol open."

The perseverations and confabulations of Barthelme and Joyce—and every other writer we cherish—constitute what we value of their style. To rethink style in terms of compulsive pathological brain operations might recall Jacobsen's famous study of aphasics and the links to metaphor and metonymy he discovered in their flawed speech patterns. His point, like mine, is that these patterns persist in nonpathological brain states as effects of compulsive organic activities. Any good writer knows this, which is why we speak so lovingly of indulging our obsessions, of making use of our compulsions to confabulate and/or perseverate. There is no normal narrative making.

At some point I hit upon the idea that what I could do for Rachel that her therapists could not do, perhaps as feelingly, is offer her help with story making, with narrative. She has always been a talented storyteller, and her language abilities and imagination have endured despite severe brain trauma. So I've become her writing teacher. Tell me a story, Rachel, I urge. Make something up. At first her stories were nonnarrative confabulations. There is Justine with a bee on her head. What about Justine? I prompted. What about the bee? Rachel smiled, shrugged. That's it, she said. That's all. The end. Eventually, the stories would acquire a narrative feel, but the narratives would be flat. Once upon a time, she might begin, but then the character Justine or a small, pale, weak girl or whoever would simply drift into some arena—the desert, the city, the mall—and stay there. These stories were shapeless, lacking destinies. Still, a sense of conflict was beginning; built into the notion of small, pale, and weak is the trajectory of its plot. Lately her stories attempt some kind of resolution: A very small weak girl struck out for the desert because she had been left alone and her father and mother had died and there was nothing she could think of to do but to go to the desert and weep under a mesquite. On the way there, however, she met a nice friend who happened to be called Charles. He had a bunch of chocolate with him, which he shared with the small, weak girl and which revitalized her. They had a great time, and eventually they went to Las Vegas. The end.

A sense, however tentative, of one idea proceeding from another, of a beginning and an ending, is not only indicative of Rachel's recovering memory but, it seems to me, is crucial in generating her memory along its circuitry of synapses. Narrative is the practice of memory and forgetfulness; it is how we accumulate experience and develop imaginative skills. Our stylistic compulsions make us utterly individual, or, to put it another way, our individuality is generated by our style. Which is to say the infinite variety of our neurons—we each have about two hundred billion—ensures our stylish individualities.

Having said all this, I confess that I'm working hard to keep this account from flying in all directions. Because these days I live in terror of the fragmentary—those blown-apart bits and pieces. I'm eschewing the loose end, the ragged transition, the unresolved thought—but, like every "unheimlich," they are poking through to haunt me. Just as in my life these days I am trying to keep everything together—Rachel, the five or six therapists who've become part of our weekdays, my students, my job, this piece of writing—and I sense from time to time a little tearing at the seams. I ignore those scratchy sounds. I proceed as if all will resolve itself. This is my assumption, my faith. In the space of a phone call my life went from a kind of random self-indulgence—I was melancholic, moody, bored—to a passionate necessary-ness. But I don't know the ending to this story, which is why the experience of writing it is so unsettling. I imagine the best because it's my only choice—it's the way I want to live.

Still, my head buzzes unpleasantly. There are worries. There are undecided questions and shaky transitions and thoughts right now that I have trouble completing. I'd like you to know that I'm writing this in my basement under these bare bulbs that hurt my eyes and that it's snowing outside and that I can hear the creak of Rachel's wheelchair overhead—she's put on rap again—and that I just quit smoking. I want to say this is not a memoir (too messy) and not a theory (too untheoretical) and not a fiction (too true); and that it occurs to me that the buzzing in my head is due to Radon, probably, and that it's cold in the basement and I detest snow and, like Rachel, I ask why why why? Why me?

Because it's unbelievable, isn't it? when life suddenly assumes the grotesque and overblown proportions of dreams. But which is the construction, the dream or the life? It occurs to me that we approach our dreams like "fiction," like impossibilities, that we've divided dream from life in order to preserve the smooth, untroubled narrative of our dailiness. Rachel, for example, frequently feels that she's in a dream or is waking from a dream. She asks: Is this reality? And I think that her reality is literally unbelievable to her—she cannot conceive of it.

I say one thing then another. I say her skirt is unfathomably beautiful. I say the wind will tear at her hairnet. I say look closely, that's me feeding the fish. Leaning over and seeing my face superimposed on the faces of the fish.

Here is my red jacket with the purple trim, my fake leopard hat, my woolen scarf, my mittens.

Here is my bad arm, which I put in first, then my good arm. Here are my feet, which no longer move.

Here is Matcha, my dear mother, hanging our clothes on the line, and here I am on a roof looking down. No wonder I feel off-balance. Such beautiful laundry! I yell. What? she says. You're not making sense.

Then she throws me something. It is a red item with a hook. A bra? I say. Something to eat?

★　★　★

Recent brain-mind theory suggests that there is no division between the brain and the mind, between, that is, biology and what we call consciousness. What this means is that there are no qualitative boundaries separating dreaming and waking, in this paradigm, just a few chemical change-ups.

The new, hypertextual theories of dreams sound oddly like postmodern theories of literature. Dreams are no longer vehicles to texts of some occluded unconscious but are themselves, postmodernly, their own writerly pastiches of significance. Harvard psychiatrist Allen Hobson calls them "virtual representations" and "the fictions we live by." If there are purposes for dreams, argues Hobson, it is that the souped-up programs of REM sleep reinforce memories and rehearse plans of action, embedding these plans and memories in rich systems of neurocircuitry, which we could call meaning or even life. Our dreams are our testing grounds; we try new things, we readjust, we plan. They are the field upon which we invent the life.

No two brains are alike. For this reason brain theory has it that no two traumatic brain injuries are alike. But, despite the heartening open-endedness of this fact, the medical profession in its practice cleaves to its old self-protective generalizations: "she may never wake up," false; "she seems acutely aphasic," false; "she will never be able to lead an independent life," don't know.

What I have found is that, just as all good narratives defy teleological, economical, linear models in favor of messy, subversive, nonlinear ones, recoveries from brain injuries create their own disordered stories. Boundaries, such as those between fact and fiction, dreams and reality, and even, in our case, mother and daughter, are dissolved in order to make a place for something new, rich, and surprising to occur. This new "something" is identity—whatever transitory fiction we call self—and the project is not so different from what we, as feminist lit crit/creative writers, have been doing for the past ten years: dissolving/subverting/transgressing gender and genre boundaries in order to assemble new subjectivities.

Which brings me back (or forth) to my dream of the dead girl in two parts, the overdetermined feature of my own messy narrative. What does the dream mean for my life? What am I meant to draw from those strangely prophetic scenes of me and Rachel looking, in two ways, at a girl who died, tragically and almost, now that I think of it, comically? One minute a ledge. Then a fall. One minute a beach. Then a wave. A rehearsal, I think, for what will come inevitably in any life and from what perspectives we are able to witness. From above, looking down at that little pile of school clothes or eye level as the wave comes even before we knew it came, that quickly. And suddenly, as I write this down, I know what that dream is about and how I am bound to be in those two places—the ledge and the shore—even as this writing seeks to conflate and distinguish the memoir from the theory from the fiction and especially as I struggle to reimagine my daughter and myself.

★ ★ ★

The sun is melting the snow between my madre and me. When I touch her hair I can feel the feel of my hands running through. Who are you, Madre? I say. Are you on the inside or the outside, because, honestly, I can't tell.

ROBERT BOSWELL

Narrative Spandrels

Evolution is a label for the creative process employed by the planet. By means of this process populations of living things change over generations. Evolution is responsible for the astonishing diversity of life on the planet.

A compelling example of evolution has been documented by Princeton biologists Rosemary and Peter Grant, who have studied the ground-dwelling finch on one of the Galapagos Islands. The finch is a seed eater and comes equipped with a strong cone-shaped bill, which it uses to crack open seeds. The Grants' widely publicized study of beak size within a single finch species from a single island documents the evolutionary process.

Until the drought of 1977 small-beaked finches dominated the island, but the drought was particularly hard on the plants that produce the tiny seeds that are the staple of their diet. These finches could not efficiently crack open the larger seeds of the more drought-resistant plants. The population of this species of finch on this single island was diminished by 85 percent. The surviving finches tended to have larger, thicker beaks than those that perished. Their offspring also had larger beaks, about 4 to 5 percent larger than what had been the norm before the drought.

Over the course of a single generation a significant change took place in the makeup of this population. The survival of the larger-beaked finch is an example of "adaptation," an unfortunate term as it may mislead one into thinking that the surviving finches adapted to their environment. The surviving finches had changed not at all; rather, their survival in the face of the extermination of the smaller-beaked among them changed the population. A shift in the environment selected the trait of being large-beaked as a positive one for survival, an example of "natural selection."

The most prominent evolutionary theorist just prior to Darwin was Jean Baptiste Lamarck. He believed in evolution, but he had much of it wrong. He had two essential arguments: (1) that organisms change over the course of their lives to the demands of a changing environment and these alterations are passed on to their offspring; and (2) if an organism has some capacity that it quits using that capacity goes away—and is lost, also, to future generations. Examining the giraffe, an evolutionary biologist might suggest that animal's long neck is an adaptation because it permitted the giraffe to nibble from the high leaves of trees, those that other quadrupeds typically could not reach, and so over generations the long neck was selected for by the environment. Lamarck believed the giraffe achieved its long neck by stretching for the leaves and then passed on that trait to its offspring. Examining the finches during the drought, Lamarck would likely have said that the survivors were the ones most successful at stretching and enlarging their beaks. In truth, of course, the finches had learned nothing. *Learning,* in fact, is a troublesome term to many evolutionary biologists, as it can be difficult to determine what is learned and what an organism inherits. Consider our concept of "learning" a language.

More than thirty years ago, Noam Chomsky suggested that the capacity for language is inborn in humans, and many researchers since have verified his assertion, documenting a wide range of innate capacities for categorizing, quantifying, making assumptions, and associating that cumulatively make up the rules of syntax. The rules are a genetic gift, a bequest of natural selection; all that people "learn" when they acquire language are the particularities and tonal variations of the locals—the complex circuitry of syntax is all hard-wired. The same is evidently true for the songs of white-crowned sparrows; their tunes appear to be inborn. They cannot learn the songs of another species of sparrow, even if denied ever hearing their own select song.

However, sometimes there are traits in organisms that don't appear to be adaptive. How does one account for such traits? The evolutionary biologist usually accounts for them by saying that we fail to understand the full context of the organism's life. A few exceptions will be acknowledged; for instance, adaptive traits may conflict with one another, and so there are trade-offs that may disguise a trait's adaptive function. Genetic drift is another possibility—the existence of a neutral change in a percentage of a population due to a genetic mutation that is neither selected for nor selected against.

Generally, though, an evolutionary biologist will look at various traits in an organism and suggest how each is adaptive. Stephen Gould has taken issue with this strategy. He and his partner, R. C. Lewontin, point to the dangers of making up adaptive stories to suit an organism's traits, to the existence of nonadaptive traits in animals and to the unfortunate willingness of the scientist to "atomize" an organism into traits. Gould's primary means of argument is an architectural metaphor. In his argument he refers to the "spandrel," which is the by-product of placing rounded arches side by side; the tapering triangular space between the top of one arch and the top of another is a spandrel. Stephen Gould:

> The great central dome of St. Mark's Cathedral in Venice presents in its mosaic design a detailed iconography expressing the mainstays of Christian faith. Three circles of figures radiate out from a central image of Christ. . . . Each circle is divided into quadrants . . . [and] each quadrant meets one of the four spandrels in the arches below the dome. Spandrels . . . are necessary architectural by-products of mounting a dome on rounded arches. Each spandrel contains a design admirably fitted into its tapering space. . . .
>
> The design is so elaborate, harmonious and purposeful that we are tempted to view it as the starting point of any analysis, as the cause in some sense of the surrounding architecture. But this would invert the proper path of any analysis. The system begins with an architectural constraint: the necessary four spandrels and their tapering triangular form. They provide a space in which the mosaicists worked.

Gould argues that if St. Mark's Cathedral were a living organism, then the beauty of the mosaic design might lead an evolutionary biologist to believe that the ornate and intricately patterned design of the mosaic dictated the necessity for spandrels, which, in turn, rounded the entryways. One can imagine a child's encyclopedia posing a question about such an organism.

Q: Why does St. Mark's have arching entryways?

A: The mosaic, which springs from triangular beginnings, is believed to attract the worship necessary for the cathedral's survival; this adaptation and its spandrel beginnings round the entryways into the shape you see.

Gould is arguing that some of the traits we see in organisms may have come into being for purposes other than the one for which they are, at present, being used; that there may by-products of traits that may ultimately serve a function. That is, the arches are a primary trait of the architecture of St. Mark's, and the spandrels are by-products of the arches; yet the mosaic so beautifully incorporates the spandrels as to make them seem primary, as if the arch had been invented by a testy and demanding mosaicist. You can see how this example serves to criticize the tendency to analyze the part outside of the whole and individual traits rather than the entire organism.

Which brings me to the writing of fiction. It seems to me that spandrels are often, if I may borrow Gould's language, the key to creating an "elaborate, harmonious, and purposeful" work of fiction. That is, the fiction writer must toil away on the primary structures, those literary arches, and in the process he inevitably creates by-products or spandrels, and very often these spandrels come to guide and shape the story and give the writer the opportunity to create a beautiful and meaningful whole.

If the dome of St. Mark's Cathedral is supported primarily by arches, the narrative of a great many stories is structured by scenes. So let us substitute scenes for arches. In the construction of any scene there are necessarily by-products, and these by-products may ultimately determine the difference between good and mediocre fiction. Moreover, these spandrels may determine the ultimate design of the narrative mosaic to such an extent that they appear to be the primary units of structure.

Think of Flannery O'Connor's "A Good Man Is Hard to Find" and the introduction of Pitty Sing, the cat, into the story. The grandmother, being who she is, sneaks the cat into the car before the family starts their trip; the action justifies itself by embodying the selfishness and self-serving dishonesty of the grandmother and by making the scene more complete and accurate—even the cat's name, Pitty Sing (as in "You're such a pitty sing!")—and the grandmother's justification for sneaking her on board (that the cat would miss her too much)—reveal character. Based on what Flannery O'Connor has said about her writing process, one can be fairly certain that this detail entered the story as a by-product of writing the scene; that is, in the process of making up the first scene, she stumbled upon this feline detail. Later in the story the cat's escape precipitates the accident that, in turn, leads to the story's astonishing conclusion.

While writing this essay, I started talking to other writers to hear about their spandrels. Steven Schwartz had his own vocabulary for it, talking about background and foreground and how elements that come into the story as background suddenly shift into the foreground, accruing meaning that he had not anticipated. Antonya Nelson mentioned a specific detail in a novella, how in the process of describing a scene involving a tornado she came up with the detail of a drinking straw being driven through a cheek and leaving a scar. Scarring, without her realizing it, became a subtext in the work and remained a subtext until the conclusion, when it moved from background to foreground. In the penultimate scene a new member of the family is bitten and scarred by another member, an action that precipitates the protagonist's final gesture and, in so doing, determines the ultimate shape of the story.

In a story of mine called "Rain" I put two women in the woods in search of a lost boy. They were close enough to civilization to hear the rapping gate of a fence but out of their element enough to lose a shoe in a muddy ravine. Those are the story's two spandrels, the gate and the shoe. Not created with thematic or structural intent, they cropped up while I was trying to convey the necessary information and completely imagine the scenes. In the story's final episode the women return to the woods, and, while I was writing this scene, the shoe and then the gate returned and guided me to the story's conclusion. Searching for the reason that she has been having some kind of breakdown since she was last in the wilderness, the protagonist instead finds her lost shoe; this and the sound of another rapping gate lead her into a kind of vision—one I had no idea was coming. I can say without any hesitation that the story would not have come together effectively without those happy accidents, those by-products, those spandrels.

Typically, scenes do indeed hold up a story, but the spandrels are often what calibrate the story's shape. The reader's primary engagement is with the characters in the scenes, and there must be adequate surface tension to involve the reader in this action while the spandrels work behind the scenes (so to speak). The surface tension is maintained by the writer because she, too, is primarily engaged with characters in the scenes. She does not anticipate that the details she creates in order to make the scene will later provide a means by which she can discover the resolution to the story.

Clearly, this is not an unusual experience among writers. In fact, that's my point: this is the way a great many writers work. What I find striking is the metaphor, provided by Stephen Jay Gould, and how it conveys the perverse complexity of the writing process and especially the narrative process, how it provides a visual representation of what I had long felt and attempted to describe. To students I have often said that the real discoveries you make about the overall story may well come while you are working on a single element of craft. My stock example is this: If you take the classic Snoopy cliché, "It was a dark and stormy night," and then try to write a better opening sentence, you might eventually come up with the following: "Lightning struck the fence post." This is not a cliché, it conveys that there was a storm, says something about the setting, and now, most important of all, you have a charred fence post in your story, which could turn out to be its most significant image; it could alter, or even determine, the final shape of the story.

The importance of spandrels as shaping elements in fiction is often most apparent in stories written without them. Of course, not all writers work in the same fashion, and any single writer may work in differing ways from one story to the next—especially, perhaps, when one writes from personal experience. But most stories or novels that use consciously imposed details fail.

Think of Hollywood films. I saw one recently in which in a woman pretends to have a husband in order to get ahead in her conservative workplace. She places his photo on her desk, although he is actually only a casual acquaintance. Circumstances force her to ask the fellow to do some acting in front of her employers, for which she offers to pay him. He stays with her, sleeping on the couch, and he falls in love with her. She also falls for him but doesn't realize it until almost too late. They reconcile, and the credits role. It's a slight twist on a very familiar story.

While he's sleeping on her couch, she tells him about a watch she used to have that meant a lot to her, a Cinderella watch. After he's gone, late in the film, she discovers that he's left her a present—a Cinderella watch. This is crucial to her realizing that he understands her and that she really does love him. The watch is meant to function as a spandrel: something introduced early on in the context of a conversation recurs in a manner that propels the outcome. However, the Cinderella watch is very clearly *not* a spandrel but a planted symbol. The watch does not come up as a means of making complete a scene whose primary purpose was to do something else (something crucial to the development of the narrative); rather, the scene has essentially no purpose but to supply an opportunity for the conversation, which, in turn, has no purpose but to plant the idea of the watch in the viewer's head. Any discriminating viewer recognizes this as a phony moment. The watch's return, then, seems (and is) a plot contrivance to force closure.

One could argue that the character having a beloved lost watch and telling her faux husband about it is a part of the plot. Isn't it, after all, a scene, and haven't I just been calling scenes the primary conduits of story? Technically, it is a scene, but in terms of its function it's a fake scene—just an excuse, a temporal place, for the planting of the symbol. The same would be true in a story even if random contemplation or philosophical pondering took place; these actions do not require a scene to exist, and so they should not represent the sole immediate function of a scene. The action of any scene should be of some immediate story consequence. This watch episode, except as a place to plant the symbol, is not really a part of the plot either. It does not advance the surface story, does not motivate the character to act, does not alter the character's behavior, does not figure in the plot in any meaningful way. One cannot believe the Cinderella watch was a by-product of the scene because the scene did nothing but introduce (and thereby point at) the fact of the lost Cinderella watch.

A scene in fiction has to accomplish many things at once. Fake scenes, when they appear in literary fiction, are usually much better done than my Hollywood example and may be able to do several worthwhile things (filling the reader in on background and providing some metaphorical sense of the character's state of mind, for example), but the actions in the scene are (typically) worse than inconsequential. Many scenes in a novel are, at the level of bare plot, largely inconsequential, but they make the character act and interact in a fashion that is, indeed, consequential and may in fact be crucial to the reader's understanding of the character. Think of Vronsky's racing the horse in *Anna Karenina* or in *The Great Gatsby* Nick Carraway's trip with Tom Buchanan and Myrtle Wilson to their apartment in the city. Scenes such as these aren't absolutely necessary to a novel's plot or story, but the reader doesn't know that while reading them; in fact, the reader must feel intensely involved in the moment for such scenes—which often profoundly reveal character—to work.

Scenes that merely plant devices are worse than inconsequential because there is no immediate involvement or payoff in the character's actions or interactions; instead, the reader feels involved in a setup for eventual metaphor, a scene that serves the needs of the writer at the expense of the immediate needs of the story.

The Cinderella watch is meant to function symbolically in the movie, but it is clear that this is an imposed symbol. The character with the faux husband discovers her true prince is the one who cares for her. The narrative, in its schematic design, is meant to play on and update the Cinderella story, with the modern Cinderella being the best worker in the organization (like Cinderella in her home) but overlooked because of her dress and attitude. There's even a ball scene wherein everyone praises her gown.

Some writers may be able to work from a schematic design and avoid the flatness that comes from fake scenes designed to plant symbols and the sluggishness that comes from a heavy-handed design. Most will fail. What makes the narrative flat is that the design comes before the story, before the characters, and the writer has been unable to disguise this fact. Planted symbols, unlike spandrels, tend to be conscious, logical metaphors that fit too neatly in a design, that merely reinforce what's going on, that neither surprise nor add, that have schematic and thematic relevance at the expense of story, plot, authority, and compression.

Unlike a spandrel, a planted symbol or device doesn't do anything in the here-and-now of the story but merely sets up some thematic business for later. A spandrel, by definition, is a by-product, and so it will always be in service of the ongoing story, the at-this-minute scene; that it will ultimately also serve a larger function in the story is what gives it its surprise and its power. Generally, that necessitates working from the detail to the discovery, rather than working from the schematic design backward, filling in the gaps in what is essentially an outline.

It may seem to you that I'm going on at great length about not very much at all. While it is a small matter, it can be a crucial one. Very often when a writer is stuck in a story, it means that he needs to go back to the beginning and either more completely imagine each scene or maybe simply give the existing material a better read, in order to identify the lurking but unused spandrels. It is why I'm often suggesting to students to "listen" to their stories and see if the material they have already written can guide their completion, to see if the evolving story already has in place the traits that will ensure its survival. Why, after all, should we believe the human creative process to be all that different from the creative process that ultimately invented us?

Recognizing opportunities within a story for its mutation into a better story is a crucial step in the development of many writers; for others this process comes as naturally as breathing, as grasping, as taking suck on a breast—all built-in responses of the human animal. There are evolutionary biologists and scientists in a wide range of disciplines who now believe that many other of our capacities are inborn, as well. Noam Chomsky's evidence that the capacity for language is hard-wired in humans, along with new discoveries about how the immune system operates, has led researchers to suggest that the infant's ability to recognize a face is innate, that a person's ability to interpret facial expressions is inborn, that our ability to make inferences, interpret feelings, are all hard-wired, that consciousness itself is the product of selection. In fact, what these researchers believe is that humans do not really learn anything; rather, what we know has already been selected for, and we spend our lives discovering our inborn capacities. Which is to say, our belief in learning is like Lamarck's naive belief that an organism can alter itself to an environment, can develop a larger beak, can profoundly stretch its neck; meanwhile, the evidence suggests that what we know is, instead, like the fortuitously large-beaked finches, a product of selection—in this case the product of millions of years of natural selection.

If we don't learn, we merely discover the range, complexity, and limits of our wiring. Selection zealots are predicting this knowledge will bring about large changes in our culture, such as the end of psychotherapy, but one of the things it makes me think of is Carl Jung's notion of the collective unconscious, how it seems that humans have powerful, innate responses to certain stimuli, as if from generational residue. Jung, of course, studied mythologies, stories, the powerful narratives that seem to touch on something intrinsic to the human being.

This, in turn, leads me to think of the automatic writing fiction writers sometimes fall into, wherein all one seems to be doing is listening to a story as it spins itself out in his mind, and the yellow hat on the girl's head in the first paragraph turns out to be important in the ultimate resolution—the spandrels leading to discoveries perhaps because they permit the writer full access to an inborn map of narrative, which may be why the conclusion of a good story, recalling Flannery O'Connor again, can both surprise us and yet seem inevitable. Readers of great fiction often report the experience of a connection so deep as to feel the narration has somehow transcended its words. Perhaps when we talk about the writerly pursuit of truth, as writers often do, in part we're talking about the ability of the writer to make contact with that pure narrative wiring, to successfully ride the inborn circuitry.

I know that there are dangers to this evolutionary argument. Racists have long attempted to prove that people of color lack the intellect of whites, and there is an excellent evolutionary argument to counter this—that the separation of *Homo sapiens* into racial groups is such a recent thing, biologically speaking, that there simply hasn't been time to produce significant differences in intellect and other higher-order capacities. I am nonetheless certain that this notion of hard wiring will be used by some for pernicious ends. But ugliness alone doesn't mean it's invalid. Just as the meretricious applications that Social Darwinists have suggested do nothing to reduce the validity of evolutionary theory.

And it's not all ugly; it suggests that our connections with the past and with each other are more manifold and intimate than we'd imagined. I find at least this one aspect of it rewarding to consider: that we may well be narrative beasts down to our very genes, that story has been selected for, that it is in the most profound sense *necessary,* and that the desire for story is a generational longing and so its fulfillment is, in essence, spiritual.

How many times have you heard writers say that it seemed as if the whole story had been in their heads from the beginning? While that might not be exactly right, what could be true is that the complex narrative structure, that ornate framework of reason and unreason, lies waiting within for us to supply the necessary particulars and tonal variations, so that we mosaicists of the word may occasionally be able to adorn a narrative so elaborately, harmoniously, and purposefully that it will seem that the spandrels and even the cut of the arches are solely of our making, rather than the product of millions of years of selection, rather than one of our truest connections with our ancestors, rather than a secular and exquisitely human embodiment of what we might fairly label the soul.

BIBLIOGRAPHY

Gazzaniga, Michael S. *Nature's Mind: The Biological Roots of Thinking, Emotions, Sexuality, Language, and Intelligence*. New York: Basic Books, 1992.

Gould Stephen Jay. *Bully for Brontosaurus*. New York: W. W. Norton, 1991.

———. *Ever since Darwin: Reflections in Natural History*. New York: W. W. Norton, 1977.

———. *The Mismeasure of Man*. New York: W. W. Norton, 1981.

———. "The Spandrels of San Marco and the Panglossian Paradigm: A Critique of the Adaptationist Programme." *Proceedings of the Royal Society of London*, ser. B. *Biological Sciences* 205 (1979): 581–98.

C. J. HRIBAL

The Scene Beast Is Hungry

In a fine essay entitled "Mistakes Were Made" Charles Baxter argues that characters need to act in the physical world. He articulates the need for action of some sort in stories, versus stories rooted in the stasis of unhappiness, where to identify the source of the trauma was to end the story. Almost as an aside, he says that the only people who want characters to make mistakes are readers. And it's from that aside that I'd like to build my argument. I'd like to talk about writing for readers and about our appetite, as readers who write, for things to happen—which I think sometimes gets forgotten, or avoided, while we're creating our characters' unhappiness.

I also came to this topic because it kept cropping up in my correspondence with two really good students who were having trouble with certain stretches of their stories. They worried that the reader might become bored, and they asked me if, while I was reading their work, I would mark those places where I felt bored. Well, I wasn't bored, ever, but there were places where I'd write in the margins, as a kind of shorthand, "The Scene Beast Is Hungry," and it was invariably in places where I felt drama had to break through a large bubble of recollection or interior reflection or explanation.

I should say, by the way, that to some extent I'm arguing against my own practice. As much as anyone, I'm a writer for whom stream of consciousness musings hold an endless fascination. But I also believe all that thinking and consciousness has to get us somewhere, and I noticed that in the examples that Baxter uses the mistakes are always physical (the recoil of a hand at a critical moment, for instance) or spoken aloud (things said that could not be unsaid), and we get somewhere because of that action.

Any action's import might be digested internally, of course, but it first has to poke through and into the physical world where we can see it. Some truisms, then:

1. That in a story, something has to happen. (E. M. Forster: "Yes—oh, dear, yes—the novel tells a story.")
2. That scenes are where things happen.

3. That good scenes are the least controllable aspects of a story and are therefore the most difficult to write.

Let's look at that last observation first. The poet Richard Ryan has observed that "in fiction, as in life, the hardest thing is when two people get together." He further observes that that's why there is so much violence on TV and in the movies. Violence is, after all, the easiest plot turn and absolves you of the need to write dialogue. *Hasta la vista, baby.*

It's also why even good writers will do almost anything to avoid writing scenes. In exposition, in summary, we are most aware of the author, or, rather, most aware of the author's control. If we ever, as writers, feel like we have a firm grip on the paddle in our narrative canoe, it's when we are, in one guise or another, *telling* things to the reader.

Conversely, in scene we are most aware of the characters, and as writers we are perhaps most aware of our *lack* of control. It's when our characters are most themselves, the least "us"—that is, if we let them go, let them be themselves, let them surprise us—that anything can happen. It is in scene that our characters shove us to the front of the canoe, the whole thing is now walla-walling, and with a Yippie! they've got the paddle and are steering us not on the placid lake of meaning and reason and explanation but toward the rapids of chaos and happenstance—and we're just along for the ride.

Or at least it can feel that way. One should recall Robert Frost's dictum, however: If there is no surprise for the writer, there is no surprise for the reader. That is most likely to happen, of course, if we're willing to let our characters be different from ourselves, if we allow them to have agendas different from our own, if we allow them to blunder into things or make mistakes, to say things we ordinarily wouldn't say ourselves.

Ask yourself how often you have your characters think of things to say, then have them decide not to say them, and, instead, make them rue and ruminate on the missed opportunity. Which is to say, perhaps, that you're having your characters act a lot like you do. Might it not be better for the story, however, if you let the character say, "What the hell," and speak his or her mind out loud, and see what happens? That's hard, of course, if you're the sort of person who more often than not bites his or her tongue. There's this general fear of letting go. But that's exactly what holds us back as writers, what paralyzes us, more than anything else—our fears. Still, fear is not necessarily a bad thing. Providing you can overcome your initial paralysis, fear is as good a motivator as any. Hence, my students saying in their letters, "Tell me when you're bored." They knew there was a reader out there expecting to be fed.

They were afraid the reader wasn't being served a satisfying meal. In fact, they knew that reader was themselves. Let's face it—our imagined readers are our own internalized fears that our stories are boring, or our hopes that our stories aren't, projected onto another body entirely.

Now, we know that. We know that there is a scene beast out there and that the scene beast has to be fed. We're also aware from popular fiction in whatever media that the scene beast can be ravenous. It bites off great chunks of sex and violence before it's happy. But we don't often write—at least not too often do we write—great hunks of sex and violence. Besides, the scene beast is not a picky eater. It'll chomp down just about anything, no matter how badly written, as long as there are active verbs and quotation marks. And that's not what we really want, is it? A scene beast not fit for polite company, with blood on the appliances and Sharon Stone on the linoleum?

So, what to do, what to do? We're like creatures out of a Beckett play—I can't go on, I'll go on. We introduce flashback after flashback into our stories, hoping this will satisfy the scene beast even if it doesn't move the story forward. Or we load up on exposition and summary, delaying as long as possible the dreaded *and then* that puts the boat in the water. Or we end scenes too soon, because we think that five or six continuous lines of dialogue look unseemly. Or how about this? You're going along, feeling your way into the scene, you're still feeling your way into the scene, you're still feeling your way into the scene, and your characters are talking, but they're not saying anything. They're just verbally twiddling their thumbs, exchanging pleasantries about the weather, while you wait for whatever it is that's supposed to happen to happen. And for a while you justify keeping this stuff in the story because "it represents the quotidian of my character's experience."

But these are coping mechanisms, and we know it. How to satiate the scene beast? We can convert large blocks of exposition into scene, compress several scenes into one scene, or develop a scene that has been arbitrarily truncated (what one of my students calls "drastic scenification"). All of those can lead to wonderful results. But we need to think about the way scenes can galvanize the whole story; we need to consider structure, or the story's architecture.

"Prose," Ernest Hemingway says, "is architecture, not interior decoration." It's probably a given that when Hemingway is on, particularly in certain scenes in *The Sun Also Rises* or in a story like "Hills Like White Elephants," there are few people who can construct a scene better than he. But it's not just scene I'm concerned with here. It's the connection between story architecture and scene, how writers incorporate scene into the structure of their stories, how they balance showing and telling, how they reconcile those two impulses, that I'd like to look at in four stories: Jamaica Kincaid's "Girl," Margaret Atwood's "Rape Fantasies," Peter Taylor's "The Gift of the Prodigal," and Tim O'Brien's "The Things They Carried." I think this is especially important because most of us write intuitively, from sentence to sentence, and it's sometimes useful to look at the relationship of the whole to its parts. I also don't think it's any accident that what propels each of these stories forward, what gives them structure and coherence, is a single scene, though how that scene is deployed is markedly different in each story.

On the surface Jamaica Kincaid's "Girl" is a dialogue, almost a monologue except for two bits of italicized interruption. It is also a single sentence. Whenever I teach this story, I ask my students to describe the scene, and what's interesting is the range of possible narrative scenarios they give: that this is happening in a kind of compressed real time—either that each clause is a separate scene and thus the story itself takes place over weeks and months and years, with the two interjections by the daughter given on the most recent day, or each clause is part of a super-speeded harangue given during a critical period of the girl's life, right before puberty. *Or* that it's all recalled by the girl—she's an adult now, and she's looking back, recalling everything her mother said to her over the years that she now understands. *Or* that it takes place in the mother's head—all the things she needs to say to her daughter that her daughter just doesn't get yet, which gives more urgency (and frustration) to the mother's demonstrations of how to do things.

What's important is that whatever the interpretation given to the monologue/dialogue—whatever context we imagine (that we are objectively watching/listening to a lovingly bitter harangue as it's happening or as it's being recalled years later), whether we are outside observers eavesdropping or inside the girl's (or the mother's) stream of consciousness—the structure of the periodic sentence, the repeated commands, and the "this is how" syntax force us to imagine the implied scene or scenes. The mother's voice, in effect, creates the scene for us; her instructions constitute a milieu in which the characters live. The lack of a specific context for this wealth of detail causes us to create one, and it's through this created context—the scene we infer or the scenes that the author implies—that we come to know the story, a story that is darker, and maybe more complex, and sadder, than just that of a mother badgering her daughter into behaving properly and learning the necessary domestic skills for a woman in this culture. The repeated lines about becoming a slut, the continual reminders to the daughter that she is not male, that hers will be a life of service in a culture filled with menacing men, the advice—sandwiched in between cold remedies and fishing advice—of how to abort a child: we catch the tone of resignation and bitterness, made explicit in the line "this is how to love a man, and if this doesn't work there are other ways, and if they don't work don't feel too bad about giving up." The mother's own life, her own experience, generates all this advice.

It is more than domestic instruction. It is a practicum on survival. It is also a warning and, sadly, an indoctrination. The mother, seeking to give the daughter the information she needs to survive, also does the culture's dirty work for it. And yet she also seeks to protect her daughter—thus the conflicting emphasis on virtue and the advice on how to perform an abortion. The mother is trying to prepare her daughter for every contingency, even that of self-assertion: "this is how to bully a man," and sometimes that self-assertion is to be found in the tiniest of gestures: "this is how to spit up in the air if you feel like it."

We are meant to see the two of them, mother and daughter (and the relationship is clear even though those words aren't used), the mother standing in the road, spitting up, then dancing away from it, the daughter watching, listening, and maybe—too late—taking that to heart, too.

Or maybe it's not too late, for, despite all the resignation, perhaps it is a dialogue that repeats itself in the ears and mind of the daughter many years later, a daughter who heard her mother's story buried in all that survival advice, who listened, and who is writing it all down now.

That's the power of the implied scene—to generate more than one reading and to have those multiple readings resonate rather than confuse.

Margaret Atwood uses an implied scene in the opening pages of "Rape Fantasies," and, by the time her implied scene becomes more explicit and particular (the story ends up a dramatic monologue), we've become included in the scene in a way we perhaps don't wish to be, thrown into a body, a persona we hadn't seen ourselves in, asked to be privy to a confession we'd just as soon not hear. This is "My Last Duchess" territory, only we're not clear how close we are to the speaker yet, and, when our exact relationship to the speaker does become clear, the intimacy that's implied startles us.

The story opens with a fairly standard dramatic monologue—dramatic rather than interior because Estelle's voice has the inflections and phrasings of spoken speech, and we as readers seem to be a part of a general audience to whom Estelle's monologue is addressed. The real scenes—we think—are going to be those recounted ones of Estelle and her four coworkers, starting with the day before yesterday, when they began talking about rape fantasies.

A couple of interesting things happen here. One is that we as a general audience get reduced to a single pair of ears, the "you" of "It's all right if I tell you. I don't expect you'll ever meet her"; the other is that once the lunch hour is over, without all the coworkers' fantasies being told, we never get back to either the coworkers or their "fantasies." We shift from that specific recalled scene to the larger dramatic monologue, from the public to the private, and what Estelle gives us next are a series of relatively comic, almost poignantly pathetic nonfantasies.

That shift reestablishes Estelle as the center of the story, yet it also sets up an expectation that we'll come back to those coworkers, that the scene left hanging will somehow be completed. Atwood—or Estelle—has created a scene beast, one hungry for the as-yet-to-be-narrated fantasies by Sondra, and possibly by the others, and it's that frustration and desire—that hunger—that helps propel the story along. We expect to be fed a particular scene, and we are fed something else instead. The recalled—and interrupted and almost arbitrarily truncated—scene with the coworkers creates a space that the rest of Estelle's narratives, her own fantasies, tries to fill. And, as the story evolves, we realize the interrupted scene, the coworkers' fantasies we don't get back to, is truncated for that very reason. Estelle wants to be the center of her own narrative. Almost all first-person narratives are really confessions for the narrator, whether conscious or unconscious, and it's often both, as it is here. Even before Estelle tells us her fantasies, we know that she probably isn't liked at work, that she snoops on her fellow employees, looking up confidential records and then gossiping about them, that she considers herself smarter than they are, that she's pushing forty, that her prospects aren't that hot, given that she's been there longer than any of them and she's still in filing, but that's all okay because she has "outside interests."

As her monologue continues, her position becomes clearer, and so does ours. The listening ears—ours now—are male, and Estelle, in all her fantasies, always feels sorry for the guy, even though what you should feel in a real rape fantasy, she tells us, is anxiety, not pity. And the one time she does have what is a real anxiety-producing fantasy, one in which real violence is threatened, she prefers not to dwell on it. She'd rather imagine her rapists as poor saps she can reason with, or fool or mother or help, and eventually they'll become friends and companions. True violence, like true loneliness, she'd prefer not to think about—she tosses both off into the realm of the other gender: "But maybe it's different for a guy."

And then we realize that we're that guy. The space created by the recalled scene, the string of fantasies Estelle spills out—we're meant to satisfy both. The dramatic monologue we've been listening to, first as a generalized listener, then as a specific listener, then as a specific male listener, has been, in the final two paragraphs, converted to a specific scene. We are having drinks with Estelle; we're at a nice place; and Estelle has told us all this as a means of getting to know us, or as a means of our getting to know her. Estelle has also probably had too much to drink—why else have we gotten this long a monologue?—and we are left in a bit of a quandary. Has she told us all this to forestall something from happening or to encourage its happening but in a "safe" way?

In either case we are now part of a scene in which we had not initially envisioned ourselves as participating. The interrupted scene with the coworkers, all talking about rape fantasies, has created in us an appetite for scene, and by the time our appetite has been satisfied we discover, surprisingly, that we are both consumers and consumed.

Peter Taylor has used a similar device in "The Gift of the Prodigal," but we are asked only to serve as invisible confidant to the narrator's monologue; we need not be characters ourselves. But even as listeners and witnesses we have plenty to do.

In the opening scene the unnamed, elderly narrator has placed us beside himself in the second-story window looking down on his son Ricky. And that is pretty much where we stay as the narrator tells us about Ricky, though, as with any repressed narrator, what he really tells us about is himself. Even his opening description, in which Ricky is equated to the washed river gravel in the drive, reveals to us the narrator's predilections and desires, however obliquely expressed.

In the passages that follow it turns out Ricky, though he's twenty-nine, requires as much upkeep as the drive. The narrator's intention, of course, is to create a sympathetic ear for himself—wife dead, one ne'er-do-well son, three older children who, while expressing concern for their father's welfare, are really concerned with maintaining their own, with keeping their own lives and worldviews sheltered and undisturbed. And it would seem that is what the narrator wants as well—maintaining "open lines of communication" with Ricky, because he believes that's what his wife Cary would have wanted. He offers this as an excuse for doing what he does—including attending Ricky's organized cockfights on several occasions, as though he himself had no interest in the matter. He also tells us he has never even looked at another woman since the day he married. He is a proper man, and his son's exploits—sexual, financial, illegal, and violent—completely baffle him, since they are the "low" sorts of activity that usually occur among a different (lower and therefore vulgar) class of people.

This, however, does not stop the narrator from reciting to us three different episodes from Ricky's colorful and scandalous past. These episodes make up the bulk of the story, and, while they are, as the narrator says of the first one, ugly, they are also related with a certain glee, the narrator's protestations of how burdensome they are notwithstanding.

Mind you, we are still fictively standing at the window while these episodes are being related, still looking down—literally and figuratively—at Ricky as Ricky decides whether or not to approach the house with his new story of woe and as the narrator decides whether or not to admit him—again, more for Cary's sake than for his own. We are meant, during all this, to assume the role of sympathetic listener, to lay our hands on the narrator's shoulder, much as one of the narrator's other children will do, and cluck at the burden this newest imposition will lay upon the narrator, the obligation to save Ricky from himself.

This would be a fairly static story were the episodes not so revealing, not of Ricky's character, though they do that, too, but of the narrator's. Like Estelle's recounted fantasies, the episodes reveal a great deal about the person relating them as well as being entertaining in their own right. The three episodes share a similar structure: Ricky gets into some kind of trouble—Ricky shoots a man in the butt who was messing around with the same married woman Ricky was messing around with; Ricky gets beaten up by the henchmen of a man who got swindled by Ricky in a horse deal; Ricky's illegal gambling racket gets busted with the collusion of a sheriff's deputy who usually attends the events for his own enjoyment—and then Ricky gets bailed out by his father. Getting bailed out means several things—keeping the matter quiet, at least as quiet as rumor will allow it, suppressing certain facts that keep the rumors from becoming reportable news, making sure no jail time is served by anyone (that it remains a financial matter, with only fines being levied), and, finally, ruining the life of the person who injured Ricky or who was responsible in some way for the matter to come to the attention of the authorities in the first place. This last bit—the purposeful disruption of other people's lives—is reported in each case almost as an aside, as a coda to each episode. There's a quality of apology to it, as though the narrator is berating himself for lacking the power and influence to do more:

We were months getting it straightened out. Ricky went out of town for a while, and the young doctor ended by having to move away permanently—to Richmond or Norfolk, I think. I only give this incident in such detail in order to show the sort of low company Ricky has always kept, even when he seemed to be among our own sort.

And:

> All we were able to do about the miserable fracas was to see to it that
> that stable was put out of business and that the man himself had to go
> elsewhere (he went down into North Carolina) to ply his trade.

And:

> Extricating Ricky from that affair and setting matters aright was a long
> and complicated undertaking. . . . All we could do about the deputy,
> who, Ricky felt sure, had connived with the federal officers, was to
> get him out of his job after the next election.

There is real power here: businesses are closed down, people are forced
to move away, perhaps an election has been fixed or at least tampered
with. Listening to these episodes, we're a little in awe of the narrator's
influence. Like the listener to Estelle's fantasies, we're hearing some
things we'd rather not hear, though, certainly, we're also titillated hearing them.

And the titillation factor is present for the narrator in each of these
episodes as well. In each at least part of the scandal hinges on the presence
of a woman whose sexuality is her defining characteristic. After the first
episode Ricky showed the narrator a picture of the woman involved.
The narrator describes her as a woman "with a tight little mouth and eyes
that burned themselves into your memory . . . the sort of intense and
reckless-looking girl that Ricky has always gone for." Despite the narrator's protestations that he's never looked at another woman since his marriage, in the aftermath of the other two episodes he recounts he spends
time imagining what the woman involved looks like, mentally compar-
ing her to the woman with the intense eyes and tight little mouth. One
is almost tempted to wipe the drool off the narrator's chin.

I don't use that image lightly. Before we think too critically of the
narrator, the episodes are followed by a recounting of the narrator's
debilitating health. Taylor, in using the first-person narrator's own both
calculating and unwitting confession, asks us both to sympathize with
and to judge the narrator. And, although the proportions might be different, I wonder if that isn't what the narrator wants, too. We sometimes
talk about not judging characters, but we do, all the time. It's a pastime
of ours. Usually we just skip to blame and finger-pointing, but the more
complex issue of judgment, and the question of proportion—judg-
ment/empathy—is a matter of tone.

As witnesses to the monologue, though, surely we catch the narrator's—and Taylor's—tone. We are drawn forward, fascinated by the goings on, while simultaneously recoiling a little by what we come to know. Up until now, though, the scene itself has been static—Ricky standing in the drive, mussing up the gravel, the narrator standing in the window, relating to us how Ricky has mussed up his life, which the narrator is occasionally called in to rake clean.

It is only after all this exposition, broken into three episodes all of a piece, that we get what passes for forward motion in the story. It begins with Ricky choosing not to go upstairs, not to approach his father. It is the narrator who moves first, calling his son upstairs. Not coincidentally, it is also the first line of dialogue in the story: "Come on up, Ricky." There are a few more lines of dialogue in the story—and they are quite important, as the narrator affirms three times his need for Ricky by saying to him, "Don't go, Ricky, don't go," after Ricky has both recognized his father's ill health and the burden these troubles place on him—but the significance of that simple action, Ricky being called up to the second floor, the first direct action in real time, is what transforms the story. We are no longer looking down on Ricky. And, while the narrator's declamations at the story's end seem to indicate he lives vicariously through Ricky's exploits, we've also seen that Ricky's exploits give the narrator an opportunity to exercise his power and influence. Oh, yes, he needs Ricky, but in ways more complex, even insidious, than simply in the way he admits.

The power of this story, the strength of its reversal, the revelations we come to understand that the narrator does not (consciously) admit, are derived from its structure: opening with a scene then holding that scene in suspension (what trouble will Ricky tell him? is he really here to ask him to bail him out again?) until all the exposition is given—exposition, mind you, that is really about the father, though it is ostensibly about Ricky. And then coming back to the scene proper, nudging the characters together via their mutual needs. In this story two scene beasts are created, the narrator's and the reader's, and they are both kept hungry— fed three tidbits—and the story ends with the promised (and much anticipated) story about to be delivered. And we don't mind too much that it's the narrator's scene beast that's about to be satisfied, not ours. We have gotten to participate vicariously in the earlier feedings anyway, and it's enough to know that supper is about to be served to the narrator. Let him eat in peace.

Tim O'Brien makes use of a somewhat similar structure in "The Things They Carried" in that he, too, creates and feeds expectation while delaying its complete satisfaction. The story is almost evenly balanced between scene and exposition, the latter being a mix of commentary and description, but it is *how* O'Brien develops that balance that's worth considering. The story's central event, for example, the event from which all the scenes will spin off or be derived, is first mentioned in the second paragraph. It is mentioned not once, not twice, but three times: "Ted Lavender, who was scared, carried tranquilizers until he was shot in the head outside the village of Than Khe in mid-April." Later that paragraph: "Until he was shot, Ted Lavender carried six or seven ounces of premium dope, which for him was a necessity." Later still that paragraph: "In mid-April, for instance, when Ted Lavender was shot . . ." The repetition almost becomes a mantra for the rest of the story. It divides the world for these characters into a before and an after. There is the world before Ted Lavender was shot, and there is the world after. It's repeated in the later sections over and over.

But what about *when* he was shot? We have this early and frequent repetition of an event that we're expecting to eventually be shown, but we don't see it in scene until the midpoint of the story. There's a reason for that. Although O'Brien has used what I earlier referred to as the simplest plot turn—violence—as the story's central event, that's not what the story is about at all. Instead, O'Brien creates an enormous tension—an appetite—by suspending the presentation of the scene itself until the meticulous and exhaustive recitation of all that they carried, from ordnance to unrequited love, has been sufficiently catalogued to generate the necessary weight that the characters in, and the readers of, the story will have to carry.

There is also a secondary story, one told in the expository sections, of Lieutenant Jimmy Cross's unrequited love for Martha, a girl back home in New Jersey. Like all good stories—that is, stories that are about more than one thing—that summarized, one-sided love is going to merge with the story of Lavender's death, and it happens—ta da!—in the scene itself when it's finally presented to us.

O'Brien, though, takes his time in getting us there. The story is divided into eleven sections separated by white space. The first two are pure commentary, description, and backfill, with the exception of naming that benchmark event—when Lavender was shot. The third block is half-description and half a scene summary of the scene we'll eventually get:

The typical load was twenty-five rounds. But Ted Lavender, who was scared, carried thirty-four rounds when he was shot and killed outside Than Khe, and he went down under an exceptional burden, more than twenty pounds of ammunition, plus the flak jacket and helmet and rations and water and toilet paper and tranquilizers and all the rest, plus the unweighed fear. He was dead weight. There was no twitching or flopping. Kiowa, who saw it happen, said it was like watching a rock fall, or a big sandbag or something—just boom, then down—not like the movies where the dead guy rolls around and does fancy spins and goes ass over teakettle—not like that, Kiowa said, the poor bastard just flat-fuck fell. Boom. Down. Nothing else. It was a bright morning in mid-April. Lieutenant Cross felt the pain. He blamed himself. They stripped off Lavender's canteens and ammo, all the heavy things, and Rat Kiley said the obvious, the guy's dead, and Mitchell Sanders used his radio to report one U.S. KIA and to request a chopper. Lieutenant Cross kept to himself. He pictured Martha's smooth young face, thinking he loved her more than anything, more than his men, and now Ted Lavender was dead because he loved her so much and could not stop thinking about her. When the dust-off arrived, they carried Lavender aboard. Afterward they burned Than Khe. They marched until dusk, then dug their holes, and that night Kiowa kept explaining how you had to be there, how fast it was, how the poor guy just dropped like so much concrete. Boom-down, he said. Like cement.

In fact, this is a summary of the rest of the story's action. But exactly why Jimmy Cross would blame himself for Lavender's death and how his love for Martha could result in a man's death—that's still a mystery. We get a partial explanation in the next section. We're told how mulling over Martha allows Cross to daydream, to feel light, to let his mind wander. But for the necessary link between action and consequences—we need the scene itself for that. Again, O'Brien takes his time getting us there. We get more description, then two references to the world before Lavender was shot, then a description of what it was like going into the tunnels—this both misdirects our attention and ratchets up the tension, and then we get this: "On April 16th, when Lee Strunk drew the number 17, he laughed and muttered something and went down quickly. The morning was hot and very still. Not good, Kiowa said." And now we are in the scene itself—a particular day, April 16, and a particular sequence of events is about to occur. And it does. We get an extended scene of the men waiting around the tunnel and of Jimmy Cross daydreaming and of Lee Strunk finally coming out of the tunnel and of Ted Lavender going off to pee. And when Lavender is shot and killed, we are told about it three separate times in that scene, as though the violence of the moment happens again and again for these men, just when they least expect it.

It should come as no surprise that the next section is a field-stripped meditation on death and whether you can draw a moral from it. The meditation is in reference to a Viet Cong death, however, and therefore slightly distances us from Lavender's—though, because it follows Lavender's death, in presentation if not in real-time sequence, we know why it's there.

The last section that is pure commentary comes next and includes some of the story's most metaphysical observations: "They shared the weight of memory." "They carried gravity." "They carried their own lives."

And then, for the most part, we're given scenes and scene summaries and projected scenes—what they'd say if they could leave, what will happen as they continue on—all of it post-Lavender's death. These other scenes are orbits of that one big scene, essentially retellings of it, as though one could make sense of the event by turning it into a metaphor. "There's a moral here," says Mitchell Sanders again. "Like cement," says Kiowa. "Boom-down."

And, rightly or wrongly, Jimmy Cross draws his own moral: I messed up. Lavender is dead because I loved Martha so much I was imagining myself there rather than worrying about perimeter security here. Whatever you want to make of that self-blaming, whether you want to judge him or empathize with him or both, what I'd like you to make of it is that the key scene is almost extruded out of the background and commentary. First it is named, then it is summarized, then it is put in suspension before being released to us. And after that scene finally emerges most of the rest of the story happens in scene, too. The story pivots right there, with Jimmy Cross daydreaming and Lavender off taking a pee. The balance between telling and showing and the shift at a critical moment from one to the other—that's worth noting. And, as with the Kincaid and Taylor and Atwood stories, to some extent telling *is* showing. Taylor and Kincaid (implicitly) and Atwood (explicitly) pull us into the scene with the narrator so that even the narration occurs in a thicket of implied scene. And certainly readers of O'Brien's book for which this is the title story are aware of O'Brien as a Vietnam veteran and writer, so that he is directly speaking to us. That feeling of one human voice talking to another is the larger context in which this story, too, operates.

If you're a writer skittish about writing scenes, take heart from how much these writers have done with not much. Each story uses essentially a single scene. The narration is largely discursive, but our interest is held because that narration is also intimate. The narrator's voice pulls us into the narration, promising us new revelations and intimacies farther down the narrative path—there's a big scene coming, my children, be patient, be patient—while at the same time delaying the arrival of that scene, the scene when all will be revealed. What Ricky's newest problem is, what those rape fantasies are exactly, why everything we do seems to convince our mother we're a slut, and *what about* that day in mid-April when Lavender got shot—that moment is coming, this voice promises us, it's on its way. But note, please, that when we finally get to the illuminating moment it *is* in scene, in action, that it happens. And it happens because the reader in all of us ultimately expects, needs, hopes for, and, yes, demands it. Note, too, that the scene, when it finally is delivered to us, provides us with something more than, even something different than, what the narrator originally promised. The scene goes *beyond* its promise, into a new place entirely. When considering the care and feeding of your scene beast, then, consider going beyond satisfaction and into the territory of delight.

WORKS CITED

Atwood, Margaret. "Rape Fantasies." In *Writing Fiction: A Guide to Narrative Craft.* Ed. Janet Burroway. 4th ed. New York: HarperCollins, 1996.

Baxter, Charles. "Mistakes Were Made." *Burning Down the House: Essays on Fiction.* St. Paul, Minn.: Graywolf Press, 1997.

Kincaid, Jamaica. "Girl." *The Story and Its Writer.* Ed. Ann Charters. 5th ed. Bedford/St. Martin's, 1999.

O'Brien, Tim. "The Things They Carried." *The Things They Carried.* New York: Penguin, 1991.

Taylor, Peter. "The Gift of the Prodigal." *The Old Forest and Other Stories.* New York: Ballantine, 1986.

PETER TURCHI

The Writer as Cartographer

> What we call the beginning is often the end
> And to make an end is to make a beginning.
> The end is where we start from.
> —T. S. Eliot, "Little Gidding"

We start with a blank: a world of possibility. Even that, though, is only *a* beginning, as opposed to *the* beginning, as there are many kinds of blanks.

There is the blank of the unwritten. The earliest "maps" in many cultures, including those of Native Americans, Inuits, and Aboriginal Australians, were created and passed on orally. In this century cartographers talk about "mental maps." These are made not only by bees doing their figure-8 dances to point their pals to the pollen and squirrels remembering, more or less, where they stored their acorns but also by you and me, as we decide how best to get to the local movie theater. Our mental maps are often not terribly accurate, based as they are on our own selective experience, our knowledge and ignorance, information and misinformation from others; nonetheless, these invisible landscapes are the maps we most often depend on. Our *sense* of where a place is or what it includes is in many ways more important than objective truth. The sense we had of the house we grew up in, the places we played as children, has little to do with the mathematical facts of a room's dimensions.

Part of every written map is the blank of the intentionally omitted. Blanks of intentional omission include the area beyond the borders of the map as well as areas left blank within those borders. While some explorers persuaded Native Americans to draw maps on paper, these were not always reliable—due not to the cartographer's ignorance but to his distrust. The sorts of things worth mapping—hunting grounds, sacred sites—were too important to be passed on to a mere curious stranger. Europeans, though frustrated, may have understood this reluctance; their ships' logs and chartbooks were often weighted or kept in metal boxes so that, if a ship were overtaken, information regarding trade routes, winds and currents, and details of coastlines and harbors could be thrown overboard and so kept safe from the enemy.

Blanks within the borders of maps have, in their way, represented many things. A blank can, of course, simply represent the unknown. It can represent the withheld, as on those drawings solicited from American Indians. It can also represent what is known but deemed unimportant. Native American tribal areas were not included on early European maps of the Americas, giving readers of those maps the impression no one lived there—at least, no one of consequence. No landowners. These are the kinds of blanks that fire Marlow's imagination in Conrad's *Heart of Darkness*—the blanks that certain minds found to be a call for colonialism and conquest.

These days we believe we're well aware of the dangers of the imperial mind-set, but there remain many who would argue that the urge to fill blank spaces is fundamental to the quest for knowledge. A tolerance for blank spaces could be a sign that our aggressive tendencies are under control, but it might also be an indication of insufficient curiosity or evidence of intense self-interest. People of the Middle East, Native Americans, and Australian Aboriginals, among many others, mapped locally. They did not attempt to map the entire world or even the places where they knew others lived. They were placing themselves. Furthermore, the oral "maps" of Native Americans and Australians, like the stick-and-shell navigational charts made by Marshall and Caroline Islanders, were deliberately encoded, as they contained privileged information. To learn how to read any map is to be indoctrinated into that mapmaker's culture.

Blanks on maps were often filled with decorations—sea serpents, dragons, griffons, hippogriffs. For a very long time decorative or fanciful maps were at least as numerous as what we might call "practical" maps. In the 1700s Jean Baptiste Bourguignon d'Anville took a radical stance, renouncing decorations, and leaving blanks in their stead: "To destroy false notions, without even going any further, is one of the ways to advance knowledge." Some of his countrymen began to call themselves "scientific cartographers," meaning they "made maps that showed only verifiable information." As one introductory text puts it, the nineteenth century saw the end of "fanciful fripperies" in the interest of stern science. It's no surprise that this corresponds with the dawn and popularity of realism in the arts—that phrase *fanciful fripperies* immediately recalls Mark Twain's venomous attack on James Fenimore Cooper. Realism, Twain argued, is more than an artistic choice—it is the truth. Thanks to Jean Baptiste Bourguignon d'Anville and his colleagues, a blank on a map became a symbol of rigorous standards; the presence of absences lent authority to all on the map that was un-blank.

The logical end to this scientific approach would be a *mappa mundi,* a detailed map of a verified world. In *A Universal History of Infamy* Jorge Luis Borges describes such a map:

In that Empire, the craft of Cartography attained such Perfection that the Map of a Single province covered the space of an entire City, and the Map of the Empire itself an entire Province. In the course of Time, these extensive maps were found somehow wanting, and so the College of Cartographers evolved a Map of the Empire that was of the same Scale as the Empire and that coincided with it point for point.

But even that world map includes only *surfaces;* there would be no indication of the layers of rock under the soil or the soil under the water. It would not include the changing angles of sunlight and shadows, the migratory paths of birds, the echo of boys' voices. To argue that sounds and smells are difficult to map, that a map is primarily visual, only underscores our acceptance of the conventions of maps—among them, that maps are fixed in time and only include features considered relatively permanent.

In the novel *A Mapmaker's Dream* James Cowan imagines the attempt of Fra Mauro, an actual sixteenth-century cartographer, to draw what he hopes will be a definitive map of the world, based not only on existing maps but on the stories of travelers from around the world. He learns that there are an infinite number of ways to depict reality. As the magnitude of this realization settles in, he writes, "My map absorbs me with what it does not reveal." Later, despite or because of his efforts to be comprehensive, he tells us, "I am left with a sense of existing in an unfathomable void, surrounded by blankness."

Whatever a map's attitude toward blanks within its borders, virtually everything is left off of a map—and must be for a map to be useful. As Denis Wood writes in his provocative book *The Power of Maps,* "No map can show everything. Could it, it would no more than reproduce the world, which, without the map, we already have. It is only its selection from the world's overwhelming richness that justifies the map."

One of the great breakthroughs of urban mapping was the work of Henry Beck, who in 1933 invented *The Way Finder* for the London Underground. Until then the map of the underground was "accurate"—it preserved the direction and distance of the train lines, listing the stops and intermediate neighborhoods. The problem was, the density of information made it almost impossible to read. Beck understood that what riders wanted to know was which trains stopped where, in what order. He color-coded the lines and drew them at neat angles, ignoring precise distances and direction, omitting virtually everything except for the names of the stations. *The Way Finder,* which has been adopted by transportation systems around the world, is a demonstration of the usefulness of leaving maps blank as well as evidence that the most accurate map, and the most detailed map, is not necessarily the best map.

I'll step out of my metaphor for a moment (with more to come) to connect some dots. Dialogue in fiction is not true to life. Even in realistic fiction, dialogue needs to *seem* plausibly conversational, and individual voices should be distinctly characterized, but as readers we have little patience with the *uhs* and *ers,* the stammers and misconstructed statements that are common in the actual speech of even the most educated of us. In writing dialogue, we create an equivalent of *The Way Finder.*

The oldest surviving map, from Mesopotamia, is five thousand years old; it seems that every culture has engaged in some sort of mapping. The question has never been *whether* to make maps but (1) what to select for inclusion, as we must necessarily omit virtually everything; and (2) how to represent it, given that, according to Mark Monmonier, "Any single map is but one of an indefinitely large number of maps that might be produced from the same data."

This latter question becomes more significant—and metaphorically more potent—when we recognize that, even on maps, there is no such thing as objective presentation. Monmonier says, "There's no escape from the cartographic paradox: to present a useful and truthful picture, an accurate map must tell white lies." The first lie of a map—the first lie of fiction—is that it is the truth. And a great deal of a map's or novel's or story's authority results from its ability to *convince* us of its authority. But as writers, and as careful readers, we must not confuse authority with objectivity or dedication to "reality."

Once we've been trained to read maps critically, alert to their implicit assumptions and omissions, we can annotate, say, a U.S. map created by Raven Maps and Images, one that illustrates the effects of conventions so common they have become, for many of us, transparent.

First, the map neatly shows us something no person or animal has ever seen. This is true not only because a curved and irregular surface has been flattened but because any eye far enough away to take in the entire continent would almost certainly have seen clouds and more certainly would not have seen the political borders of states or place names. The colors of the land have been carefully, conventionally selected to indicate elevation. This "clear" image, then, is of a place that does not exist in nature. It is an intellectual construct.

We must recognize, too, how the unavoidable act of selectivity affects the map. Raven's *Map of the United States* is in fact a map of the *contigu-*

ous United States. Alaska and Hawaii, the locations of which make them inconvenient to include, are simply excluded. For roughly two million Americans, these are disturbing omissions. And, while location has played a crucial role in determining what is included, the mapmakers have decided that proximity alone isn't enough. Mexico and Canada are not, of course, among the United States, but their absence—or the presence of white spaces in their stead—makes them seem invisible, inconsequential. Their absence on Raven's map makes this an explicitly political document, as national interests, not natural landforms, are the primary determining factor. But, while the waters off the coast are, for political purposes, considered the nation's to protect, defend, fish, and drill, the Atlantic and Pacific Oceans and the Gulf of Mexico have been erased. Land is, implicitly, more important than water.

The cartographers have chosen to include "Cultural Information," which, they say, consists of "cities, highways, airports, and other information independent from the landforms but of interest to the viewer." Which viewer? If we fork over the money for one of Raven's beautiful maps, we're buying something quite different from the objective document we may think we want. We are, instead, buying a visual statement, a way of seeing—one that asserts tremendous authority and which few viewers are likely to question.

Words can never be a simple reflection of life. Our very limited set of symbols, the letters of our alphabet, are forced to translate all the unspeakable data of our senses, all of our thoughts, and all of our emotions.

This is why it is important for all of us realists, damned by that word *conventional,* to remember, always, that we have chosen a particular projection—one that seems to us to minimize distortion and to speak powerfully. *This is our choice.* And to simply learn how others have done it, to pick up the graph paper and begin plotting our lines, limits us from the start. Realism, like every other artistic endeavor, fails when it becomes an exercise in filling in the blanks. Realism succeeds when the author remembers to question his or her assumptions. Why do we represent dialogue the way we do? Why are smells so often absent? What is the relation of chronology to the way we think? What are we doing when we imagine a character's consciousness, the flow of thoughts through her head—and then render them on the page in some particular order, in a particular syntax? How are we manipulating the data? To what ends?

The same holds true for surrealists, experimentalists, modernists, postmodernists, and romantics, hopeless or otherwise. *All* of our approaches are possible projections. "How to choose?" Denis Wood asks. "This is the question, for the answer determines the way the earth will look on the map." One projection distorts shapes while preserving relationships; another preserves distances near the equator but completely loses the poles. "The selection of a map projection is always to choose among competing interests," Wood asserts, "to take . . . a point of view."

If no map is objective, we must reconsider what we mean when we ask if a map is "accurate." Under the most rigorous examination, no map is accurate. On the other hand, I can easily draw what is called a Sketch Map that will lead you from my office to my house. "Accuracy," then, must be judged against the map's stated purpose. When "usefulness" is not so easy to judge, as in the case of art, we might ask why we should bother to create something inevitably incomplete and inaccurate.

Wood argues that maps give us "a reality that exceeds our vision, our reach, the span of our days, a reality we achieve no other way. We are always mapping the invisible or the unattainable . . . the future or the past." He adds that through the map we "link all [our] elaborately constructed knowledge up with our living." Whatever our beliefs with regard to God and science, for many of us a belief in God and a belief in the combustion engine are not so far removed. Try explaining to a child why she should believe in the Immaculate Conception or Moses bearing the Ten Commandments but not in Santa Claus; in the benefits of fluoride but not in the Tooth Fairy. The most profound questions of our existence cannot be answered through a mere collection of concrete evidence; at some point, whether we are theologians or automobile mechanics, dentists or draftsmen, each of us reaches a border of the verifiable world—and every one of us leaps. A great deal of what we know, we know only through our imagination—and that knowledge is crucial to our lives.

But I digress. When making a map, we must keep in mind our purpose.

We must also consider which conventions to employ and how. Will we include water? Will we give any indication of neighboring lands? How will our map be oriented?

One of my earliest remembered classroom humiliations occurred when an elementary school teacher asked who could point to the North. I raised my hand and, when called upon, simply extended my forefinger; North was Up. In every map I had ever seen, including the ones tightly rolled above the top of our fourth-grade classroom's chalkboard, North was at the top. What I didn't know then, as even our teacher laughed, is that the practice of orienting maps to the north is a convention; orientation is entirely arbitrary. There is no "up" or "down" in space; the term *orientation* comes from the practice of locating the Orient, or the East, at the top of maps. Many Islamic maps were oriented to the south, as was Fra Mauro's world map, and today Australians happily promote a map not only oriented toward the South, giving the Southern Hemisphere the superior position but locating their continent in the center.

These alternatives are not only dis-orienting to those of us who think of North as up, or ahead; they seem *wrong*. The modern convention is so strong, and as Americans we are so used to seeing the United States in the visually dominant position, as if this were the most obvious choice in the world, that we may find it difficult to make sense of a differently designed map. One Northern Hemispherean looked at my Australia-privileged map and asked, "Do they really *use* this?"

The convention of orientation is not to be treated lightly; if we decide to orient our map to the west, or the south-southeast, we had better make that clear, and we must anticipate a good deal of misreading.

Some maps actually ignore compass orientation yet are quite easy to follow. In 1675 John Ogilby produced the first road maps of England and Wales in long strips, thus inventing the route map, or TripTik. When I'm driving long distances, I appreciate having my hand held, every turn clearly marked. Critics of realistic narratives might compare those of us who write them to the AAA employees who confidently move bold markers over narrow maps, clearly charting the route of the traveler's choice—shortest, fastest, most scenic. But, unlike the auto club employees, even those of us who write realistic fiction are rarely interested simply in getting our clientele from one point to another. Rather, like another travel-oriented enterprise, we aim to provide an adventure in moving; we want our readers to find good (or bad) company at rest stops, overhear interesting conversation at roadside diners, have the occasional breakdown. We want them to be followed, like Humbert Humbert, by cars with drivers they only gradually identify. When we caution them about falling rocks, we fully intend to push a few into their path.

Even I, a self-proclaimed conventional realist and map clutcher, appreciate a certain amount of disorientation. It is not for nothing that those of us who are passionate about reading can talk about being *lost* in a book. Years ago I entered my studio apartment one afternoon with a stack of freshman essays I was being paid to grade and a new novel by Italo Calvino, whose work I had never read. I opened the book to its disarming first sentence: "You are about to begin reading Italo Calvino's new novel, *If on a winter's night a traveler*." The first chapter is not the beginning of a story, as we expect, but a description of our own preparation for reading, a description both comically accurate and, the narrator acknowledges, mildly unsettling:

> Perhaps at first you feel a bit lost. . . . But then you go on and you realize that the book is readable nevertheless, independently of what you expected of the author, it's the book in itself that arouses your curiosity; in fact, on sober reflection, you prefer it this way, confronting something and not quite knowing yet what it is.

Hours later I closed the covers. When I opened the book to reread a passage, I could not even find the words on the page; through my window stars shone in a black sky. I had read the entire novel without once getting up, without even turning on a light. I had, gloriously, been lost in a book.

As readers, we are content, even delighted, to be lost, in the sense that we are both absorbed and surprised, as long as we feel confident we are following a guide who has not only the destination but our route to it clearly in mind. John Barth's short story "Lost in the Funhouse" suggests that a prerequisite for finding a way through a story or novel is to be lost; the journey can't begin until we've been set down in a place somehow unfamiliar. And part of a reader's willingness to be led is a willingness to be betrayed, outwitted, jumped from behind.

In that modern labyrinth we call the mall, a thoughtful reader both appreciates and rejects the assertion of the message beneath the arrow pointing to a red circle on the mall directory, the message that insists, You Are Here. No, we think, looking down at our feet—I Am *Here*. The directory reduces the mall to rectangles and corridors, number and color coded, simplifying the world around us, all for the purpose of getting us from here to there with as little confusion as possible. Barth tells us that the point-of-view character in his story, a fiction writer in the making, "envisions a truly astonishing funhouse, incredibly complex yet utterly controlled." While we tolerate some amount of dislocation, at some point we need to know where we stand in the world of a piece of fiction or a poem. With its opening line(s) the work asserts: You Are Here. Trust me in this, and we may proceed. "You don't know about me without you have read a book by the name of *The Adventures of Tom Sawyer*," Huck explains, immediately placing us, and himself, in both the real and fictional worlds—a dash of metafiction long before its time. "In my younger and more impressionable years . . . ," Nick Carraway begins, while Tolstoy insists "Happy families are all alike. . . ." Shakespeare, who left no metaphor unturned, claims, "Thus is his cheek the map of days outworn, / When beauty lived and died as flowers do now," and we are firmly placed. Every piece of writing has its basis for assertion, its orientation, and must immediately begin to persuade us of its authority, its ability to guide.

My son recently received as a gift one of those hand-held electronic game-playing machines. Nearly all of these games show the player a very limited portion of the physical "space" depicted in the game. The key is to avoid obstacles and discover entrances and exits—to find your way through its landscape, which is revealed only in fragments, creating mystery and suspense. This is a sort of disorientation we also find in writing—though the limitations of our "view" are, in prose, usually imposed by the linearity of syntax, the fact that words are read one at a time, left to right in our language, and in sentences, or grammatical units. Poets have the additional tool of the line and its companion, blank space.

We all know the satisfaction and delight afforded by those works that send us spinning back out into the world, dizzy and exhilarated, disoriented and newly oriented. Alain Robbe-Grillet's "The Secret Room" is unusual not only because it does not offer us plot, action, scene, or character in their most familiar forms but because its primary mode of development is to disorient and orient us spatially—not just once but again and again. "The first thing to be seen is a red stain, of a deep, dark, shiny red, with almost black shadows. It is in the form of an irregular rosette, sharply outlined, extending in several directions"—thus the story begins. In the rest of that paragraph, and the next, the claustrophobia and disorientation are relieved a bit as we're given context: we're told the room is "a dungeon, a sunken room, or a cathedral." Given the extraordinary range of dungeon to cathedral and the wholly ambiguous "sunken room," it's a wonder we feel any relief, but we do. The *appearance* of information is comforting, even when it is as useless as an earlier map's hippogriffs and monoculi.

In the second paragraph we're allowed perspective—we see some columns "repeated with progressive vagueness." In the third we learn that the original image was a bloody wound on a white body; in the fourth, plot and story enter as we see "a black silhouette . . . a man wrapped in a long, floating cape . . . his deed accomplished." We return to what we are now told is "a fully rounded woman's body . . . lying on its back" on the floor. That cold, distant *its* seals off any hope of action.

One paragraph is devoted entirely to colors, another to the size of the room, yet another to light, as "no clue . . . suggests the directions of the rays." A paragraph describes the "vaguely outlined" stairs in the distance;

another focuses on the escaping man's cloak. We keep returning to the body of what is now called "the young sacrificial victim," the implications more than enough to tempt us to imagine the morbid scenario. In the final paragraphs even the narrator seems compelled to speculate; just when we have surrendered any expectation of movement, the characters move, albeit in the past. The repetition of details—the staircase with no handrail, the man's cape—begins to provide rhythm, even structure.

The story's final sentence is also its last paragraph:

> Near the body, whose wound has stiffened, whose brilliance is already growing dim, the thin smoke from the incense burner traces complicated scrolls in the still air: first a coil turned horizontally to the left, which then straightens out and rises slightly, then returns to the axis of its point of origin, which it crosses as it moves to the right, then turns back in the first direction, only to wind back again, thus forming an irregular sinusoidal curve, more and more flattened out, and rising, vertically, toward the top of the canvas.

Ah-hah, we can hardly resist thinking. No wonder the narrator seemed so unconcerned about this poor naked woman chained to the floor with her legs spread, stabbed in the breast, and the man in black already escaping.

But wait, the better reader in us says. Didn't we know from the beginning that this was "only" a short story? Why would we worry about a murdered woman in a story and not a murdered woman in a painting?

The second remove of art in the story's final sentence changes our perspective forever—just as it changes our reading forever to know all that is withheld in the beginning—but the word *canvas* is no answer. It is the electric shock that sends us running back through the story, reconsidering what we read, remembering our reactions. One reading is that the corpse is itself a map, a story—mysterious at first, then made sense of, and finally familiar.

The movement of "The Secret Room" is movement through space and time; we are allowed so close a look at the wound in the first paragraph that it has no meaning—we don't know what we're seeing. As we back away, we (think we) begin to understand. We look back at the wound, understanding more. We look away, notice a new detail, look back. Understanding rises like a diver in murky water. We are reading a map—at least, this is about as close as words printed on a page come to re-creating an experience of encountering a graphic image. At the same time, this story stresses one of the significant differences between the linear unfolding of words on a page and a visual image. Sequence, or the release of information, is one of the writer's most powerful tools.

Postmodernism and metafiction take on as their subject our curious ability to imagine ourselves in a world created entirely by the placement of ink on a page. "Lost in the Funhouse," with its constant asides discussing the techniques and conventions of fiction, engages us in both worlds at once—or in neither, completely. "Why do you insist on believing?" the narrator implies. It isn't just that we *can* imagine a world created through words; the power of tales, tall and short, is that we *want* to enter their world. This includes nonreaders; we are all storytellers and story listeners.

In *Arctic Dreams* Barry Lopez reprints a map of the Alaskan coastline drawn by a Native-American fisherman. The product of years of mental mapmaking, the coast is drawn from above—that is, it offers a view the fisherman had never seen—yet the map is extraordinarily accurate. His knowledge came from walking the shoreline. "The map presents us with the reality we know," Denis Wood explains, "as differentiated from the reality we see and hear and feel." Similarly, as writers, we are able to— *we need to*—project ourselves, so we can re-create what we have never seen or experienced.

Our ability and need to project ourselves into the world of a piece of writing is not confined to narrative. Robert Hass has written that the "confusion of art and life, inner and outer, is the very territory of the image; it is what an image is." Hass continues, "Often enough, when a thing is seen clearly, there is a sense of absence about it . . . as if, the more palpable it is, the more some immense subterranean displacement seems to be working in it; as if at the point of truest observation the visible and invisible exerted enormous counterpressure."

In the Buson haiku

> Apprentice's holiday:
> hops over kite string
>   keeps going

the kite itself is invisible—never seen, never noted—yet it is absolutely present. The kite is a powerful blank; the kite *string* is held taut by the unseen. Good art, like an image, evokes more than it represents; it draws the imagination outward.

Hass goes on to say, "It is . . . some feeling in the arrest of the image that what perishes and what lasts forever have been brought into conjunction." Every map goes out of date; every map asserts a truth that it can never attain. This conjoining of "what perishes and what lasts forever" is at the heart of the universality of art. People who deny art its power, or don't understand it, often focus on the specific, the literal, the perishable; when we learn to read beyond the literal, we understand how art can offer truth, can guide our lives.

It is the artful balance of detail and blankness, suggestion and opportunity, that fires the imagination. The art of short stories is, in part, the art of selecting what little the reader needs to know. Kate Chopin's "The Storm" is not only highly selective, but it employs white space, disorients us twice in quick succession, and propels us into the world of the unspoken.

It begins with a man and his son at the store. Chopin announces her metaphor in the second sentence, as the husband, Bobinôt, "called the child's attention to certain somber clouds that were rolling with sinister intention from the west, accompanied by a sullen, threatening roar." We get it; it's the Metaphorical Storm—but Chopin is explicit because she's setting us up for a sucker punch. (Good writers trust good readers enough to be able to fool them this way.) The storm breaks out; they decide to wait until it passes before walking home. Bobinôt is afraid of his wife's temper, so he buys her a can of shrimps while they wait.

In the next section Calixta, the wife and mother, is "sewing furiously," oblivious to the weather. When she realizes why it's suddenly so dark, she hurries out to get the laundry, only to find Alcée, whom "she had not seen . . . very often since her marriage, and never alone." Alcée, eager to be of service, grabs her husband's trousers. The storm arrives, beating violently at the house; Calixta is in a panic. There follows a bit of overheated prose ("face . . . warm and steaming," "lips . . . red and moist," "bosom . . . full, firm"), the result of which is that "they did not heed the crashing torrents, and the roar of the elements made her laugh." The prose mirrors their passionate spasms for a few sentences, until "the growl of the thunder was distant and passing away." Realizing Bobinôt and their son will soon be home, Calixta sends Alcée off, both of them aglow. From their perspective we see "the rain was over; and the sun was turning the glistening green world into a palace of gems." (This, the second section of the story, and by far the longest, runs, in my anthologized version, just over two pages.)

Section 3 finds Bobinôt and Bibi, the boy, "trudging home" then pausing at the cistern to remove "the signs of their tramp over heavy roads and through wet fields." No palace of gems here. Bobinôt is "prepared for the worst," but Calixta rushes to greet them, kissing first her son and then her generous husband. When they sit down to dinner, "they laughed much and . . . loud."

And then everything is given a ninety-degree turn: in section 4, a single paragraph, Alcée writes to his wife, who is in Biloxi with their babies, and tells her "not to hurry back[;] . . . though he missed them, he was willing to bear the separation a while longer."

And then again: in the final section, a paragraph plus one sentence, we shift to Alcée's wife's point of view. She is charmed by the letter and relieved at the invitation to extend "the pleasant liberty of her maiden days." The final sentence tells us, "So the storm passed and everyone was happy."

The story is under four pages long—a study in omission and selectivity. Like a game of crack the whip, it flings its omniscience far from its narrative center, in part to support Chopin's final assertion, removing the burden of proof from the narrator. Even so, I have taught the story to students who refused to believe that a woman could violate the bonds of her marriage, gain momentary pleasure, choose not to destroy her marriage, and not be destroyed. They had been shown a map of a world that included none of the monotonously simple-minded moral repercussions that loom so large in the products of popular culture, and they refused to believe that such a place could exist.

Whatever we make of its final assertion, "The Storm" is a provocative demonstration of Chekhov's suggestion that a writer's job is not to provide answers but to pose important questions. Chopin *seems* to be ending with an answer—"everyone was happy"—but she wrote that sentence knowing the reader would immediately supply the question: *Everyone was happy?* Good writing can blindside us with inarguable brilliance. *This is contrary to everything you know,* the story or poem says, *yet you cannot deny it.*

It's common enough to say that good writing gives us a new perspective, whether that means taking us somewhere we've never been or, more often, showing us one of the familiar places in some new way. The question, always, is how to do it. A very different kind of selectivity is employed by Robert Coover in "The Babysitter." In the tradition of a Way Finder, Coover guides our attention to sequences of events, emphasizing sequence over characterization, setting, and other elements. The story demonstrates the economy of convention by grounding us in the familiar—even in cliché and stereotype—so that it can simultaneously challenge one of the most fundamental conventions of narrative.

"The Babysitter" concerns a suburban couple going off to a party who leave their children in the care of a babysitter. More accurately, it offers us several stories—about the husband, the wife, the children, the babysitter, that girl's boyfriend, that boy's boyfriend, and, notably, the television. Coover hooks us with the familiarity of the scene and characters. Everyone in this story wants to have sex with someone, or is afraid to, which may amount to the same thing. The narrator shifts attention like a store security guard monitoring all nine cameras at once—but when the characters begin to act, various passages begin to contradict one another. It soon becomes apparent that all of the things we're told are happening can't be happening—which is to say, they can't be happening if we insist on clinging to our worn notions of time and space. Coover even tells us the time at the beginning of some of the sections, just as if we were watching through that security camera—but our security is false; that clock is a magician's decoy.

Some readers of this story cling to convention, insisting that one chain of events in the story is the *real* one and the others are "imagined" by the characters. And there is Coover's great success—he forces us to confront our desire to believe in "the real one." I have asked students to consider the possibility that there *is* no real one; *all* the stories are real—they are all going on at once, in the minds of the characters, and we can't cling to an objective reality. If I teach the story again, I will tell them: "*This* is the real story: You reading a book, all of us arguing over it. When we read fiction, we agree to be *there,* in the world of the story; but we are always *here.*" Or I will tell them: "This is how it is *for the writer.* The story could be any of these things. Why pick one over another? Why not tell them all?" Or I will tell them, "Reading this, we are Alice falling through the looking glass."

"The Babysitter" is a map of many trails, all beginning and ending at the same place, or it is a map with no trails, only familiar territory. We can easily imagine any of a number of paths from here to there or from another here to that other there; we can imagine them all. None of them and all of them are on the map.

Gwen Diehn, an artist and colleague of mine, spent most of a year making what she calls "artistic maps" of the area around our campus. They all depict trees and the river, some include contour lines, many include written descriptions. One she calls "The Bovine Walk," a map of a pasture with tiny herds of rectangular-stamped cows in the places they congregated as Gwen watched them, night after night, from her house. Her walking maps, confoundingly, don't include paths or trails. She says paths are too limiting; they take you where *they* want to go so determine what you see.

This is the mystery of meaning in art. Meaning is there, but not the way Exit 55 is *there;* meaning is there, somewhere; there to be found.

But it isn't buried treasure. It is more like an energy line apparent to a feng shui master.

Feng shui, the ancient Chinese art of divining energy in the landscape, is still used to site buildings so that all who enter will benefit from the good *ch'i,* or vital energy, as opposed to suffer from bad *ch'i.* My colleague the mapmaker has pointed out to me a land form on our campus that is considered both rare and remarkably fortuitous: where dark, lush grass grows above an underground stream or at the site of an old riverbed, the feng shui initiate can make out a form known as The Frolicking Green Water Dragon. I have walked by and driven past the pasture before the sawmill for years; the Frolicking Green Water Dragon was always there—or, a nonbeliever might say, it was never there and still isn't. But now it is there for me.

Meaning in art is there all the time, or it is never there; it can be seen from a particular perspective, but only if we have been prepared to see it. It isn't that a map *creates* a Frolicking Green Water Dragon; the map chooses to include it. There is nothing in the landscape itself that would assign those words to a characteristic of the land. To be able to imagine the dragon is to see the familiar anew. It is not the only way to see the pasture, and, unless we are culturally or spiritually predisposed toward it, there is no reason to assume it is the best way to see the pasture.

I'll put it another way: Starting in England, three friends and I once resolved that each of us would make our way to Fez, in Morocco, where we would meet and buy a fez. We slept on cold cement floors, our lives were threatened; it was one of the great trips of my life. But standing in the center of the old city, preparing to negotiate with yet another merchant, we understood there was no need to buy a fez. As travelers through fiction and poetry, we need to distrust the urge to scoop up theme and meaning, as if the things we can neatly pack are necessarily the things we came for.

Is there anything new to map or map anew?

I believe there is, though my evidence is metaphorical. Only in recent decades have we begun to map the land under the ice of Antarctica (the psychological implications of which are almost insultingly clear), the ocean floor, and the ozone layer. Satellites revealed new islands in the Canadian Arctic as recently as the early 1980s. And the last ten years have seen the introduction of cosmic mapping.

Cosmic mapping, using radio emissions and other sources of radiation, involves time as well as space. Cosmic cartographers have mapped parts of the visible universe back as far as 15 billion years, or to within a few hundred thousand years of the Big Bang. Thanks to a modern version of an old tool—the Hubble telescope—astronomers are charting new cosmic territory every day. A recent *New York Times* headline announced: "Data Suggest Universe Will Expand Forever." Tools such as the Hubble don't just allow us to see what we know more clearly; they give us a new sense of all that we don't know.

How do we know where to start?

If we are mapmakers, we are also explorers; and we must remember that a great many of the fruits of exploration were considered, by someone, to be evidence of failure.

As one text obligingly puts it, Alexander Dalrymple's "biggest contribution to geography and mapmaking came about because he believed in something that did not exist." Terra Australis, or the Southern Land, appeared on maps for sixteen hundred years. Much larger than Australia, it was thought to balance the weight of Europe and Asia in the Northern Hemisphere. Dalrymple made such persuasive arguments for the ways this enormous southern continent could benefit Britain that his government sent Captain James Cook on three voyages. Cook never found Terra Australis, but as a by-product of his search he produced the first comprehensive maps of the Pacific, the world's largest ocean.

And then there's the lesson of Christopher Columbus. Columbus died insisting he had reached India, or very nearly so. Never once did he claim he had found a new world—because to say as much would have been to admit failure. Centuries later T. S. Eliot commiserated:

And what you thought you came for
Is only a shell, a husk of meaning. . . .
Either you had no purpose
Or the purpose is beyond the end you figured
And is altered in fulfillment.
　　　　　　　　—"Little Gidding"

In *Back Roads to Far Towns* Basho recalls apologizing for having to leave early, hastily, a temple where he had spent the night, without doing the customary guest's work of sweeping the yard. The "young priests" ran up, not to reprimand him but bearing paper and ink so that he would leave them a poem. He tells us, "At that moment willows in the yard were shedding leaves:

sweeping the yard
let me leave the temple
the willows' failings.

Sandals already on, jotted it hastily down for them." This is the writer as explorer, pausing just long enough to leave his words behind.

How important is this mapmaking?

In the 1980s, Beaver Indians in Northeastern British Columbia presented officials from the Northern Pipeline Agency with what they called a Dream Map. They explained that the map depicted heaven and its opposite, animals, trails to follow and paths to avoid—all of which had been revealed through dreams. A Dream Map would be buried with the man who made it, to guide his spirit.

Such a document may seem distant from our own experience, but very recently a new generation of cartographers has been mapping cyberspace, a world William Gibson has described as "a consensus hallucination." The term might also describe the worlds we create in stories, poems, and novels—worlds of "consensus hallucination." Readers talk about the "suspension of disbelief." As writers, our job is to sustain belief in a world of the imagination, one as real to us as our computers, as day-old bread and tomorrow's newspaper, as our fears and our dreams.

We start off either with some sense of what we want to find or with curiosity and patience, trusting our imaginations to show us a path that exists, though no one has ever seen it. We stare at our own backyards, hack trails through the rainforest, paddle through overgrown rivers, wade into swamps even as something pulls thickly at our boots. When we reach what feels like a destination, we turn and map the way for others. But will we show them the trail or force them to negotiate a muddy slope? Will we label the poison ivy, indicate where the river is shallow enough to cross? Or will we add serpents dangling from the trees? We cannot be trusted. We tell our readers, *Trust me.*

At our best we don't make road maps so much as chart the territory, creating the stories of Frolicking Green Water Dragons and lost cities, the stories of constellations, finding order in the very stars—the uncountable but finite bodies that glimmer above us, always in view, always out of reach. In *A Mapmaker's Dream* Fra Mauro decides the search for the ultimate map ends with the individual. "Wise men contemplate the world," he thinks, "knowing full well that they are contemplating themselves." It may be folly to imagine anything more universal, more objective, more true. Each of us stands at one unique spot in the universe, at one moment in the expanse of time, holding a blank sheet of paper.

And this is where we begin.

WORKS CITED

Basho. *Back Roads to Far Towns*. Trans. Cid Corman and Kamaike Susumu. Hopewell, N.J.: Ecco Press, 1996.

Cowan, James. *A Mapmaker's Dream: The Meditations of Fra Mauro, Cartographer to the Court of Venice*. Boston: Shambala, 1996.

Hass, Robert, ed. *The Essential Haiku: Versions of Basho, Buson, and Issa*. Hopewell, N.J.: Ecco Press, 1994.

Monmonier, Mark. *Drawing the Line: Tales of Maps and Controversy*. New York: Henry Holt, 1995.

———. *How to Lie with Maps*. 2d ed. Chicago: University of Chicago Press, 1996.

Stefoff, Rebecca. *The Young Oxford Companion to Maps and Mapmaking*. New York: Oxford University Press, 1995.

Wood, Denis. *The Power of Maps*. New York: Guilford, 1992.

ANTONYA NELSON

"Mom's on the Roof"

The Usefulness of Jokes in Shaping Short Stories

*A man goes on a trip to Europe, leaving his brother at his house to take
care of his cat. When he arrives in Europe, he phones home to see how things
are.*

His brother says, "Your cat's dead."

*The traveling brother is stunned. He says to his housesitting brother,
"That's a really rotten way to tell bad news. I can't believe you'd ruin my
vacation that way. I'm going to show you a better method. Listen up: See,
what you could have done was, the first day I called, you could have said,
'The cat's on the roof and we can't get her down.' Then the next day I called,
you might have said, 'Well, we got the cat off the roof—firefighters, ladders,
the whole nine yards—but it doesn't look good, it's touch and go.' Then on
the third day, you would say, 'We did our best, the vet tried hard—I V drips,
surgery, etc.—but the cat passed on.' See how that's a better way to tell me?"*

*"Yes, yes," says the brother at home. "You're absolutely right. Brilliant.
Thank you."*

*"You're welcome," says the traveler. "So how's everything else? How's
Mom?"*

*At home, his brother hesitates, then says, "Well, Mom's on the roof, and
we can't get her down."*

I wanted to explain to myself why my favorite narratives are short stories and jokes. Why I seek them out, why I write them, why my favorite
friends are the ones who can shape our conversations around the structure of joke and story. I decided to conduct a formal investigation into
my pleasure. I went looking for the connection between jokes and short
stories. I wanted to learn something about each by comparison with the
other.

First, I should mention that I don't think all stories operate like jokes,
nor is *humor* one of the prerequisites of the story end of this comparison
(humor is, of course, essential to the joke side). I also know that not all
people are as enamored of jokes as I am. I would suggest that, by following my path in this quest, the interested student of writing might
establish her own aesthetic. That is, what is it about jokes, metaphori-

cally speaking, that permits a writer to best apprehend the job of creating a story? Alice Munro thinks of stories as houses, and, in considering her work, it's not hard to envision her toddling from room to room until the place feels complete. Denis Johnson makes use of the terribly associative realms of both poetry and pharmacology to inform the shape and content of his work. Flannery O'Connor relies on the heavy dictates of Catholicism. These are some obvious selections. I have a feeling that most personal aesthetics are vaguely obscure to anyone other than the writer herself, and possibly to her too.

I would like to be able to write stories that work in the way jokes work. That surprise and delight in precisely the manner that jokes do. That amuse and seduce and hold up on retelling. That make deadly serious political or psychological points while appearing to be playful and carefree. That have been reduced to their most economic and necessary length. That have at the center some ineffable intelligence.

Or maybe I like jokes because they work in familiar familial ways: deviously, passively aggressive, indirectly. As an example, I have chosen Deborah Eisenberg's story "The Girl Who Left Her Sock on the Floor" precisely because of its quirky and unpredictable progression toward closure, because it defies paraphrasing in the way a joke does, because its ways and means hold tension in the reader the way a well-told joke does in its listener. When the story succeeds, the reader does not laugh but, instead, experiences that comparable physical effect: the satisfied sigh, the thrilled risen arm hairs, the brief tear-filled eye.

Great short stories and great jokes work toward a moment of insight. We call that either a punch line or an epiphany, depending on whether we're Henny Youngman or James Joyce. This is the most luminous of similarities between a joke and a story: narrative with a firework built in.

An epiphany is described as "a spiritual flash" that has the power to change the way one views oneself or the world. Joyce's concept was that an epiphany occurs when a story's elements have reached critical mass. Flannery O'Connor calls it a "moment of transcendence," and I think we all understand the term as applied to fiction. We also understand what a punch line is. I would not go so far as to claim a punch line to be the equivalent of a spiritual flash, not really, since I don't think a good joke can change your life. A good joke just changes a lightbulb. But I would say that the visceral response is similar in apprehending each of these, the punch line and the epiphany, and that response has something to do with the way they're used in their respective venues. A punch line, like an epiphany, serves to realign our understanding of characters, relations, situations, or events. It insists on an absent logical step in the process of cognition. It forces the listener or reader to leap not forward but sideways, or vertically, in order to follow. *"Mom's on the roof,"* the homebound literal-minded brother claims. For an instant we are puzzled—then, nearly simultaneous with that puzzlement, light dawns: our castigating traveler has gotten exactly what he asked for, though not what he expected. We laugh, having just experienced a sudden cognitive reorganization.

This reorganization is triggered by the perception of an *appropriate incongruity,* an oxymoronic-sounding term I hope to make clear as this proceeds. Humor is rooted in what is called "appropriate incongruity," the understanding of an appropriate intermingling of elements from domains that are generally regarded as incongruous. *When is a door not a door? When it's ajar.* We know that the door is not a jar, but the pleasure is in the brief recognition of cleverness. A flash of insight pops. The punch line to a joke reveals that what is seemingly incongruous is appropriate, or what is seemingly appropriate is incongruous. The punch line must link or align two domains that otherwise occupy separate planes.

In Deborah Eisenberg's story "The Girl Who Left Her Sock on the Floor" the competing planes of reference in the story are the known and the unknown. Francie, the story's protagonist, is informed at the story's opening that her mother has died. This blunt fact sets her on a journey ripe with subtle and not-so-subtle fictions. It becomes the story's point to merge the factual with the fictional in order to arrive at the truth. The punch line, predictably enough, depends on the reader's ability to apprehend the junction of fact and fiction. "The Girl Who Left Her Sock on the Floor" is not unique among stories that I like, in that, when reading it I enjoyed it, had no idea where it was going, found it surprising, funny, believable, and, ultimately, supremely moving. I could not chart its reason for pleasing me so; it was a story whose design, on first reading, eluded me yet moved me. That is, I responded emotionally rather than intellectually—and I'm a highly intellectual, which is to say jealous and critical, reader, which is, as you're probably well aware, a crippling and annoying feature of being a writer. Anyway, I couldn't figure out why the thing was a story. A lot of my undergraduate students are in that position most of the time, so I put myself in their collective shoes and worked to wrangle elegance out of the thing. That is, what gave the story shape, power, force, etc? Why did it make the hairs on my arms stand up? In evaluating it, I discovered why, and the fact that the shaping device was invisible to me on first reading is one of the reasons I love this story. It has a bit of magic in it, a sleight of hand.

"I often ask myself what makes a story work," Flannery O'Connor says, and then answers herself by stating that "it is probably some action, some gesture of a character that is unlike any other in the story, one which indicates where the real heart of the story lies. This would have to be an action or a gesture which was both totally right and totally unexpected." Could there be a more fitting definition of an *appropriate incongruity?* The *inevitable surprise?* In her own story "A Good Man Is Hard to Find" O'Connor cites the moment of the Grandmother's transcendence as the one where the old lady reaches out to touch the Misfit, claiming him as one of her own children. The Misfit uses her transcendent gesture as the lead-in to his "punch line" when he later asserts that the Grandmother would have been a good woman if there'd been someone there to shoot her every moment of her life. It's a better story when the full truth is given its due; Grandma is, indeed, revealed to be a Christian, but, let's get one thing straight: it cost her her life to demonstrate it. The story isn't a great story, not a satisfying joke, until the Misfit gets to put in his two cents. Like the overwhelming majority of punch lines in narrative jokes, the epiphany here is expressed in dialogue or in some other kind of performed action: a gesture, a noise, singing. A punch line is rarely more than a line. Frequently, it is much less—a noise, an exclamation, a word, a gesture, or even a musical tone.

"What's time to a hog?"
"You're ugly, too."
"How about a little head?"
"You ain't so smart. I been believing in nothing ever since I was born."
"Strange day, huh? Starting with the blimp."

This compactness is directly related to the function of the punch line as a technical device. The punch line must effect a sudden transformation in apprehension. Nothing more thoroughly kills a great moment, in a story, than the overexplanation of that moment, the lingering and loitering, the little love-in the writer might be having with her transcendent insight. Because an appropriate incongruity must, to some extent, be discovered by the listener or reader. Discovery is an experience, an experience that can only be shared by engineering a situation in which someone is allowed to repeat that discovery. Being shown the solution to a puzzle is qualitatively different from discovering it oneself. Consequently, the joke must establish a balance between revealing too little and revealing too much. If a joke shows too little, the discovery of an appropriate incongruity will not be achieved. If it shows too much, the appropriate incongruity will not be discovered so much as displayed.

Humor depends upon surprise, but that surprise must be crafted. This seeming paradox is at the heart of great humor. Humor is *fundamentally* ambiguous. It is grounded in an ambiguous system of relations—relations that are simultaneously incongruous *and* appropriate. To recognize the joke, weight must be given to both. Jokes, like stories, rely on the creation of and belief in a wholly fictional world, complete with its own rules of subordination and primacy. Unlike many other forms of narrative prose—newspaper articles, historical texts, morality tales—the "point" is elusive. In fact, the intention of jokes and stories is precisely the opposite of that of the newspaper or the history book. Jokes, for instance, do not deliver information directly. And the information that they do deliver is often impractical and/or whimsical. At best its benefits might be labeled "emotional intelligence," the identical response that short stories engender. I might justify my utter fascination with fiction and jokes—to the exclusion of almost any other discourse—by saying that from them I have learned immeasurable information concerning character and human nature.

The best jokes depend on the creation of character, by which I mean, when we hear them we recognize ourselves or someone we know or human nature in general within them. A universal truth must be revealed. It can be a small universal truth, and its terms are no doubt idiosyncratic. The cloddish brother who blurts out that the cat has died is familiar, as is the bossy superior brother who reprimands him, and then too is cringingly familiar the beautiful moment when the superior brother gets precisely what he asked for—a refined version of very bad news—and discovers he must amend his thinking. Characters in jokes are in situations. In jokes, as in stories, reversal and just deserts, gained by means that are surprising, please us. We like to be surprised.

This surprise often comes at the intersection of a pairing of complementary characters—the fool and the wise man, the Misfit and the Grandmother, two characters who, taken together, represent some whole creation—whose roles complicate, often by use of upheaval. Francie, in "The Girl Who Left Her Sock on the Floor," encounters a variety of escalating complements in her journey "home": her roommate, her mother's nurse, and, finally, Iris Ackerman, her seatmate on the bus. Each supplies a missing link in her quest for knowledge; each embodies an aspect of the "other" for Francie to either adopt or reject as facets of her ever-shifting character; and each also serves to dislodge or rearrange a previously gained insight.

Complementary characters disrupt complacency and therefore dictate a necessary unpredictability in both jokes and stories. How is it that we can continue to tell the same old stories—and jokes—and continue to make them fresh? Most stories, as is the case with most jokes, stem from a series of models and classic shapes: you've got your heroic quest, you've got your guy walking into a bar. This argues for the constant reinvention of the form; there's nothing more unfunny than a dated joke. We have expectations of short stories, as we do in jokes, and those expectations are essential. We have to have context for understanding that what we're about to receive is a joke. Our narrator clues us in, changes the pitch of his voice, begins at the beginning. But, paradoxically, whatever expectations we bring to either the short story or the joke must also not be simply met but exceeded. We don't want to hear the same joke, but we don't mind variations on a theme—in fact, we appreciate the self-conscious mastery and reworking of certain themes. We reward cleverness in both stories and jokes. We applaud the moment when the familiar kind of story takes off, when the type of joke transcends itself, is funny in spite of being familiar. Perhaps that is the difference between a competent short story and a masterful one. It is not the degree of surprise but the degree of the correctness of the surprise. *Of course* the bible salesman in "Good Country People" must steal Hulga's leg. *Of course* his final words to her are precisely what she must hear: he hasn't believed in anything for a long time, and he didn't have to obtain a Ph.D. in philosophy to know it. He commits the perfect punch line, unpredictable as it is *hermeneutically radiant.*

Hermeneutic radiance, as I understand it, is akin to inimitability. A moment of hermeneutic radiance is one that is perfectly itself, a phrase or image that cannot be described or better illuminated than the way it is presented. Its effect is ineffable. "A story," says Flannery O'Connor, "isn't any good unless it successfully resists paraphrase." She also claims that a story "is a way to say something that can't be said any other way. . . . You tell a story because a statement would be inadequate." This inimitable quality is one common to both short stories and jokes, and it is directly attributable to the fact that, in jokes and stories, every word counts. Unlike many other forms of written or spoken discourse, you cannot skim a good story or joke. They are two forms that value both brevity and precision, traits to be admired.

In the absence of these traits a joke or story goes terribly awry. Consider the following: "A man named Fred goes on vacation in Italy. He'd visited Italy in the past, and was eager to return to Venice, where he'd had an affair with an exotic Italian woman. So he leaves his house in Rochester, and he also has this brother in Rochester. His brother is taking care of the house while the man is in Italy. The house is a large house, with a pitched roof. The brother must take care of the bills, the mail, the phone messages, the cat. . . ." There are dangers in overdeveloping joke narratives. A listener trying to keep track of so many potential details is in danger of overlooking the single one necessary to the comprehension of the punch line. Similarly, overdevelopment in short stories tends to dilute, divide, and distract from the central source of power.

And how to know that central source of power?

> *A doctor, as he left a woman's bedside, said to her husband with a shake of his head, "I don't like her looks."*
> *"I've not liked her looks for a long time," the husband agreed.*

If the doctor says, "I don't like her looks," and the husband says, "I think she's ugly," the joke is ruined. Not unlike the storyteller who does not recognize the significant moment, the emphatic structure, the right detail. One is forever encountering people who say: I love jokes, but I can't tell them. In jokes we recognize that the telling is everything—the sequence, the timing, the inflection. We have fewer cues in the instance of short stories because, typically, we don't have the immediate gratification of a hearty guffaw from our audience. Moreover, jokes are repeated narratives, whereas short stories are original works. We often recognize the power of the *material* but can't figure how to *shape* it, how to emphasize it, how to weigh pertinent against irrelevant information, how to get to the punch line in a way that neither over- nor underexplains. We want to give someone else our pleasure, our intelligence. We want to remember the joke and fashion the story in order to tell it right.

And, on the other end of the transaction, the audience has to be able to receive jokes and stories, to understand them. Jokes depend on idiomatic understanding (if you don't know the word *ajar,* then you will miss the open door); jokes depend on cultural savvy (of a variety of levels, depending on what TV programs you miss, which newspapers you don't read, what history you forgot); and stories, often, depend as well on a developed aesthetic. It's easier to understand simple irony or to recognize the point of overwhelmingly plot-driven fiction than to weasel meaning out of more elusive stories. I read "The Girl Who Left Her Sock on the Floor" to my eleven-year-old daughter and my seven-year-old son. My son confessed to not "getting" it at all; my daughter's response mimics a great many others', I imagine: she believed that the story was not yet over when the author had chosen to end it. She believed that the father had to come through the door for the story to achieve proper closure. A certain level of sophistication is necessary to appreciate this story fully, and, after I explained my theories on why it was shaped the way it was, she accepted that shape as suitable, interesting even. My son still didn't get it; when I said that the parents were purposefully offstage, he said, "Oh. You didn't say it was a *play*."

I've marked the development of my children by their ability to "get" things. The same obstacles pertain in their understanding of jokes or stories as they do to all people. For example, a great deal of humor does not translate well. Oftentimes the social order of the world we're reading about—whether we are distanced from it by place or time or ethnicity or religious bias—prohibits our fully getting it. Jokes are understood within cultures, adhering to that culture's sense of taboo, rules, hierarchy, etc., and frequently depend on the social and cultural conventions that a group shares. Our current shared paranoia-disguised-as-disdain concerning Internet technology now drives a great deal of our humor, while one of our oldest, fondest unified comic images—the staggering drunk—has been relegated, alongside Amos and Andy, to the category of dated humor.

In joke theory there are things named "scripts." We hear a certain sort of joke and succumb to the premise: blonds are dumb; various individuals are dead and facing their maker at heaven's gate; here's that desert isle, once more. We don't believe them, but we indulge the scripts. We suspend disbelief; we step willingly into their premises. Similarly, there exist story types: war stories, relationship stories, coming of age stories, strangers riding into town stories, men or women embarking on journeys stories. Coming of age, for example, often occurs in American letters when a boy goes into the woods to bag his first deer. Or when a girl discovers her stained underpants. These are scripts too. The joke or story then has a whole background of expectation behind it, a history, its own rarefied atmosphere. How funny a dumb blond joke will it be? How clever a coming of age story? This has nothing to do with the realism of the situation, because dumb blond jokes depend on shallow stereotype, and coming of age stories depend on a deadly serious truth, but they do share the weight of predecessors, of expectation on the part of the listener. They share baggage, a social construct. In Sweden, perhaps, dumb blond jokes do not work. Internationally speaking, it's possible to envision the reader who will not understand killing a deer as a mark of manhood or stained underpants as a traumatic developmental stage.

Some people will not buy into scripts but will choose to embrace the fictional construct as a stereotype—perfectly valid, a lot of what feminist and other criticism is about—and necessary to recognize now and again. Racial stereotyping, in jokes or fiction, is now beneath us as a cultural audience. And yet those characteristics we have historically assigned to lawyers, to blond women, to African Americans, to Jews, while false *stereotypes,* represent true *human* types. And so we must refigure our methods of broadcasting those human truths. To defuse stereotype and reclaim the useful human truth, we cast the script characters as animals: the hyena as scam artist, the elephant as ponderous drudge, the owl wise, the rabbit randy, the cat snottily self-absorbed, the dog moronically loyal, the snake devious, the monkey clever, etc. What's important in both instances—jokes and stories—is pegging universal human characteristics in such a way that we respond to the truth of the characterization. We laugh with, rather than at. There's a fluidity to the subjects in art that are deemed unacceptable by its audience, which is determined by the historical moment; brainiac computer moguls, for example, are fair game right now in the way that, once upon a time, all sorts of ethnic groups were.

As often as subjects are deemed offensive by a group, there will be ones deemed personally sensitive. Many of us might individually characterize certain jokes as offensive, certain writers as offensive, some material simply off-limits for whatever personal wound it opens. So be it. My point is not to argue your taste or aesthetic—in fact, I would encourage you to study that which offends you, to get to the heart of the offense, since it is such a powerful emotion. Offense is not indifference but anger, and anger is never a bad emotion to study. Like fear, it involves mystery, and mystery is what drives great fiction.

Furthermore, in order to joke about some things that we might deem "unfunny," the person involved must take a step backwards from the material. An emotional tie to a particular topic may produce the feeling that the subject should not be joked about at all or, at the very least, that the joke must avoid the use of certain categories, images, and linguistic expressions. A joke that fails to live up to these standards may not be regarded as funny. The emotional attachment to the topic overpowers the appreciation of the intellectual structure of the joke. "That's not funny!" is a reaction that recognizes but discounts the joke structure and categorizes the expression as some form of serious statement—an insult or obscenity. This is not to imply that a person cannot joke about people or events that are important to him—he can. To do so, however, he must be able to suspend his involvement with them. For the purposes of the joke he must detach himself sufficiently from these personages and events to recognize them as ideas that can be manipulated for some particular semantic value.

People will joke about anything. Maybe that's the point. Maybe it is some people's way of saying that nothing is sacred. True, almost all jokes are based on someone else's misfortune. That is the basis of humor. Do we joke about the truly horrible as a way of distancing ourselves from it? As a way of isolating ourselves from tragedy? By joking, do we make it unreal? Is that the same as fiction writing? Maybe. But maybe we joke about such things for a different reason. Maybe we do it to satisfy some deep, dark urge within us to speak the unspeakable, to push against the limits of decency. And that, of course, is not really an attempt to be funny.

Jokes and stories contain truths. They are often discomfiting truths. The man who finds his wife ugly is revealing a terrible truth: a long marriage often becomes one in which a man finds his wife physically repulsive. Part of our laughter is the recognition of truth; as with stories that are elegant and great, we respond to the painful tragic beauty of raw truth, the forbidden (often) or the unquestioned (a man *ought* to find his wife lovely, conventional wisdom declares—jokes are often the antithesis of little needlepoint niceties, wherein the wife would be "beautiful on the inside"—and the truth very frequently forces us to question assumptions). Questioning assumptions and investigating paradoxes is the backdrop of short fiction and jokes. Why is Chekhov's "Lady with a Pet Dog" a great story? Because love is supposed to make you happy, and, the truth is, love makes Dmitri and Anna miserable. It's a great story because it nails that particular paradox directly on the head, in doing so shattering that "love is happiness" nonsensical conventional wisdom into a thousand pieces. We have to remember that all expressive forms—myths, fairytales, songs, rituals—serve to disguise forbidden impulses so that they can be expressed in a socially acceptable fashion.

A businessman was going bankrupt and needed to fire some of his employees. He had three secretaries, two of which he'd have to let go, but he didn't know which two to fire and which one to keep. So he explained his dilemma to a friend, who had the following advice: "Listen, this may cost you a little money up front, but it will be well worth it and will pay for itself in the long run. Next payday, add an extra five hundred dollars to each of their paychecks and see how they respond. That will let you know who to keep."

The next payday came around and the businessman took his friend's advice. The first secretary looked at her check and said to herself, "The boss overpaid me by five hundred dollars. I'd better get that extra money back to him right away. I know the business is in trouble, and he can't afford such errors." The second secretary looked at her check and said to herself, "He overpaid me by five hundred dollars. He will eventually discover the error, but in the meantime I'll bank the money. When he asks me to give it back, I'll return it, but I will get to keep whatever interest accumulates." The third secretary looked at her check and said to herself, "He overpaid me by five hundred dollars. He'll eventually discover his mistake and ask for the money back, but I won't give it to him. I'll just quit. The business is not doing all that well, and it will probably go under. At least I'll be five hundred dollars ahead."

Which secretary got to keep her job?
The one with the big tits.

This joke reveals the particular truth that jokes and stories frequently reveal: that instinct triumphs in overwhelming proportion to reason. Various philosophers give us the following dicta: Man is the moral animal; man is the only animal who knows he's going to die; man is the laughing animal. Still and all, big-brained as we are, dressed in clothes and writing rules, we succumb, more often than is comforting, to our animal instincts. We are guided by our hearts far more often than our heads. It's *funny* when we say that men think with their little heads. Funny and *true*. Jokes and stories address the constant battle raging between reason and instinct.

A man is sitting at a bar when he's startled to see his friend walk in—his head totally shrunken, the size of a tennis ball!
"What happened?" he exclaims.
His friend answers in an unnaturally adenoidal voice: "Well, it's like this. I came upon this mermaid yesterday, stranded out of water. So I helped her back into the sea, and she was really grateful; she said I'd saved her life. She asked if there was anything she could do for me in return to express her gratitude. I figured, what the hell, and asked, 'How about a little fuck?' And she says, 'Mmm, physically impossible,' kind of flipping her tail. So I said, 'OK then, how about a little head?'

Humor is, first and foremost, play. As writing a story is. A grownup, articulate, intellectual form of play. Intellectual emotional processing. A process, for me anyway, not unlike being given a discordant set of objects and abstractions—a sock, a bus, a window, History in both upper- and lowercase letters, platitudes, erosion, a blimp, a dead mother—and making a piece of art out of them.

"The Girl Who Left Her Sock on the Floor" has a rambling, seemingly aimless narrative punctuated by non sequiturs and ludicrousness, much like a joke. But, also like a joke, it is deviously shapely. In it Francie performs the tidy trick of losing a mother and gaining a father. The story takes place in the time when she has neither, the region of transference, flight, falling through air from one swinging bar to another, although she's mostly riding the bus rather than a trapeze, as it turns out, going from one destination to another in the company of random strangers who offer their sagacious and/or spurious pieces of advice. She is wholly on her own, exposed like an open wound, and completely without resources other than her own character. She takes in platitudes and advice without discriminating about their appropriateness, applying them as she finds necessary, which attribute—her openmindedness—eventually convinces the reader she will survive. This journey is the test of her character, and her vulnerability—of which the reader is more aware than Francie herself—is what makes the story suspenseful. We read not just to find out what happens but to make sure she is okay. We like her, in spite of herself and ourselves. She triumphs, which also makes the story satisfying. She makes it to her father's. She is forced off the relative safety of her mother's trapeze swing, free-falls for the course of the story, bouncing from one advice giver to another, then grasps the father's swing as the story closes.

It's important to note that the reader never sees either of these parents. They are literally absent in the story, so that we, like Francie, must use conjecture to create them. Further, their absence permits Eisenberg's readers to inhabit the same emotional and physical space as Francie: orphaned. Where are the grownups? Who is in charge of this child?

Every time Francie looks out the window she sees a different cast of disintegration. First it is the physical aspect of spring, "faint crumblings and tricklings," as she watches Cynthia come up the hill to her. Next she sits on the bus observing the "failing farms. Rusted machinery glow[s] against the sky in fragile tangles." The third and fourth windows described are in memory, one a car window shattered by a rock, and the other the apartment window through which Francie has for years envisioned her father's death. From the hospital Francie observes the wrecking ball and other signs of destruction—and construction, resurrection—that mark the center of this story. There are ghosts through the glass of television screens, "predatory machines" through the hospital windows. On her final bus journey she seats herself once again at a window seat. When she arrives in New York she sees "enclaves of people wrapped in ragged blankets huddled against the walls of the glaring station." Her final episode with a window is the one she imagines her father looking up at, the one that will reveal her on its other side. The reversal—one viewing the other in imagination from building to street, from street to building—is what gives the last moment of the story its weight.

Francie's roommate Jessica says the worst thing is that anything can just happen. And Francie says it's worse even than that. What she means, I think, is that things can *unhappen*. Things can not have been at all. Her history, in the course of the story, has become a fabrication and therefore is without substance to pull her through. Throughout the story objects or people fall; the atmosphere and noises within it crumble to the ground. Time is given physical presence, the ability to coalesce and then shatter like glass.

Once Francie lands in New York, we have no confidence that her life will be good, that her father will want her, that he will be any more nurturing or acceptable than the mother (he could hardly be less so), but we are satisfied with her grasp of the swing, tentative as it is. We feel we have delivered her, that she has delivered herself. We can leave her because she has arrived. And of course this literal arrival replicates the story's thematic interests. Francie is beginning to understand history, even as it opens the floor beneath her feet. She slams shut World History on page 1, being given no choice but to discover her own history in its place. This is a coming of age story that feels distinctly honest: the truth complicates rather than simplifies. And, despite the pain of complication, there is the consolation prize of truth. That is the bitterest and sweetest of paradoxes. The truth will not only set you free; it will chain you down.

Francie grows up by losing her mother. It's quite mythic, classical, in its terms: the girl who cannot ascend to the throne of adulthood until her mother the queen has died. And yet its icons and features are uniquely contemporary and mundane. The nasty bus, the frigid headmistress, the secret cigarette smoking and general surliness of a teenage girl, the cloying nosy neighbor, the crazy/not crazy woman on the bus. The timely reality of a gay father. The mother's beautifully unsentimental character. The bus is the deft symbolic agent of both destruction and salvation: it killed her father, and then it delivers Francie to his door. It carries inside of it a microcosm of civilization, a band of human tribesmen each with his own "situation" and history, each with a "tendril of plausible reality now generating tendrils of their own." Also traditional in the story's structure is the use of a sustained metaphor: the rock of event shattering the window of a life. I appreciate the story's blend of archetypal incident, traditional methodology, and contemporary situation. Together they provide the solid integrity of the story.

And still it bears resemblance to a kind of joke. The world Francie once believed in has been shaken apart, revealing another, also uncertain, and the moment when Alex, her father's roommate, echoes the woman on the bus about the blimp is the story's subtle punch line, aligning the parallel planes Francie has been battling since story's beginning. "Strange day, huh? Starting with the blimp." His words echo, ratify, announce, in their hermeneutically radiant way, that there is truth in conjecture, in the power of imagination, in the impossible event of a blimp crashing into a building or a dead man being suddenly alive, and this epiphany/punch line permits Francie to finally envision her living father, who is on his way to her.

This is not an obvious epiphany, but the art in jokes and stories must be, to some degree, hidden. Bad jokes are met with groans rather than laughter. Bad stories are met with indifference instead of the utterance of that little sigh that Bill Matthews named "the gerbil orgasm"—you know, that noise we hear, or make ourselves, after the reading of a great piece of writing: "Mmm." We respond, as we have been moved, emotionally, intellect bringing up the rear. A joke is bad, in general, because its listener is superior to it—perhaps responds intellectually but feels no emotional transcendence, no pleasing surprise, present. A story is bad, in general, for the same reason.

Finally, how do we writers access superior insights? By according our unconscious minds as much respect as our conscious ones, by valuing the quick interplay between them, by making our appropriate incongruities, by writing up to rather than down to both our characters and our audience, by upending conventional wisdom, by risking offending someone.

> *A man is eating a bald eagle. He gets caught by forest rangers, and they go, "Yo buddy, don't you realize it's a federal offense to eat a bald eagle? We're gonna have to lock you up." So they cuff him and haul him away, driving him to jail, and pretty soon one of the rangers can't help himself; he leans over and says real quiet, "Hey, just between you and me, what's a bald eagle taste like, anyway?" And the guy thinks for a minute then says, "Something between a whooping crane and a trumpeter swan."*

PART THREE   *Facing Up to the Reader*

MICHAEL MARTONE

Ruining a Story

The following is the first aesthetic argument I can remember having.

I was in the third grade and had just seen, with a group of my friends, the movie *A Hard Day's Night*, starring the Beatles. We were much taken with the movie and the Beatles, so we decided to put on a show at Bill Stuckey's house using the garage there because it was the only one we knew that opened automatically. We could employ the door as an impressive and professional curtain, revealing to the neighborhood kids sitting in the driveway our version of a lip-synched concert. Mark Taylor would be Paul. He was left-handed. Bill Stuckey would be Ringo. Slightly more affluent than the rest of us, he had a drum kit along with the mechanized double garage. A quiet kid named Charlie would be George. His perfection in the role is now supported by my inability to remember his last name. And Rick Blaine would be John because he actually had a guitar he could play and was serious about growing up and playing in a band. He still plays in a band today. For reasons that reveal a lot about me then and now, I wanted desperately to be Brian Epstein, the manager.

Together we set about recreating the concert footage we had recently seen, building the set while listening to the music we would pretend to sing. The yin and yang of the Capitol 45 spun on Bill Stuckey's turntable. A stack of records dense as a devil's food cake floated on the spindle. "Love Me Do." "Please Please Me." "She Loves You, Ya, Ya, Ya." As we worked, we heard the screams too, imagined our escape routes through the backyard gardens and alleys, our stage overrun, before we could get the garage door down, by hysterical little sisters acting their parts in our kooky adventures.

The falling out with my friends came over the issue of wires. Our imitation microphones, amplifiers, and electric guitars were connected by means of pilfered extension cords of various gauges and colors. Though these carried no load and were plugged into painted cardboard boxes and disguised coatracks, my colleagues in the band paid too much attention, in my mind, to safety. They channeled the cords away from

From the *Southern Indiana Review* 1, no. 1 (1994).

traffic patterns, taped kinks down, even ran lengths of them under throw rugs. My vision of the archetypal scene of the Fab Four included a carpet of crisscrossing wires dangerously coiling around the tapping Beatle boots. Indeed, the power of the image for me was generated by all those mysterious connecting wires that were the physical residue of the sound. I liked the way they appeared so randomly, so spontaneously, about their own business. The performance of the band would be so good you wouldn't notice them. But I did notice the style of their mess.

I couldn't convince the band, the parental lessons of electricity running too deep perhaps. Besides it didn't matter. The shake of Ringo's head, the way Paul and George leaned into the one mic, the elevation of John's chin, those things mattered. I can still remember how mad I was, storming out of the garage. I was so angry that other people didn't see the way I saw things. I was even more upset that I wasn't able to put into words why those wires should be so important.

As you can see, I have been thinking about this for a long time, and I'm a bit surprised to see now that the way I look at things has been with me so long. I understand years later that both camps had a unified artistic vision, but where my friends made points in their scheme of things with neatness and order, I was more interested in the order of neat clutter.

I have found, too, that I like to read stories and write stories that have this quality of clutter. Stories, as something different from novels, are particularly suited to a special type of ruin. Situated as they often are near the moment right before or right after things change utterly, stories can detail the stuff of life in a way the novel can't. The sheer bulk of things in a novel suggests an operator's manual to me. A story is much more microscopic, its fragments used to reconstruct, to imply what has happened. Because of the story's slightness, its intimacy, the explosive acts of violence a novel can build cannot be carried. A story for me, then, is often a littered landscape of parts of things. Where a novel is a forest fire, the story is rust.

Both a novel and a story are maps of life, of course, and distort the world by amplifying selected details. The novel's ambition is to create a world from the ground up, while a story grinds the earth down to its atoms. The world of the novel is a moon, a satellite, of the one we inhabit. The world of the story is an impulse, scrambled pixels, bounced over the horizon, sorting themselves out on the screen of the retina.

Novels murder and create. Stories are the scenes of crimes. I find, when I talk about stories, I often use the metaphors of detection, archaeology, pathology, forensics of all kinds. Collecting the evidence often is enough in a story. As a reader, I am satisfied on the periphery of my nerves. Instead of its solution, the vibrations of the crime itself, its harmonic, are encoded in the air.

Finally, a novel seems to me to depend upon the predicate of sentences. There is so much to move. A novel is a kind of western expansion, manifest destiny. A story can thrive on the nominative, nodes of names that the reader wires together into patterns, jerry-rigged, Dr. Seuss contraptions. The name itself contains a little story, the list of names on paper becomes a tissue of living tissue.

If you have been to Greece, then you know, or, if you haven't, you can begin to imagine, its ruins. The white marble of its classical period is characterized by the acropolis in Athens. Currently, the Parthenon and the other buildings are being restored to a state of previous ruin to combat the accelerating deterioration from modern air pollutants. They are not restoring it to its original condition but to that moment of ruin right after the Turks blew it up. Shrouded in scaffolding, the temple's repair to disrepair brings us face to face with essential questions of why we look at this most looked at of buildings. But there are also the red brick ruins of Byzantine Greece, not as popular perhaps as their ancient cousins but still evocative in their own way. Monemvasia is a kind of Port Townsend or Key West or Provincetown of Greece. Its unfinished and deteriorating old mansions are slowly being restored and lived in. Walking through the rubble, you stumble into a garden patio, geraniums blooming in blue painted olive oil tins.

But I am most taken by the contemporary ruins I have found everywhere else in Greece. Each new house, apartment block, villa of reenforced concrete is topped by an unfinished floor—a nest of tangled rebar at the tip of each corner column, the plumbing and electrical conduits roughed in, and visible sometimes the framing for some rooms or a door. A stairway leads up to nothing. All of these floors are left unfinished for tax reasons. You pay property tax when you finish the house. So the top floors of all those buildings have the look of destruction, as if the whole country had collectively exploded, mimicking the exploding powder magazine in the Parthenon, a whole nation topped with a jagged crown.

To think about ruins is necessarily to begin to think about inertia, entropy, decay, rot. Stories, as illuminated moments along the time lines of these inevitable processes, should at least indicate this potential destruction. Encapsulated within the story, attached to it, are the signs of the larger story of life that the story is part of, is commenting upon.

When I bought my first house, I also bought a how-to-fix-it book. Its first line was: *Water is the enemy of the house.* As I write this, it is raining. The gutter above my window leaks. I can hear the big drops of water splashing on the walk below. The spray of water has kept the foundation wet on this the north side of the house. The bricks are now grouted with moss.

What will happen and what has happened is as important as what is happening now.

A story contains its weather and its weathering. The irresistible course of human events is contained in your reader. Add a little water, a lichen blooms.

Before looking at three stories and their techniques for ruining, the spoils of their spoiling, I'd like to stick with real architecture for a bit. It is hard to make physical the verbal. And I find it hard to talk about story writing anyway. It is easier for me when I am able to attach the extra dimension, the density, to stories as I think about them. If they were only made up of Lego blocks, Tinker Toys, I'd feel a lot better. So, for a while longer, I'd like to regard two architects who practice, in their more solid work, types of ruining analogous to what I find wonderful in stories.

Frank Gehry recently completed his first building in Boston. It was actually a renovation of an existing box office tower. During the work the building was sheathed in scaffolding, which was then draped in a scrim to protect the workers and prevent accidents by keeping debris and tools within the envelope it created. The sidewalk, in part, was closed off at the building's base—the yellow tape, the chain-link fence, the Day-Glo orange netting. Other sidewalks tunneled beneath the scaffold, walled in with unfinished flaking plywood. After the new tenant moved in, Tower Records, the work continued, building the building around the building. The skin of the construction expanded and contracted as another floor was added and then an overhanging roof. If you know Gehry's work, part of the fun is sorting out the appliances of the actual construction and the constructed thing itself. After the building was finished, part of the scaffolding remained in place. Sheets of plywood, lengths of chain fencing sat there. With Gehry's work, you never know if that will be that.

Perhaps Gehry's best-known project is his own house. Starting with a pink asbestos-shingled bungalow, Gehry "ruined" his house. First, he wrapped most of it with mismatched sheets of corrugated steel, bringing the asphalt of the driveway into the new house as a floor. The house, in his words, was "edited," with interior parts highlighted—a finished window is set in the stripped-to-the-lath wall. The ceiling is removed and the framing exposed. The original house, manipulated in these ways and housed in the shell of the new structure, becomes a kind of knickknack, a museum object. Openings are cut everywhere. A window is encased in a window. Chainlike fencing boxes out ghostlike rooms. Open the front door to The Front Door. The outer walls are deteriorating plywood, and the inner walls are refinished siding of shingles or clapboards. There are studs and untaped, unskimmed drywall.

Gehry explains the house this way:

I was concerned with maintaining a freshness in the house. Often freshness is lost in overfinishing houses, their vitality is lost. I wanted to avoid this by emphasizing the feeling that the details are still in process: that the building hasn't stopped. The very finished building has security and it's predictable. I wanted to try something different. I like playing at the edge of disaster.

Much could be said about Gehry's "deconstruction," dreaded word. That's not my focus now. Nor is it centered solely on the self-consciousness of the self-referential techniques. My interest is less theoretical, more practical, when it comes to houses and stories. I see Gehry as a *camoufluer,* one who disguises a house with parts of other houses and in so doing distorts our perception of time and space. Gehry said he liked *playing* at the edge of disaster, and that is what I'd like to spark in the writer of future stories, this sense of play with the materials at hand as one works.

In his book *Art and Camouflage* Roy Behrens traces the principles of concealment in nature, art, and warfare. To understand the principles of concealment, he argues, is also to understand how things are revealed. Acts of creation, he writes, always involve treating two things as if they are one, a kind of feigned confusion. He continues (paraphrasing Arthur Koestler): "An act of creation is not something out of nothing; it uncovers, selects, reshuffles, combines, synthesizes already existing facts, ideas, faculties, skills. The more familiar the parts, the more striking the new whole." The play in Gehry derives from feeling comfortable in such confusion of parts, the ordering of disorder.

If Gehry is a camoufluer, what can I say for Richard Rogers? Perhaps that he is a coroner or pathologist. The British architect's buildings are vast rooms or bays suspended from trusses and bridge work. The service areas—lighting, air ducts, stairs, restrooms—are attached to the *outside* and brightly colored like the drawings of arterial systems in anatomies. Rogers's buildings do look as if they have been turned inside out. The thing we are accustomed to have hidden in a building is exposed.

Rogers is often the guy Prince Charles attacks when he is criticizing new buildings as cold, industrial, impersonal, and lacking in artistic ornament. But Rogers's buildings are loved. His most famous building is the Pompidou Center in Paris, a grid of steel suspension that looks from the outside like a huge machine and where close to twenty thousand people a day ride the glazed escalator, which worms its way up the plaza facade to catch views of the city. These buildings have been thought of as High-Tech architecture, but they really are a kind of nostalgia for the low-tech girders and glass of the nineteenth-century machine age. The Pompidou Center is closer in feel to the Eiffel Tower than the silent microchip wafer of sand.

Rogers's work keeps the metaphor of the machine going in the age of information. In this way his buildings are ruins. Though they are shiny bright and new, they strongly suggest that passage of time, the whole time line, by means exposing the guts of an old wind-up clock.

In a book of photographs called *Dead Tech: A Guide to the Archaeology of the Future* there are pictures of blast furnaces from the Ruhr and abandoned power plants of Lorraine that look like the Pompidou Center. Along with Prince Charles, writers, I think, often resist what has been or has the feel of being mass produced or machine made in favor of the unique and handmade. But this mechanical world is like the natural one to Rogers. Machines are not only things that make other things but are made things themselves. His buildings are visitors (as perhaps our stories are visitors as well in this age of information) from a Newtonian universe, alien to the world of light, byte, and bit. Stories composed of junk, of hunks of stuff, and set in motion to do real Work with a capital *W*. They, too, are little clockworks that keep a strange kind of special time.

In the plaza of the Pompidou Center there is a fountain designed by the Swiss sculptor Tinguely. Being from Switzerland, the country Graham Greene reminds us in *The Third Man* perfected, after five hundred years of peace, the cuckoo clock, Tinguely is an apt choice for the site. His work combines the two processes I have been hinting at here. His sculptures are mad cuckoo clocks of exposed gears and pulleys in kinetic frenzy, machines whose functions, often, are to fly apart. His work simultaneously invokes the unfinished tasks of creation and decay.

We live in such a world. Walking around Boston, I slalom around sawhorses with blinking lights. Riding on the elevated expressway the city now wants to bury, I see exit ramps fly off to nowhere. Inconvenienced, I often chant to myself that this will be a great town when they're done with it. This will be a great town when they are done with it. But they will never be done with it. They will never be done with it.

Certain aesthetic choices a writer makes can render such a world served up on the half shell of immortality.

I want to look briefly at three stories: Ernest Hemingway's "In Another Country," Donald Barthelme's "At the End of the Mechanical Age," and Janet Kauffman's "Machinery." They share an actual setting of ruins—the rear area of a world war, the end of an age, farms turning into factories. They also all use The Machine thematically and structurally. The Machine I am trying to get at here is the old metaphor we have lived with a long time. It colors our vision of the world and allows us to see ourselves as chemical-electrical machines as well as imagining our stories as purring, tuned engines. Workshops are as much a product of the mechanical age as are garages. I'm interested here in the organic unity, the fit, of a machine used dramatically in a story and how it then machines that story. How the therapeutic machines in "In Another Country" lurch. How a story meters the grace in Barthelme. How combining corn parallels the story's digestion of itself, the kernel of truth in "Machinery."

In "In Another Country" an American volunteer recounts his recuperation at an Italian hospital with other officers invalided out of the Great War. The narrator is truly in another country, alienated by culture and language, by class, by being badly, that is unheroically, wounded. He spends the story seeking connections while enduring a sham therapeutic rehabilitation. The major, a fellow patient, who has been teaching him grammar at the hospital, instructs the narrator about life and death as well when his, the major's, wife dies freakishly.

How does Hemingway ruin the story?

It meanders. It meanders like the walks along the river to the hospital, the walks the young soldiers take through the communist quarter. It digresses to the meditation on medals and heroic language, which leads to the grammar lessons of the major and his vernacular outburst at his wife's death. The best example of meandering comes when we follow, into the future, the little story within the bigger story about one of the soldiers and his nose.

> He wore a black silk handkerchief across his face because he had no nose then and his face was being rebuilt. . . . They rebuilt his face but he came from a very old family and they could never get the nose

right. He went to South America and worked in a bank. But this was a long time ago, and then we did not any of us know how it was going to be different afterward. We only knew then that there was the war, but that we were not going to it anymore.

The ending of that paragraph leads us on to another technique to consider. The story's meanderings actually curve back upon themselves, an oxbow. That is, the story repeats. It repeats itself, in this case, in the phrase about the war always being there, which takes us back to the story's famous opening:

> In the fall the war was there, but we did not go to it any more. It was cold in the fall in Milan and the dark came very early. Then the electric lights came on, and it was pleasant along the streets looking in the windows. There was much game hanging outside the shops, and the snow powdered in the fur of the foxes and the wind blew their tails. The deer hung stiff and heavy and empty, and the small birds blew in the wind and the wind turned the feathers. It was a cold fall and the wind came down from the mountains.

And from here it goes forward to what will happen years from now. Words repeat. Sentences repeat. Parts of paragraphs are made up of repeated words and sentences. Here in the opening paragraph not only are words and phrases repeated and varied, but the nouns are seldom replaced by pronouns. The strong effect, in context of the story, is that the story itself is a bad, almost elementary translation from a foreign tongue. By repeating *war* and *was* and *fall* and *cold* and *and,* the story emphasizes the detachment the narrator speaks of, the rhythm of the machines he is attached to, and the mechanics of grammar conscious in the narrator's conversations with the major. In the major's final outburst there is repetition as well. It is a different kind of grammar lesson. An exercise in dread as he declines the words *loss* and *marriage* and *must* and *cannot.* Strapped to the lurching machines, the language stutters.

Though there is a forward movement to the story, the devices of meandering and repetition work against the line of action. We begin to see the story as a type of ink stain spreading on cotton rag paper, like blood on a bandage. Something happens all at once *and* over and over again. Truly, another country.

"At the End of the Mechanical Age" tells the story of the meeting, marriage, and divorce of the narrator and a Mrs. Davis. In the background

God is dressed as a meter reader, measuring the depletion of grace in the household by reading the meter in the basement. Barthelme has rewired the story in such a way that everything lights up except the lightbulb. Everything but what happens is illuminated.

> I went to the grocery store to buy some soap. I stood for a long time before the soaps in their attractive boxes, RUB and FAB and TUB and suchlike. I couldn't decide so I closed my eyes and reached out blindly and when I opened my eyes I found her hand in mine. Her name was Mrs. Davis, she said, and TUB was the best for important cleaning experiences, in her opinion.

The plot is sketched in a few sentences:

> At the wedding Mrs. Davis spoke to me kindly.
> After the marriage, Mrs. Davis explained marriage to me.
> After the explanation came the divorce.

That is the action of the story. Its weight has been redistributed to detail; ground and background are reversed.

Barthelme also imposes other artistic forms on his stories. In this case, opera, and in one of Mrs. Davis's arias, "The Song of Maude," she trills of tools:

> It was Maude who thought of calling the rattail file a rattail file. Maude who christened the needle-nosed pliers. Maude named the rasp. . . . It was Maude who named the maul. Similarly the sledge, the wedge, the ball-peen hammer, the adz, the shim, the hone, the strop. The handsaw, the hacksaw, the bucksaw and the fretsaw.

And so on for a full page.

Barthelme said he saw himself on the leading edge of the junk phenomenon. So, not only is the junk highlighted and exposed; it is juxtaposed. Here, in the introduction of God, he takes seriously the mundane and flattens the heroic once again.

> God was standing in the basement reading meters to see how much grace had been used up in the month of June. Grace is electricity, science has found, it is not like electricity, it is electricity and God was down in the basement reading the meters in His blue jumpsuit with the flashlight stuck in the pocket.

Note the capitol *H* of *His* and the attention paid to the detail of the flashlight and the jumpsuit.

The story also explodes cliché from the inside instead of fleeing it: "That is the kind of man I like, a strong and simple-minded man. The case method was not Jake's method, he went right through the middle of the line and never failed to gain yardage no matter what the game was. He had a lust for life and life had a lust for him." And so on.

In his stories Barthelme often bangs together blocks of such stuff with such force and volume that the reader finds the wreckage inhabitable. Strangely familiar and familiarly strange. The effect is to capture, realistically, our age of stuff, an age of no context where everything matters.

In "Machinery" Janet Kauffman continues to employ methods she used before in stories such as "Patriotic." Fragments, fragmentations of compound sentences into their component parts, short paragraphing. Unlike Hemingway, who jams together scenes without transitions, Kauffman employs white spaces while jumping just as far out of sequence. Combined with her first-person present-tense narration is her use of questions. Her stories have the feel of a draft of an essay.

Little happens in "Machinery." The farm woman narrator establishes the estrangement of her teenage son, Harry, from the family. The musing on what her son needs takes over the story. The only recounted action is her annual ritual of riding in the cab of a combine with Pat, a neighbor, its owner and driver. They must shout to be heard, and they pick up the conversation from where it ended last year during the harvest. The narrator tries to talk about Harry. The story then is all shouted. Exclamation marks are everywhere, adding a visual vibration to the short sentences and paragraphs. Kauffman is not afraid to digress into neat stuff. Here she tells us about a combine. The language is just technical enough: "The machine cuts into the corn, pulls the stalks inside, runs the ears between rollers to shell them, joggles it all on a sieve, then augers the kernels into a bin, and fans out the husks debris like exhaust." The act itself, that is the combining of a cornfield, is interesting enough to propel the story along. Pat shouts out a story of seeing a UFO in a cornfield that turns out to be another combine running with its lights on at night. The bigger story is made up of such stories, told to fill the time during work, to let your companion know you are still there. These stories are tips of submerged thoughts.

"Machinery" ends with just such a floating paragraph. The narrator in the cab of the combine watches as her son, her source of worry, drives along the field, paralleling them in the dark, an echo of Pat's UFO story: "I see two lights, car lights, turning our way. The car moves slowly; the lights hover. . . . It must be Harry, with no license, out for a drive." Kauffman overplays all her parallels. With the brevity and quickness of the story, her conceits seem forced, too apt, even arty. The story reads as an idea of a story. It is a story combined. That is, all the separate acts of dramatization and exposition are swept up at once into one swift gesture. The story is like this conversation in the cab. It is being constantly built up and then torn down.

> I notice it every year. Sometime we have so much to say to each other. And sometimes we have nothing. "Margaret's moved to Fennville!" Pat says. . . . Margaret is his daughter. He describes her house—how she is fixing it up, building a stairwell. She works in a hospital, we talk, the new machinery there but half of what we say gets lost.

The story is about losing half of what you say. And Kauffman's strategy in its construction is to do just that too. She ruins it. She tools out half of the story itself.

In the process of making a story, we have a desire to get it just right, and a workshop contributes to that urge to finish a story, to polish it off. It is said that the thing needs "polishing."

The frustrations I felt as the manager Brian Epstein so many years ago resulted from the same drive to get things not just right but perfect. Though the aesthetic of the unfinished and the ruined was, and still is, a good one, I was unable to translate that vision of incompleteness, spontaneity, sloppiness, and randomness into a vision of the world.

I would urge you to resist that impulse in yourself that urges you to get the thing perfect. Incorporate the instinct to tinker as a structure not as something you employ to get to an end. Proceed comfortably knowing that things, no matter how much you handle them, will not fall exactly into place. Walk away not in anger but knowing that writing many short stories, one flawed sputtering attempt after another, can accumulate into a whole junkyard of wrecked vehicles that attest to what it is you were driving at. It is a type of calculus. You are always approaching, by means of an equation with multiple X's, the absolute.

One last model for all of this.

I come from Indiana, which is, among other things, the double-wide, RV, van conversion, mobile home capital of the world. Everywhere there are those stubby little trucks hauling halves of houses, the open side wrapped in plastic. Wide load. Flashing lights. Fields of mutating vans.

Fiberglass and Plexiglass. I grew up on a vast flat plain where houses and parts of houses shuttled back and forth between factories made of pre-fabricated parts. Where cars transformed into houses. Where house found wheels.

In this landscape of impermanence, who carpenters together the mobile homes and vans? The Amish. They come from their farms, eighty-acre oases in the shifting sands of mobility. They bring their skills, their craft, honed for a life of subsistence and sustainablity, to an enter-prise that is cheap and quick. I like to think of this uneasy marriage, the symbiosis of care and expedience, craft and crate, greed and gift. I like to think of my stories as these hobbled habitats, finished by hand, cruising the interstates, oversized loads, still settling.

KEVIN McILVOY

The Editor Comes Clean at Last

(A Tale of One Rejection Letter and One Acceptance
Letter to Stephen Crane)

Writing and writing—thousands of pages between the age of twenty and twenty-nine—often unemployed, always struggling financially, Stephen Crane had to self-publish *Maggie: A Girl of the Streets.* He received the support of William Dean Howells (the single most significant editor in the American literary tradition) for publication of *The Red Badge of Courage,* and, when all was said and done, he earned less than a hundred dollars for the book. As a result of writing *The Red Badge of Courage,* one of the greatest Civil War novels ever (written without Crane having experienced one minute of the Civil War), he was assigned by editors as a war correspondent. In this capacity he was constantly placed at the front lines in extremely dangerous circumstances, which ultimately seemed to help him none at all in writing "authentic" war fiction.

His single greatest professional good fortune was being present for the sinking of the steamer *Commodore* while headed to Cuba. It would not have been in keeping with poor Crane's luck for him to have been *returning* from the chaos of that place. He and three others, an oiler, a cook, and a captain, spent thirty hours in a life raft before swimming for shore. Crane's newspaper report of the episode was his most famous piece of journalism; his short story "The Open Boat" brought more fame. In a manner typical of him Crane's follow-up effort to make a little more money, just a little more, with a kind of "Open Boat II" entitled "Flanagan and His Short Filibustering Adventure," was his most critically damned work. He recovered fully from that criticism but never quite recovered physically from almost drowning. He died of tuberculosis at twenty-nine, his family in dire financial need.

For the sake of this essay, let us assume that Stephen Crane, determined to make the big bucks he never could while he was alive, leaves the grave, secures a job with the Alamogordo *New Mexican Daily News,* avoids all battlefields (knows better now), makes no contact with the dead William Dean Howells, rents a boat but parks it in his apartment garage. He and others newly arisen from the dead, Faulkner, Eliot, Conrad, Poe, and company, begin submitting all their greatest works—multiple submissions, of course—to contemporary literary magazine editors.

It is painful to consider how many rejection letters they will receive from well-meaning but immature editors. As a short story writer and novelist for twenty-five years and as an editor of a literary magazine for twenty years, I am keenly aware of the kinds of letters such editors write early in their careers, and I know firsthand about the effects of those letters upon authors. In an effort to constructively reckon with my own conscience about the manner in which I have responded to manuscripts, I offer these two imaginary letters, written twenty years apart. The first letter is by the inexperienced editor, and the second is by the experienced editor who has learned well from his teachers, that is, from the many writers whose work he has rejected and the few whose work he has accepted.

I.

October 10, 1981

Dear Stephen Crane,

Thank you for submitting yet *another* short story. I apologize once more for losing your novella manuscript, *George's Mother*. And I apologize for the five months it has taken for us to respond to each new story you have sent.

I appreciate the sentiment you expressed in your cover letter that, after all, some writers live short lives. As you know, your previous submissions, "The Black Dog," "The Octopush," and "An Experiment in Luxury," were not well received here. Nothing you have sent has been well received here.

I admire your persistence.

I will list my reservations about this newest, long submission, "The Red Badge of Courage."

1. The characters are without color. You offer no thorough description, no significant background, almost no names: the youth, the loud young soldier, the tattered man. You insist on us knowing them exclusively *in the moment*.

2. The characters' speech is cryptic one moment, one moment colloquial, in the next moment biblical, prophetic, and, in the next, incoherent.

3. The proportions of the plot are strange. *Should* the spectacle of war be presented as a set of redundant skirmishes while the preclimactic and postclimactic moments of plot, especially the moments of *in*activity, are given so much more attention than the climactic battle moments?

I recently received a similarly redundant story about a family repeatedly uprooted, a boy repeatedly confounded in his loyalty to his father who burns one barn after another. A Mr. William Faulkner sent it. His work, like yours, has not been well received here.

4. "Badge" is overloaded with ironies that insist on moral truths but make them so damn complex that the reader who wishes at least *some* truths could be only true, feels frustrated.

5. The writer seems unable or unwilling to hold stable any element of the work. The point of view continually shifts and, with it, the narrative distance. The reader feels historically distant, and then relationally distant, and then intimately close.

The narrative voice is   what is it? Aphoristic in the manner of Ben Franklin. Imbued with the "intellectual calculus" Baudelaire so admired, with the unclothed and exalted rhythms of Whitman. At times the voice in this tragic story is oddly comic, disturbingly comic. Many times while I read the story, I had to ask myself, "Is this funny?"

The story structure, especially the chaptering, seems determined by time, then by thematic emphasis, then by de-emphasis, by passages of interior journey, and by interruptions of exterior development. It shows the writer's insistence on intuition instead of authorial control.

6. The story *wanders,* as I have said. It has at its heart a kind of innocent *wonder* also, as if each action that occurs is unprecedented, each uncovered personal or public truth in it has never been revealed. Is the writer too much in awe of the work, too little in awe of the reader?

7. Too often, your sentences spin their wheels, and even the wheels are of questionable shape. Should so much poetic diction be present in a work of prose? Are the sentences too ambitious? Why, at the story's beginning, do the sentences labor so often to express the psychological state of the whole group instead of fixing on Henry Fleming or focusing on his closest relationships?

What clarity results from sentences like this one? *Near where they stood shells were flip-flapping and hooting. Occasional bullets buzzed in the air and spanged into tree trunks.*

I wish you well with "The Red Badge of Courage" and all your work.

Respectfully,
The Editor

II.

October 10, 2001

Dear Stephen Crane,

Thank you for sending "The Open Boat." This remarkable story does exactly what a fellow named Joseph Conrad always says in his cover letters *his* work will do: It will speak "to our capacity for delight and wonder, to the sense of mystery surrounding our lives, to our sense of pity and beauty, and pain; to the latent feeling of fellowship with all creation; and to the subtle but invincible conviction of solidarity that knits together the loneliness of innumerable hearts: to that solidarity in dreams, in joy, in sorrow, in aspirations, in illusions, in hope, in fear, which binds men to each other, which binds together all humanity—the dead to the living, the living to the unborn."

Can you *imagine* someone writing that in a cover letter? Happens all the time. Until recently, Mr. Conrad's work has not been well received here. I have had to learn to delight and wonder in order to value it. I have grown in the twenty years you have been submitting your work and I have been responding to it.

"The Open Boat" offers all the aspects of storytelling I once least appreciated and now love most:

1. The characters are without "color," yet I find them unforgettable. You offer no thorough descriptions, no significant background, almost no names. They are: the cook, the captain, the correspondent. The oiler, Billy, seems to pay with his life for being named. Your characters are, by definition, superficial. To each other they are only mysterious surfaces. At the dangerous moments when it appears each man might be revealed to the others, what is revealed instead is the face of humanity, a face they know but have not recognized in its full complexity and mystery before these hours adrift.

That, anyway, is how I receive the invitation of the story's opening passage:

> None of them knew the color of the sky. Their eyes glanced level, and were fastened upon the waves that swept toward them. These waves were of the hue of slate, save for the tops, which were of foaming white, and all of the men knew the colors of the sea. The horizon narrowed and widened, and dipped and rose, and at all times its edge was jagged with waves that seemed thrust up in points like rocks.

And how do they *develop,* these noncharacters who scarcely add up to one collective personality? The three who survive do not have epiphanies, moments of clarity; they do not have Aha! reactions though they sometimes have Ha!Ah! reactions. We are constantly reminded of what they individually and collectively do not know and do not learn: *The process of the breaking day was unknown to them. They were aware only of this effect upon the color of the waves that rolled toward them.*

On the same page—is that thing that they *maybe* see a house of refuge or a life-saving station? Which do we all most hope for—salvation or refuge? They argue about it. They don't know.

And in the absence of facts what do the men *feel?*

> *The crest of each of the waves was a hill, from the top of which the men surveyed for a moment a broad, tumultuous expanse, shining and wind-riven. It was probably splendid, it was probably glorious, this play of the free sea, wild with lights of emerald and white and amber.*

I love and admire this passage, which I quote back to you, its own author, only to invite you to celebrate it with me.

The three who survive at the end have neither answers nor progressively more articulate questions, only the question as repetitious in the story as the waves:

> *If I am going to be drowned—if I am going to be drowned—if I am going to be drowned, why, in the name of the seven mad gods who rule the sea, was I allowed to come thus far and contemplate sand and trees?*

This passage is the prayer of every writer who receives a handwritten response at the bottom of a rejection letter, isn't it?

I must comment that the "If I am going to be drowned" refrain is mercifully more abbreviated in some parts of the manuscript than others. At the risk of repeating my old mistakes, I have made editorial recommendations about the form of it in section 4, especially the passage,

> *Was I brought here merely to have my nose dragged away as I was about to nibble the sacred cheese of life? It is preposterous!*

Would you agree with me that it is a preposterous passage? Will you consider throwing out the cheese, sacred or not? Perhaps you would consider throwing out "the old hen" and the "old ninny woman, Fate" in the same passage.

In any case the repeated question, "If I am going to be drowned" multiplies our sense of everything the characters do not and cannot know. Is that "character development"? Yes!

As if to challenge my conventional ideas of character development and my own motivations as an editor and writer, you present this goliath passage that is brilliantly slain by one puny phrase—and only at the end of the sentence's rampage:

The correspondent wondered if none ever ascended the tall wind-tower, and if then they never looked seaward. This tower was a giant, standing with its back to the plight of the ants. It represented in a degree, to the correspondent, the serenity of nature amid the struggles of the individual—nature in the wind, and nature in the vision of the men. She did not seem cruel to him then, nor beneficent, nor treacherous, nor wise. But she was indifferent, flatly indifferent. It is, perhaps, plausible that a man in this situation, impressed with the unconcern of the universe, should see the innumerable flaws of his life and have them taste wickedly in his mind and wish for another chance. A distinction between right and wrong seems absurdly clear to him, then, in this new ignorance of the grave-edge, and he understands that if he were given another opportunity he would mend his conduct and his words, and be better and brighter during an introduction or at a tea.

Those last twelve words, "and be better and brighter during an introduction or at a tea," deflate entirely the ballooning drama of the one hundred and fifty-six words before them. The character is given a certain kind of wisdom and is given surprising opportunity to contemplate its small ultimate value. The terms of the reading experience are wonderfully contrary.

2. The characters' speech is cryptic one moment, one moment biblical, prophetic, and, in the next, incoherent. It is always repetitious, as in section 6:

> *"Billie!" There was a slow and gradual disentanglement. "Billie, will you spell me?"*
> *"Sure," said the other.*

And two sentences later:

> *"Will you spell me?"*
> *"Sure, Billie."*

Four paragraphs later there is, at last, an exciting promise of real conversation:

> *At last there was a short conversation.*
> *"Billie! . . . Billie, will you spell me?"*
> *"Sure," said the oiler.*

Likewise, how many times in the story is some form of this conversation in section 2 replayed?

> *"See it?" said the captain.*
> *"No," said the correspondent, slowly; "I didn't see anything."*
> *"Look again," said the captain.*

In a story so preoccupied with *unknowing* it seems right that the dialogue reminds us about seeing, and looking again. It seems right that in a story in which one character cannot truly puzzle together another, one "spells" the other. It seems right that in a story in which all the characters are so cursed, the word *spell* should be given such incantatory repetition.

I am newly convinced by this rendering of the routine, pointless, recursive private speech of characters (especially these male characters) which is so uniquely different than their public speech. Perhaps as a person I have sometimes been too afraid of such private speech, and as an editor I have been too guilty of counseling restraint—for instance, advising against too many *fucks* and *shits,* though I have certainly known many memorable ones—in manuscripts that have not been well received here.

Your storytelling reminds me that the true speech of characters is sometimes what *would be* said (private speech) and, at other times, what *should* be said (public speech): *"If we don't all get ashore," said the captain, "if we don't all get ashore, I suppose you fellows know where to send news of my finish?"*

Is this eloquent, noble speech as expressive as "Will you spell me?"

I am happy that the story presents such instances of private *and* public speech and that private speech predominates.

3. The proportions of the story's plot are undeniably strange. And splendid! I am sure, now, that I should not have rejected so much work by this fellow Poe. In his indignant responses to rejection he has often impolitely reminded me of Bacon's maxim—he is overfond of it: "There is no exquisite beauty without some strangeness in the proportions."

As I reread your story, I begin to appreciate that the sections are in waves, seven waves, each of different pitch and force, varying in tensions that might be read as dangers; yet you give the greatest proportion of each section to the rising or falling face of the wave and not the crest—in other words, the drama and not the spectacle. The sections end not with predictable crescendos but decrescendos:

> *"Billie! Billie, will you spell me?"*
> *"Sure."*

The sections begin unpredictably: the pattern of the section endings complements the variety of the section openings. Another writer might have hurried to the part of the story in which the characters must abandon the dinghy. In this story the writer trusts the routines and rituals of the moments of *inactivity* for what they will reveal. My personal favorite moments of "The Open Boat" do not involve the men in capital-*C* Conflict with the mighty ocean, but in lower case-*c* conflict with their own bodies and minds and souls. I admire this moment in midstory, which receives the emphasis of a section ending *and* a section opening:

> *The cook's head was on a thwart, and he looked without interest at the water under his nose. He was deep in other scenes. Finally he spoke, "Billie," he murmured dreamfully, "what kind of pie do you like best?"*
>
> *V.*
>
> *"Pie!" said the oiler and the correspondent, agitatedly, "Don't talk about those things, blast you!"*
> *"Well," said the cook, "I was just thinking about ham sandwiches, and—"*

I can hardly express my appreciation for the deadpan sentence immediately following:

> *A night on the sea in an open boat is a long night.*

The comic deflation of the spectacle permits simple drama to take precedence. Because the drama takes place in the repetitious ways I have mentioned earlier, there is no obvious sense of what is conventionally called "plot development."

Henry James—a writer recently returned from the dead to work on our magazine staff—a prickly and distant fellow, but smart—calls this manner of plot "stable variation" and says it is not necessarily preferable to "progression." Mr. James is only an assistant editor, and we're considering sending him back to the grave.

4. As in "Red Badge," "The Open Boat" insists on moral truths. They are confounding moral truths, and many readers will be frustrated that the wisdom of the work cannot be distilled, the themes stated plainly. I gather that you have already experienced this reader reaction as I remember the part of your cover letter that responds to our rejection letter for "Red Badge": "It seems to me that you cut all the ethical sense out of the book. All the anarchy, perhaps. It is the anarchy which I particularly insist upon."

The ironies dawning upon the men offer "problematic moral truth," to borrow a phrase from William Dean Howells, who has, sadly, remained dead since 1920.

The opening of section 6 offers an example of your authorial anarchy. You present the choral refrain of the work:

> *If I am going to be drowned—if I am going to be drowned—if I am going to be drowned, why, in the name of the seven mad gods who rule the sea, was I allowed to come thus far and contemplate sand and trees?*

You then speculate about its meaning:

> *During this dismal night, it may be remarked that a man would conclude that it was really the intention of the seven mad gods to drown him, despite the abominable injustice of it. For it was certainly an abominable injustice to drown a man who had worked so hard, so hard. The man felt it would be a crime most unnatural. Other people had drowned at sea since galleys swarmed with painted sails, but still—*

You evaluate the meaning:

> *When it occurs to a man that nature does not regard him as important, and that she feels she would not maim the universe by disposing of him, he at first wishes to throw bricks at the temple, and he hates deeply the fact that there are no bricks and no temples. Any visible expression of nature would surely be pelleted with his jeers.*

The men are becoming "interpreters," as the last sentence of the story says they will: "they felt that they could then be interpreters." The moral truths they will interpret will not be reductive. They will, in fact, be unstable. The story inspires "the active soul" R. W. Emerson (a spiritual force transcending the biases of academics who continue to try to bury him) said literature should strive to create.

5. The point of view, narrative voice, and story structure—all three are unstable. Why did I ever believe that it was a fault and not a virtue in storytelling to have the quality of multivalence, that is, the capacity for the story's point of view, narrative voice, and structure to change in value, to dynamically evolve through the course of a single work? The answer: editorial immaturity.

I thought respect for the reader was communicated by holding these elements constant while other elements were in dynamic process. "The

Open Boat" proves me wrong. The viewpoint continually shifts and, with it, the narrative distance. The story vacillates between a very distant panoramic omniscience, the men "viewed as if from a balcony," and an omniscience that has as its central intelligence the *collective* observations and even the *collective* thoughts of the men. It sometimes enters the anonymous third-person viewpoint, as in section 6, mentioned earlier:

> *During this dismal night, it may be remarked that a man would conclude.*
> *. . . For it was certainly an abominable injustice to drown a man.*

The story only begins to reside exclusively in the correspondent's point of view in the final section, and his point of view is sometimes reportorial, sometimes intimate, and then a blend of both, as in section 7, when he observes the swamping of the boat, his own curious responses, and then the situation of all the men:

> *The January water was icy, and he reflected immediately that it was colder than he had expected to find it off the coast of Florida. This appeared to his dazed mind as a fact important enough to be noted at the time. The coldness of the water was sad; it was tragic. This fact was somehow mixed and confused with his opinion of his own situation so that it seemed almost a proper reason for tears. The water was cold.*
> *When he came to the surface he was conscious of little but the noisy water. Afterward he saw his companions in the sea. The oiler was ahead in the race. He was swimming strongly and rapidly. Off to the correspondent's left, the cook's great white and corked back bulged out of the water; and in the rear the captain was hanging with his one good hand to the keel of the overturned dinghy.*

The narrative voice naturally shifts in complement to the point of view changes. The varying stresses of each moment are conveyed in shifts within the same narrative voice—changes in tone, rhythm, syntax. Like the men in the boat, we feel optimism *and* absolute despair; we feel the horrifying *and* amusing ridiculousness of it all and the wrongness of it and the strange goodness and rightness—and we feel all of these things at once.

The story structure, particularly in the chaptering, is linked to but not bound by the *developing* point of view and narrative voice. Authorial intelligence *and* authorial intuition decide this story structure. The reader's intelligence is not underestimated. The reader's intuition is not undervalued.

I begin to appreciate, at last, that narrative voice, story structure, and point of view should not be designed to make the work all engine nor to make it all enigma but to make it engine *and* enigma. I am only just now learning.

None of them knew the color of the sky.

The sentence only barely encloses the reader. The sentence throws the reader from the boat.

What a way to treat a reader.

6 and 7. I am almost at the end of this long letter in which I wish to offer you back the vulnerabilities your own open story invites.

I appreciate the path of the sentences: the wandering of the story that takes the "stance of wonder"—a term I borrow from a literary brother to you, a Mr. Berryman. I like the sentences throughout the story that derail our expectation that we might be given simple knowledge and which invite and inspire, instead, wonder. I value that *now* because your work has taught me how to value it, one submission after another, one rejection after another.

In the past I wanted a sentence to be all engine, on the tracks, accelerating and breaking smoothly, and I would not welcome a sentence that was enigma, not welcome at all a sentence that was *all* enigma. The more my own life, at middle age, has become all enigma, the more I question any sentence that is all engine. *None of them knew the color of the sky.* The perfect example.

And here is another simple example:

He had, on a certain star-lit evening, said wonderingly and quite reverently: "Deh moon sure looks like hell, don't it?"

It is, now, one of my favorite sentences in all of literature. It is from your story, "Maggie: A Girl of the Streets," which was not well received here.

I will be happy to read the new story you mentioned, "The Blue Hotel," the one you said was recently rejected by *Atlantic Monthly*.

You have been patient with me, Stephen, willing to tolerate my inability to meet your work on its own terms, ever willing to submit more work in order to foster my education as an editor.

Your story "The Open Boat" will appear in the newest volume of our magazine, only a little over one hundred years after you wrote it.

Payment, I am sorry to say, will be in copies (2).

Sincerely,
The Editor

PABLO MEDINA

Literature and Democracy

> Did you, too, O friend, suppose democracy was only for elec-
> tions, for politics, and for a party name?
> —Walt Whitman, *Democratic Vistas*

North American culture exhibits a certain predilection for labeling its
people, both the native born and the immigrant. The first label applied
to me, almost immediately upon my arrival in the United States, was the
term *refugee*. Other labels followed, slowly at first, and then they rained
in great profusion. At one point or another I have been called Cuban,
Latin, Latino, Hispanic, Spic, Dago, Jew, and once, even, Nigger. I did
not mind these labels very much while I was growing up. During those
days in New York everyone called you something in New York, and
you were supposed to call them something back. Besides, unaware of
the negative connotations these terms carried along with them, I had little emotional investment in being called one thing or the other. My
innocence was bliss.

When I became a writer and started publishing my work, the labels
narrowed, and I was called a Hispanic-American writer or a Cuban-
American one, or, occasionally, a Latino writer. Suddenly, the labels
bothered me, perhaps because the people using them did not know me
personally, and I had the distinct impression that I was somehow being
manipulated. I wanted to be known simply as a writer, a good writer
preferably, and all other labels seemed to detract from and diffuse that
ambition. The feelings persisted, even increased through the years, as the
literary community, driven by the vanity and silliness of political correctness, started labeling everything and everyone, hyphenating the
terms in an attempt to account for every possible racial and ethnic
configuration.

My reaction against labels is no longer ill defined. It is based, rather,
on the conviction that ethnic labels in literature are undemocratic and
that they separate rather than unite, marginalize rather than celebrate.
My purpose in this essay is to look at the ways in which ethnic labels are

---

From the *AWP Chronicle* 30, no. 4 (February 1998).

used and misused and to offer valid alternative perspectives from which to look at contemporary literature.

European writers have learned the hard way that ethnocentric writing, if taken far enough, can light the fire of hatred and destruction. Danilo Kiš, the Yugoslav writer, once wrote, "All the nationalist sees in others is his own image: the image of a nationalist. . . . The nationalist feels not only that hell is other nations but also that everything not his (Serb, Croat, French . . .) is alien to him. Nationalism is the ideology of banality. It is a totalitarian ideology. . . . Nationalism is also kitsch." As has become all too clear in Kiš's former homeland, there is a very brief and slippery step from nationalism to ethnocentrism and all that goes with it. Nationalist literature is literature that relies heavily on the adjective that precedes it for its identity. Kiš called this phenomenon the tyranny of the adjective, a tyranny he reacted against quite strongly with regard to himself when critics tried to label him a Yugoslav or a Jewish writer (he was part Jewish).

To say that the nationalistic and/or ethnic labeling of literature is strictly a reductionist exercise, however, is itself reductionist. The tendency to label or name for the purposes of classification seems inherent in literary criticism of all nations irrespective of time period. Reading American literary critics of the first half of this century, for example, one notices the tendency to categorize writers according to their geographical origins. Thus, the terms *Southern writing, Western writing, New York* and *New England writing,* etc., came into being. It was a simple and objective approach. All a critic needed to do was to place the author within a net of geographical correspondences, most of which were evident, if not obvious. Easy to do this with writers such as Willa Cather, William Faulkner, Carson McCullers, even John Steinbeck, in whose works place is central to story.

A writer like Hemingway, however, offered a thorny problem. Born in Illinois, he spent much of his growing-up years in Michigan, lived in Europe, Florida, Cuba, and wrote about everywhere and everything he experienced. What to do with him? Hemingway, a great writer despite all other labels that may be applied to him, said this: "The essence, when it is the essence, can be in a plain glass bottle and you need no fancy labels, nor in Madrid do you need any national costumes; no matter what sort of building they put up, though the building itself may look like Buenos Aires, when you see it against that sky you know it is Madrid" (*Death in the Afternoon*).

It is important to note here that literary classification in and of itself can be a harmless, even a beneficent, exercise. In the 1960s new terms were created in an effort to accommodate points of view that differed from the mainstream, or so the story goes, and to allow a space for underrepresented voices in the literary life of the United States. In the very least these terms, mostly ethnic and gender related, help us to see the distinctive characteristics of each writer in relation to others as well as their points of convergence. The general grouping that we can call North American writing can presently be divided using the ethnic model into Hispanic-American, Asian-American, African-American, Arab-American, and so on. If you bring closer focus on, let's say, the Hispanic-American group, you can subdivide that into Puerto Rican, Mexican, Cuban, Dominican, Colombian, etc. For example, Cristina García and Ana Castillo are two fine writers living and working in the United States, both of whom write novels in English about people of Hispanic background, and so they can be classified as Hispanic-American writers. But to stop there shows us only very general similarities between them. Their work is quite different, and the nature of some of those differences becomes clear when we realize that Ana Castillo is of Mexican ancestry, while Cristina García was born in Cuba. So, one is a Mexican-American writer, while the other is a Cuban-American writer. If you decide at this point to narrow the focus even further on Cuban-American writers, you could choose to divide that group according to gender, sexual orientation, political outlook, or any other criteria.

Now a curious thing happens here: the narrower the gauge of your focus and the farther away the classification gets from the general categories you started with (for our purposes Writers or Writing), the dimmer the criteria for including people in your group to begin with. To be more specific, by the time you get down to Cuban-American White Female Heterosexual Anglophone Liberal, you have moved so far away from the factors that led you to consider García as a serious writer that those factors become meaningless, when they should be the most meaningful. Suddenly, the person's worth as a writer is of secondary importance to the social labels we, as critics and as readers, are able to tag on her. The tyranny of the adjective rears its ugly head.

If one of the purposes of ethnic classification is to give credit where credit is due and to show the great variety of writing that exists in this country, an equal but opposite result is that ethnic labels tend to separate and exclude. As a reader, I must admit that, whenever a book is advertised as a gay novel or an African-American novel or a feminist novel, my decision whether to read the book is based on the adjective appearing before it and not so much on its promise as a good book. I don't know how many books I have failed to read this way, but there are many other books I have read because I approached them on their promise, not on their color or sexual orientation or political affiliation, and have learned in the process that what matters about truly great literature is the totality of its human content.

I remember reading James Baldwin's *Giovanni's Room* when I was a teenager because a friend touted it as a great book. Had he said that it was a gay novel, I don't know that I would have read it. But he didn't, and I approached the book without any preconception; it was the unqualified reading that allowed the beauty and passion of the story to unfold for me. Furthermore, it allowed me to see, clearly, without the stereotypes that were then rampant among heterosexual teenage boys, how love between two people of the same sex was moving and powerful in all the right ways. I have not returned to *Giovanni's Room,* and so it is hard to say what I would feel about the novel now. But I can say this: that small novel taught me more about homosexuality than anything I had read up to that point precisely because it had not been labeled for me in advance.

All too many critics and editors tend to rely on labels because they make easier what is, essentially, a very difficult task: the evaluation of literature. The editor of a well-known book review explained to my own editor that she had not assigned my novel for review because it was hard to get people to do "that kind of book." She never bothered to explain what "that kind of book" meant, but I doubt that she was referring to the quality of its writing. When I heard this from my editor, I had the curious sensation that my novel was being pushed aside not because of anything the book said—it was evident that the editor in question had not so much as cracked the spine—but because of the way it had been labeled, that is, a Cuban-American novel, though Cuba itself is never once mentioned in the text.

As ethnic labels gain currency, it becomes more convenient for critics to compartmentalize literature and, as a consequence, to marginalize much of it. James Baldwin once said, "When you say you are white, you force yourself to call me black." In other words, one label begets another. When you call yourself American, everyone else is an outsider. What is to be gained by the use of such labels that hasn't already been accomplished? Convenience? The purpose of literary criticism is not convenience but understanding, and understanding is no more contained in labels than it is in a bottle.

Many of the writers who blossomed in the 1970s and 1980s, in their attempts to gain acceptance, began to write to fit the labels. It was, after all, the "in" thing to do. In a disturbing number of cases they helped the critics along by slapping the labels on their foreheads themselves. The anthologies are now filled with their writing. For these writers the only way to get published is to be as ethnic as possible, and to a degree they are right, for their work would otherwise not arouse any interest, either because it lacks the polish or "glitz" or marketing angle that appeals to editors or, frankly, because it is badly written. Every word in their pages announces their ethnicity, in fact, blares it from the rooftops, as if this and this alone legitimized the writing as serious literature. Much of this writing tends to be heavily autobiographical, that being the easiest way to deal with ethnicity, and is also highly sentimental. Ethnic writers, then, become shackled by the label they have come to accept and avoid writing anything that is not somehow related to their background. In a curious reversal they must themselves label everything around them, reluctant to or incapable of dealing with literature on its own terms, without the filter of an adjective. As Danilo Kis pointed out, they also deny the value of any piece of writing that does not trumpet its background on every page. In short, the so-called ethnic writers become subjects of the tyrannical adjective, gaining in intolerance as they themselves are marginalized by the so-called mainstream, appropriating everything before them in a desperate attempt to break out of the isolation imposed by the label.

In May 1995 Julia Alvarez, the Dominican-born author, published an article in the *Washington Post Book World* in which she argued that "William Carlos Williams was—as he would be termed today—'a Hispanic-American writer.'" The evidence for her argument comes from discovering in a collection of Williams's poems a half-dozen Spanish titles and learning that Williams's mother was Puerto Rican (hence his middle name Carlos). Her strongest bit of support, however, is also the wildest. Referring to Williams's famous poem, "The Red Wheelbarrow," she translates the opening line of that poem, "So much depends . . . ," into the common Spanish figure, *Todo depende,* which she had heard so often as a girl in the Dominican Republic. In so doing, Alvarez implies that there is some deep unconscious ethnic connection that drew her to Williams's poetry. No mention is made in the essay that she was moved by the poem simply because it was a great poem that spoke to her as a human being. The problem here is not that she is relying on an ethnic connection to validate her response—poems affect us in a multiplicity of ways—but that that ethnic connection is based on a blatant inaccuracy in translation. The Spanish *Todo depende* is the equivalent of an equally common English figure, "It all depends." "So much depends," the actual phrase of the poem, is more accurately rendered as *Tanto depende,* a strange, unfamiliar syntax both in Spanish as in English. But *tanto depende,* or "so much depends," is not at all what she used to hear as a child, and so the accurate translation of the phrase, which is essential for the poem to function in either language, would rob Alvarez's argument of its sentimental appeal, or of its kitsch, as Danilo Kiš would have it. After all, she begins the essay by saying that her encounter with Williams was love at first sight. That love, she maintains, was ethnic in nature. The idea that William Carlos Williams is in any imaginable way a "Hispanic American" is as silly to me as saying that he is an American Hispanic: in the end manipulative, debilitating, and destructive. Williams is as quintessentially and unhyphenatedly American as Walt Whitman or José Martí or Julia Alvarez, for that matter, but beyond that he is a poet whose work transcends nationality and ethnicity and affects us on a human level.

Jorge Luis Borges wrote about these issues in an essay titled "The Argentine Writer and Tradition." In it he said,

> Some days past I have found a curious confirmation of the fact that what is truly native can and often does dispense with local color; I found this confirmation in Gibbon's *Decline and Fall of the Roman Empire*. Gibbon observes that in the Arabian book *par excellence,* in the Koran, there are no camels; I believe if there were any doubt as to the authenticity of the Koran, this absence of camels would be sufficient to prove it is an Arabian work. It was written by Mohammed and Mohammed, as an Arab, had no reason to know that camels were especially Arabian; for him they were a part of reality, he had no reason to emphasize them; on the other hand, the first thing a falsifier, a tourist, an Arab nationalist would do is have a surfeit of camels, caravans of camels, on every page; but Mohammed, as an Arab, was unconcerned: he knew he could be an Arab without camels. (*Labyrinths*)

William Faulkner said that the artist (and the artist's background, including his ethnicity, is part of the artist) "is of no importance. Only what he creates is important, since there is nothing new to be said. Shakespeare, Balzac, Homer have all written about the same things, and if they had lived one thousand or two thousand years longer, the publishers wouldn't have needed anyone since." And Nabokov said, "There is only one school of literature—that of talent," while the Colombian poet Jorge Zalamea suggested that in poetry there is no underdevelopment. The easy way is to wave the ethnic banner, let yourself be labeled and convince yourself that you have said something profound. The hard way, and the true way, is not to deny ethnicity but to transcend it so that you can reach for and connect with other humans. To understand this is to come to terms with the fact that the artistic process is, by its very nature, universal and democratic. Ethnicity is one of many platforms on which the writer stands and, as such, a secondary concern in the writing; it is in the reaching, in the connecting, where art lies.

Some weeks ago, while I was trying to think coherently about the topic of democracy in literature, I reread Sandra Cisneros's *The House on Mango Street*. This book consists of a series of vignettes that take place in a working-class neighborhood of Chicago, told from the point of view of a girl named Esperanza. Each of the stories deals with a different aspect of the neighborhood, from the time Esperanza's family moves onto Mango Street until she decides to leave someday and find her way in the world. There are stories about Esperanza's friends, about her family, and about several of the neighbors, most of whom happen to be Hispanic. The language is clear and direct. The voice handles Spanish names and phrases deftly, but it is very much at home in English. Come to think of it, English seems its primary language, while the stories and characters in it are only incidentally Hispanic. The problems and issues Esperanza and her family face—learning English, getting used to a new environment, fathers who leave and never come back, health problems, celebrations to keep despair at bay—are universal to Italians, Jamaicans, or Vietnamese settling in Chicago, Brooklyn, Los Angeles, or any major city in the United States. I'm not sure how inherently Hispanic Sandra Cisneros's *The House on Mango Street* is, but I have the distinct impression after reading it that it is a very North American book.

This leads me to two interrelated questions: How Hispanic is the so-called Hispanic-American writing? And, second, what is the connection between literature written by Hispanics in the United States and the literature written in Latin American countries? Look at Cisneros again. To find the sources of her writing, her rhythms, her characters, and her stories, one has to look to the streets of American cities and at the literature that arises from there. She is much closer in style to a Toni Cade Bambara or a Grace Paley (if she is close to anyone) than, let's say, Isabel Allende. Cisneros's themes are firmly, sharply North American—people making it in alien urban surroundings; people, kids especially, coping with poverty, trying to overcome the odds against them; and women asserting themselves in a society that is doubly stacked against them. Here is an excerpt:

> The eskimos got thirty different names for snow, I say. I read it in a book.
> I got a cousin, Rachel says. She got three different names.
> There ain't thirty different kinds of snow, Lucy, says. There are

two kinds. The clean kind and the dirty kind, clean and dirty. Only two.

There are a million zillion kinds, says Nancy. No two exactly alike. Only how do you remember which one is which?

She got three last names, and, let me see, two first names. One in English and one in Spanish. . . .

And clouds got at least ten different names, I say.

Names for clouds? Nenny asks. Names just like you and me?

That up there, that's cumulus, and everybody looks up.

Now take a look at this passage from Grace Paley's "A Man Told Me the Story of His Life":

I wanted to be a doctor. I wanted to be a doctor with my whole heart.

I learned every bone, every organ in the body. What is it for? Why does it work?

The school said to me: Vicente, be an engineer. That would be good. You understand mathematics.

I said to the school: I want to be a doctor. I already know how the organs connect. When something goes wrong, I'll understand how to make repairs.

The school said: Vicente, you will really be an excellent engineer. You show on all the tests what a good engineer you will be. It doesn't show whether you'll be a good doctor.

Both passages exhibit sharp, staccato sentences, suggesting rapid, multiple observations. In both the language moves contrapuntally, with the narrators' statements contrasted by those of the people around them. The grace of the writing in both cases lies not in the elegance but in the brevity and accuracy of the sentences. It is not my intention here to show Grace Paley's influence on Sandra Cisneros. For all I know, Cisneros has never read Paley. But I do want to illustrate a point, namely, that similar surroundings inspire similar writings, regardless of the writers' backgrounds.

A few years ago a congress of Mexican and Mexican-American women writers was convened in Mexico City. A friend who attended tells me that all the participants awaited the gathering with great anticipation. Everyone expected that there would be instant rapport between the two groups and that they would easily join ranks. The results? The two groups had little to say to each other. The Mexicans were daughters of privilege. Most of them came from the upper-middle or the upper classes of their country, and their writing, in language, in style, and in theme, tended to reflect their backgrounds. The Mexican-American women, by contrast, came mostly from the middle and working classes in the United States. Their work clearly mirrored that. I would not be fair if I didn't explain that since that congress there has been a real attempt on the part of both groups to reach each other and understand each other's work. As a matter of fact, Elena Poniatowska, one of Mexico's most distinguished writers, was the translator into Spanish of Sandra Cisneros's *The House on Mango Street.* It is nevertheless significant that the understanding, far from being spontaneous and instinctive, has had to be worked at.

Oscar Hijuelos, whom a number of critics have labeled a "Cuban American," is another interesting case of a writer whose work appears to be more influenced by his immediate surroundings than by his ethnic background. Born in New York of Cuban parents, he is the author of five acclaimed novels. His first, *Our House in the Last World,* deals with an immigrant Cuban family's attempts to adapt to life in New York. Sound familiar? His second, *The Mambo Kings Play Songs of Love,* for which he received the Pulitzer Prize, is about a couple of Cuban musicians trying to make it in New York and the attempt of the son of one of them to understand their life. His third, *The Fourteen Sisters of Esteban Montez O'Brien,* is the story of a Cuban-Irish family in a small Pennsylvania town. His fourth, *Mr. Ives' Christmas,* is a study of how a man copes with grief over the death of his son. Though the Cuban motif resounds strongly in his first two books, it weakens substantially in *Fourteen Sisters* and is all but nonexistent in *Mr. Ives' Christmas.*[1]

I remember distinctly when I first read *Mambo Kings* my feeling that I had before me a North American, not a Cuban, book. If there are any echoes in Hijuelos's work, they come from Dreiser, Dickens, perhaps even Hemingway, but there is very little of Alejo Carpentier, Lezama Lima, Cabrera Infante, Severo Sarduy, and the other great Cuban novelists. The Cuban baroque seems not to have touched Hijuelos, but North American directness certainly has. Here is the beginning of *Mambo Kings:*

> It was a Saturday afternoon on La Salle Street, years and years ago when I was a little kid, and around three o'clock Mrs. Shannon, the heavy Irish woman in her perpetually soup-stained dress, opened her

---

[1]This essay was written before the publication of Hijuelo's fifth novel, *The Empress of the Splendid Seasons.*

back window and shouted out into the courtyard, "Hey Cesar, yoo-hoo, I think you're on television, I swear it's you!" When I heard the opening strains of the *I Love Lucy* show I got excited because I knew she was referring to an item of eternity, that episode in which my dead father and my Uncle Cesar had appeared, playing Ricky Ricardo's singing cousins fresh off the farm in Oriente Province, Cuba, and north in New York for an engagement at Ricky's night-club, the Tropicana.

The language, "Hey, Cesar, yoo-hoo . . ."; the setting, an apartment building in what appears to be a U.S. city; Mrs. Shannon, the heavy Irish woman in her perpetually soup-stained dress; and, finally, the reference to "I Love Lucy," all fix this novel within the North American tapestry. Cuban novels—and, I might add, Latin American novels—begin with great drama or great satire or sweeping historical vision. North American novels begin with the narrator's feet firmly planted in everyday reality: "Call me Ishmael."

Another pertinent case is that of Junot Díaz, a young Dominican-born writer with an MFA degree in writing from Cornell University. I first saw one of his stories in the autumn 1995 issue of *Story* magazine. Soon after, two of his stories appeared in the *New Yorker,* and in 1996 another appeared in a subsequent issue of *Story*. In the fall of 1996 Grove Press published his first collection, titled *Drown*. His appearance on the scene is nothing short of meteoric; his talent is undeniable.

The curious thing about Díaz's work is that, though his stories treat the lives of Dominicans both in the island and in the United States, his style is distinctly North American. At times his narrative voice has an academic ring to it, as if the stories told were being passed through a filter. The story titled "Drown," for example, is a first-person account by a young drug dealer told in present tense, very much the tense in vogue among academic realists. Indeed, there seems to be a dichotomy in the diction between the use of studied, almost poetic words and col-loquialisms and street idioms. Notice this sentence, which describes the narrator's reminiscence of a visit to a public swimming pool: "We lunged from the boards and swam out to the deep end, wrestling and farting around." I was particularly struck by his use of the imagistic, lit-erary verb *lunged* at the beginning of the sentence and the colloquial par-ticipial phrase *farting around* at the end, as if the speaker here is, on the one hand, working for literary effect and, on the other, trying to tell a story plainly, in street language. Notice this other passage in which the narrator speaks of his mother: "She's so quiet that most of the time I'm startled to find her in the apartment. I'll enter a room and she'll stir, detaching herself from the cracking plaster walls, from the stained cabinets, and fright will pass through me like a wire." And this passage: "Nights I drink with Alex and Danny, and other friends who remain. The Malibou Bar is no good, just us washouts and the sucias we can con into joining us." Junot Díaz wants to tell street stories, using the language of the street, with its sharp edge and its jazzy rhythms and the smart diction of *washouts, con,* and the Spanish *sucias,* used here to refer to loose women; but he also seems to want to please an audience out there composed of very studious people who are comfortable with and use words such as *lunged* and *startled* and *detaching* and *fright.* Make no mistake, I think Díaz is a fine writer, but he has clearly slipped into the North American current, such as it is. The problems of his diction are North American; they are problems that surface when the intellectual training of the writer runs head on against his need to tell a story democratically, instinctively, using the immediate language of experience, not the studied language of the academy.

We can think of Western literature as having two branches. The first of these is the aristocratic branch, which arose out of the courtly poetry and the monastic writings of the Middle Ages and which in the United States became the intellectual branch and had its blossoming in the writings of Emerson, Thoreau, and the other transcendentalists. The second is the democratic branch, which originated with jongleurs and minstrels in the streets of medieval Europe. This democratic branch has naturally been very strong in the United States and can be traced in English literature at least to Chaucer, but it finds an eloquent and convincing champion more recently in the figure of William Wordsworth. In the preface to the 1800 edition of the *Lyrical Ballads* he writes, "The principal object, then, in these Poems was to choose incidents and situations from common life, and to relate or describe them, throughout, as far as was possible in a selection of language really used by men." One takes his phrase *the language used by men* to mean common everyday unadorned speech. Though Wordsworth was not always successful in writing in plainspeak, the fact that he tried to do so seems to have opened the way for the grounding of much future poetry in the English, not of the learned few but of the common majority as they went about their daily business. In the United States the attempt to write a democratic literature finds suitable homes in the work of Whitman, with his expansive and inclusive verse, and also in the work of Mark Twain, especially in *The Adventures of Huckleberry Finn,* which is told in the voice and point of view of an unidealized and unsentimentalized boy. One of the many things that Mark Twain taught writers was that the voice of indigence had its own eloquence and narrative drive derived not from its weakness but from its strength and that it was better suited for telling American stories than the stylized, literary English imported from Victorian England.

By contrast, Latin American societies are, if not aristocratic, then certainly oligarchic. The disparity between the upper social levels and the lower ones is immeasurable by North American standards. Even now, at the end of the twentieth century, a good education is a privilege reserved primarily for the upper-middle and the upper classes. The vast majority of the population receives the most basic education, if they get any at all. Economic survival stands at the center of most people's lives, while the writing of literature is left to the privileged and, thus, curiously absent from daily life, even when the writers themselves are well-known and lionized as national heroes. Layered over this social stratification is an age-old distinction, inherited from Spanish letters, between literary language and the language of everyday affairs. This distinction, highlighted in Spain by the creation of the Royal Academy of the Spanish Language, fixed the canon of proper written language and presented its version as the true one in opposition to colloquial and colonial mongrel versions. Such rigidity left its indelible mark on the literatures of Spanish-speaking countries of the Americas, where, in the absence of an aristocracy in the European sense, the bourgeoisie flourished and took over political rule at the end of the colonial period. The great themes of Spanish American literature are bourgeois themes, and the stories around these themes are told in a refined, stylized bourgeois language. A good analog for this may be found in French literature of the nineteenth and twentieth centuries, to which many Latin American writers looked for their models. And so we can say that the aristocratic branch of literature in Latin America metamorphosed into a bourgeois oligarchic one.

Populist democratic literature exists in Latin America, that cannot be denied, and writers have tried to write in clear, unadorned language. In the second half of the nineteenth century, for example, the Cuban modernist poet José Martí wrote his "Versos Sencillos," poems free of the weighty rhetorical language of much Spanish language poetry of that century. Two movements, which arose from oral traditions in their respective countries, also come to mind: Afro-Cuban poetry, a subgenre of Cuban poetry; and the gauchesque movement in Argentine literature, from which arose the national epic of Argentina, *Martín Fierro* by José Hernández. The democratic branch, however, has been left untended compared to the oligarchic one, and these movements have been seen as colorful curiosities. Both gauchesque literature and Afro-Cuban poetry are considered anachronisms in the regions where they once thrived, and few writers nowadays concern themselves with those forms.

The fact is that in Spanish America the language and themes of serious literature tend to be removed from the speech and concerns of common people. Two important conditions further solidify this dichotomy. First, the Royal Academy of the Spanish Language, to which I referred earlier and which has branches in every Spanish-speaking country, maintains, like its French counterpart, a very strong grip on literature. From a young age children are taught at school that there is a "proper" language, which they must learn if they want to advance socially. Given the social rigidity of Latin American society, there is enormous pressure on the children of the middle class to master this language, which morphologically speaking, is identical from country to country. Under these circumstances the language of the streets is disavowed, and the young writer has little room for experimentation and for exploiting different varieties of linguistic experience as well as the points of view associated with them.

Second, there has never existed in Latin America a tradition of social and historical criticism independent of literature. Spurred on by their social conscience, writers, both poets and novelists, have taken on the critical role and often use their creative works as vehicles for critical analysis. The language that results from these endeavors tends to have a heavy intellectual content while falling short on local color. Coupled with the emphasis on "literary" language, it is easy to see why Latin American fiction is so poor in dialogue (refined stylized dialogues run contrary to the premise of modern fiction—the pursuit of realism) but rich in omniscient narrative. Think of Borges, García Márquez, Vargas Llosa. The examples are numerous.

My point then is this: that Sandra Cisneros and most other so-called Hispanic-American writers are closer to a North American style or a North American tradition than to a Latin American one. Putting aside for a moment the obvious—that these writers write almost exclusively in English—the North American tradition, with its strong democratic branch, has given their voices an authority they would have lacked in the societies their families came from, where their parents or grandparents were oppressed economically and/or politically and kept from all but the most basic education, with literary expression for all intents and purposes beyond their reach. Second, the themes and concerns, the scenery and the characters, the voices and the vistas, of Hispanic writers of English, as a group, are North American. The theme of urban displacement is, for example, a North American theme. So is the theme of discrimination, which makes its presence so abundantly felt in an already thriving African-American literature. The attempt to write in the language and rhythms of the street, of the common people—Wordsworth would say, "in the real language of men"—this, too, is as American as apple pie and, more globally, an interest and concern of English-speaking writers, as we have already seen. In effect, Hispanic writers in the United States are acting as the mouthpieces of their forebears, mostly poor but ambitious immigrants, and thereby giving space on the page to their human concerns—their drives, their fears, their longings and their hatreds, too. These writers are doing so within an existing tradition, and what they are discovering is that their themes are not much different from those of Twain, Steinbeck, Paley, Morrison, Ellison, and Dreiser, who sit eminently in the canon of the North American tradition. Amazingly, it is not only economic opportunity that has been provided to immigrants of Hispanic countries but literary opportunity as well. And it is that literary opportunity that is embodying the spirit of a whole group of people who had been, up until the twentieth century, spiritually disenfranchised in their countries of origin.

Once we understand this phenomenon in relation to English writers of Hispanic origin, we may perhaps be able to see the damage that is done to them by labeling and marginalizing them. Until critics do away with labels and, using the highest aesthetic standards, look rigorously and caringly at the literature being written by these groups and until the writers liberate themselves from the tyranny of the adjective, ethnic labeling is not only undermining them as artists but also undermining the democratic tradition in literature. Finally, it is all to the good that, rather than retrench in the safety of the academy with its elitist and exclusionary tendencies, North American letters instead open themselves up to the voices of all the dispossessed and oppressed peoples who land on these shores. I want to believe that beyond a sense of what is right, legal, and politically correct there can be a concurrent understanding on the part of the literary establishment that there exists a direct line of development from Whitman and Twain to Emily Dickinson to William Carlos Williams to Langston Hughes to Oscar Hijuelos to Sandra Cisneros to Junot Díaz and that, rather than undermine North American literature, writers of Hispanic backgrounds, and by extension all underrepresented writers, are enriching and multiplying its perspectives.

WORKS CITED

Alvarez, Julia. "On Finding a Latino Voice." *Washington Post Book World,* 14 May 1995, 1, 10.
Borges, Jorge Luis. *Labyrinths: Selected Stories and Other Writings.* Ed. Donald Yates and James E. Irby. New York: New Directions, 1964.
Cisneros, Sandra. *The House on Mango Street.* New York: Vintage Books, 1991.
Díaz, Junot. "Drown." *New Yorker,* 29 January 1996, 78–83.

Faulkner, William. *Writers at Work: The Paris Review Interviews*. Ed. Malcolm Cowley. New York: Viking Compass, 1957.

Hemingway, Ernest. *Death in the Afternoon*. New York: Charles Scribner's Sons, 1932.

Hijuelos, Oscar. *The Mambo Kings Play Songs of Love*. New York: Farrar, Straus and Giroux, 1989.

Kiš, Danilo. *Homo Poeticus*. Ed. Susan Sontag. New York: Farrar, Straus and Giroux, 1995.

Paley, Grace. "A Man Told Me the Story of His Life." In *Later That Same Day*. New York: Penguin Books, 1986.

Wordsworth, William. *Selected Poems and Prefaces*. Ed. Jack Stillinger. Boston: Houghton Mifflin, 1965.

JUDITH GROSSMAN

Thinking about a Reader

In many fiction-writing workshops the conventional wisdom is to warn apprentice writers against any thoughts concerning possible readers of the work-in-progress. The point here would be that a writer needs, above all, to keep the mind's eye focused within *this* scene, the very moment of *this* story—for how else will we achieve that desired intensity of conviction, that integrated mesh of detail? Indeed, how else will our story even come to pass on the page, or screen, given the notoriously chilling effect of a critical presence in the area, a suspected eye peering over the shoulder?

Then there's the plausible consideration that all too-deliberate efforts to please an audience are doomed to be futile. To quote Donald Barthelme, wickedly out of context: "It does no good to *mash down* on the button." One fatal hint of trying too hard, of crass manipulation, and it will be that most desirable reader whom we lose.

So, do we subscribe outright to the conventional wisdom, that is, that if we don't focus exclusively on being inside the flow of a credible imaginative world the writing will surely suffer? It seems as if we must. And yet, the moment I use words like *conviction,* and *credible,* I'm already implying that there is some kind of awareness of audience going on, somewhere. For who is to be convinced—to whom must the story be credible? Not, I think, the writer alone: there is an outside to the whole situation. To face this issue directly threatens to put us in a serious double bind. I would like to try and defuse the problematic confrontation, by nominating two key moments in the process of making fiction when a writer can legitimately bring to mind the sense, and interests, of a reader.

The first of these comes at the start of a fictional project, when we are recommitting ourselves to the work and learning once more what the practice of fiction means to us—what we think we're doing. This would be especially true when we undertake the larger project of a novel. Right then, even the most reclusive minded of writers might consider

---

Originally published, under the title "Thinking and Not Thinking about the Reader," in the *AWP Chronicle* 31, no. 2 (October 1988).

the late-Victorian observation by George Saintsbury that "it is the first duty of a novelist to let himself be read."

When I came across those words, quoted in some random review a while back, they took me by surprise, like an uncomfortable reminder of a truth stuffed way back in the closet: that writing is a solitary practice that has a sociable destiny. Gertrude Stein put it succinctly: "I write for myself, and strangers." Safe behind the closed door of our study or bedroom or converted garage, we are (however subliminally) opening another kind of door—toward an implied presence, the distant yet oddly intimate stranger.

Such a realization becomes easier to handle if we can understand how an internally buried audience is always and already there. In what follows I'm drawing, in a general way of course, on psychoanalytic sources. (Those who have studied Freud, Winnicott, and Lacan may make more particular connections, as for instance with Lacan's theory of the "mirror stage.") My point would be first to recall that the self, especially the self as displayed in language, is a *collaborative creation;* the old-fashioned image of the artist as pure, self-begotten isolate seems to me by now thoroughly enough discredited. Second—again not a new idea—I would say that fiction with communicative power reflects certain early encounters that confirmed *this* particular vocation for the writer. Early on there would have arisen a key relationship with somebody close— parent perhaps, relative, or older sibling—who actively acknowledged in a child not simply her curiosity about the world but her drive to interpret the experience of it in words, and, not least, she would have shown a strong tropism toward language-play for its own sake. Later, when the written word came in, it could be a teacher, or anybody who gave that vital response—whatever served to validate and secure the direction taken. And even as writers in adult life, I believe, we still draw on that sequence of confirmations when taking the risks of new work.

What I'm putting emphasis on here is the fact that the initiation into writing, as with speech, has a social character and that sociability gives the fiction its presence for a reader. "Presence" is a hard thing to define, but the playwright Alan Bennett's remark about reading Proust describes the unmistakable effect: "It is as if a hand has come out and taken yours." We can expect, and many discerning biographies of writers, from Henry James to Franz Kafka, support the expectation, that distinct traces of those early relational moments will show up in the lasting personal agenda writers bring to their fiction—in that sense we often get of a constantly recurring, ground-bass thematic. Our own obsessions, resurfacing year after year, even when we thought they were exhausted.

There's something more to add, relating to the plain oddity of writers' specializing in communication at a double distance, via the printed word rather than by letter, phone call, or face-to-face. I have a friend who used to write me terrific letters, now sends me terrific e-mails, and has always been a great talker. She communicates with an unimpeded immediacy that I lack, and yet, with all the other kinds of work she's done, she is decidedly not a writer. What I've finally come to believe is this: that writers are, in general, driven to perfect what was originally an *incomplete,* partly successful, but also partly failed communicative act—and, in doing so, to transcend its limited and specific personal frame.

To cite one famous literary example, it's clear from the opening chapters of James Joyce's "Portrait of the Artist as a Young Man" that Stephen's father is his first initiator into the art of telling stories but that afterwards the father deteriorates into alcoholism and fades out at his end of the conversation. When Stephen goes into exile at the book's conclusion, he makes his famous invocation thus: "Old father, old artificer, stand me now and ever in good stead!" And we know, of course, that the all-too-human father has been subsumed into the mythic patron, his namesake the Greek Daedalus. Stephen—and Joyce—required sufficient distance from the actual father to complete their original communicative mission.

When I mention the writer's need for distance, this is not to deny that many writers can deploy at least the effect of public geniality. Nabokov called himself "a social cripple," but he managed those fine college lectures, to make a living. And now that we have to go out and sell books, well, it's surprising what necessity will produce. Still, the key ritual of the writer's metier is, typically, to withdraw from the social scene and, by means of the art's resources, amplify the voice so that it will carry across space and time. An important correlative note: we always hope to make up for the insult of our withdrawal from others through the compounded interest, true grace, of what we bring back. Because withdrawal, even while it marks the scar from that childhood failure, *is always an insult,* and an offering of compensatory value must be made.

The way writers talk about their personal agenda in fiction, and their sense of an audience, can be additionally revealing about the range of possible configurations. Scanning through some of the *Paris Review* interviews collected as *Writers at Work,* I've found several telling examples. Here, for example, is Robert Stone on writing as an exercise in power—benign but nevertheless coercive: "What you're trying to do when you write is to crowd the reader out of his own space and occupy it with yours, in a good cause" (8th ser., 349). It is a matter of record that

Robert Stone, as a young child, lived under the care of a mother who suffered from schizophrenia. The effort to pit his still developing grasp of normative reality against her delusional illness might well be reflected in Stone's own commitment to a strong form of realism: the real, corrected truth of the world out there.

And here is Joan Didion going a step further, admitting an aggressive element in the design of writer on reader: "It's hostile in that you're trying to make somebody see something the way you see it, trying to impose your idea, your picture." But then she qualifies the position: "I am always writing to myself. So very possibly I'm committing an aggressive and hostile act towards myself" (5th ser., 342). This interesting qualification seems to take the sting out of the fictional invasion of a reader's mind by disclaiming the reader as primary target. Is it a concessive gesture of the female-masochistic type? Or does it go beyond that, to an imagined merging of writing and reading selves? Either way, it's a teasing provocation.

This authorial disposition toward the exercise of dominance can be traced as directly, of course, in certain fictional styles. Consider, for instance, the declarative opening sentences for which Hemingway was famous, as here in "Big Two-Hearted River": "The train went up the track out of sight, around one of the hills of burnt timber. Nick sat down on the bundle of canvas and bedding the baggage man had pitched out of the baggage car. There was no town, nothing but the rails and the burned-over country." That's the master's voice, directing the reader's vision without any weak solicitations to believe—just telling us the way it is. Hemingway clears a space with his vanishing train, his burned-off hills; then he directs our attention onto the single figure in this landscape who is to engage us: Nick.

Or consider Gabriel García Márquez's abrupt opening, in the story "A Very Old Man with Enormous Wings," which opens the door on a world of unexplained and unexplainable strangeness: "On the third day of rain they had killed so many crabs inside the house that Pelayo had to cross his drenched courtyard and throw them into the sea, because the newborn child had a temperature all night and they thought it was due to the stench." Márquez immerses us—it is a characteristic move for him—in a world completely outside our normative, literate experience, and in this way he makes us entirely dependent on its author as exclusive, privileged witness and mediator.

These writers demonstrate, in related but distinctive ways, their command of authoritative speech, and their insistence on *this* version of the world. By contrast, here's an example from Doris Lessing of another way of proceeding, though almost as self-confident. It is the opening sentence of Lessing's famous story "To Room Nineteen": "This is a story, I suppose, about a failure in intelligence: the Rawlings' marriage was grounded in intelligence."

Lessing, with this flat, analytical tone, her casually speculative *I suppose,* is refusing the obvious kind of fictional authority, in line perhaps with her egalitarian politics. The reader she wants—we could say, whom she constructs—is more like a fellow thinker about the contemporary scene, in which the Rawlings can function almost as a case study. As the story builds, so will the dramatic involvement, but always within the limits of Lessing's sense of an implied reader of active and independent rationality.

By contrast again, in the matter of having designs on a reader, Philip Roth goes much further. Asked by his interviewer whether he has a reader in mind when writing, he answered: "No. I occasionally have an anti-Roth reader in mind. I think, 'How he is going to hate this!' That can be just the encouragement I need" (*Writers at Work,* 7th ser., 273). Here is the writer as rebel, whose work has always been fueled substantially by anger and the anarchic joy of playing Lord of Misrule. Whereas for Stone, Didion, and others, the literary roots run back at least to a nineteenth-century novelistic tradition of opening up an instructive world, for Roth there is an alternative subversive lineage, going back in part to Eastern Europeans, the Dostoevsky of *Notes from Underground,* and in part through *Tristram Shandy*—with maybe a touch of de Sade?—to Rabelais.

On yet another side there is Stephen King, who likes to say in newspaper interviews (though not the *Paris Review*): "What I want is to reach through the paper and grab the reader. I don't want to just mess with your head, I want to mess with your life. I want you to miss appointments, burn dinner, skip your homework. . . . Compulsive reading is a sickness, and I've always wanted to be 'Typhoid Stevie'" (*Baltimore Sun,* 13 September 1997). Here, the hand reaching out is merrily sadistic, armed with a needleful of addiction. And, perhaps because so much of what really oppresses us in daily life is the officially benign routine concealing its dreadful horrors, many of us take what he offers with relief.

Then there's an entirely different cluster of writers whose communicative agenda stresses intimacy, the courtship of the reader either as phantom-surrogate for the original, far-back listener or (associatively or narcissistically) for a past state of the self. Muriel Spark describes this approach through the advice of her character Mrs. Hawkins, in *A Far Cry from Kensington:*

"You are writing to a friend," was the sort of thing I used to say. "And this is a dear and close friend, real—or better—invented in your mind like a fixation. Write privately, not publicly, without fear or timidity, right to the end of the letter, as if it was never going to be published, so that your true friend will read it over and over, and then want more enchanting letters from you."

Saul Bellow puts it this way: "I have in mind another human being who will understand me. I count on this" (*Writers at Work,* 3d ser., 186). And here is John Updike: "When I write, I aim in my mind not towards New York but towards a vague spot a little to the east of Kansas. I think of the books on library shelves, without their jackets, years old, and a countryish teenaged boy finding them and having them speak to him" (431). Updike's description of his imagined reader is very close to the small-town Pennsylvania teenager he himself once was: he seems to be pitching his voice back toward his own beginnings as a writer, making that act of reconnection I have described but to a fully self-assimilated hearer. And in very similar words Richard Ford says: "I want to write, partly at least, for the kind of reader I was when I was nineteen years old" (*Paris Review* 140:96).

Thinking of writers with a gift for offering this intimate, immediate presence to a reader, Grace Paley comes to mind, and here I quote the opening of her story "Wants":

I saw my ex-husband in the street. I was sitting on the steps of the new library.

Hello, my life, I said. We had once been married for twenty-seven years, so I felt justified. (*Enormous Changes at the Last Minute*)

This speaker is at home with us; she has no need to explain who she is, who her ex-husband is, or where this library is located. The story she tells comes across as much closer to us than any narrative situation in which names might matter. Incidentally, in an interview Paley gave for the collection on women writers, *Listen to Their Voices* (edited by Mickey Pearlman), she says she has "never been writing-ambitious the way some of the younger women are." She goes on: "The word *career* drives me crazy for some reason; I hate it in men as well as women." Writing and the private social world belong together for Paley; and in fact her public work of political action, notably in the Vietnam era, has been kept distinct from her writing life, although the values espoused are present in both.

Of this grouping, though, it is perhaps Jack Kerouac who tied the intimate social life most thoroughly into the work, giving priority to the former. In his *Paris Review* interview he gives this account: "You think out what actually happened, you tell your friends about it, you mull it over in your mind, you connect it at leisure, then when the time comes to pay the rent again, you force yourself to sit at the typewriter . . . and get it over with as fast as you can" (4th ser., 383). For Kerouac the first draft is crucial to the integrity of the communicative act. By this means, he says, "you simply give the reader the actual workings of your mind during the writing process" (364). Thus, the reader stands in as directly as possible for Kerouac's friends—with whom, obviously, he'd rather be shooting the breeze.

A few writers, it's true, do disclaim all awareness of a reader as destination for the work. Eudora Welty states: "I don't write for my friends or myself either; I write for *it,* for the pleasure of *it."* Actual publication, she adds, "gives me a terrible sense of exposure, as if I'd gotten sunburned" (*Writers at Work,* 4th ser., 275). Edna O'Brien also places her work in an impersonal frame: "A story comes to me, is given to me, as it were, and I write it" (7th ser., 261).

In these instances my impression to date is of a gender factor operating; I've not so far located a male writer who makes such thoroughgoing disclaimers. Both Welty and O'Brien grew up in societies where traditional feminine roles were well defined, and it's possible that they prefer not to consider any demands their work might make on the attention of others. Welty speaks of writing as something like a private act of devotion, in which, to be sure, she takes pleasure. O'Brien (like Alice Walker with her dedication of *The Color Purple* to its characters—"Thank you for coming") asserts only the status of a medium, writing down what "is given." There is a marked impersonality about Welty's and O'Brien's emphatic use of the term *it* to denote the work, which indicates to me a self-protective distancing from the conscious sense of power in relation to a reader.

Nevertheless, when I read the opening of Welty's much anthologized story "A Worn Path," I *hear* an unmistakable tone of authority, specifically that of a storyteller still linked to and supported by folktale traditions: "It was December—a bright frozen day in the early morning. Far out in the country there was an old Negro woman with her head tied in a red rag, coming along a path through the pinewood." These sentences are, in their way, no less confidently declarative than Hemingway's. However, where Hemingway will tend to place a self-surrogate at the center of his narrative space, Welty is bearing witness to what can be known of the life of her community—seen clearly but at a tactful degree of distance. The emphasis here is firmly on the pictorial image, the small dark figure with its red head-wrap, against a bright wintry landscape: no accident that Welty has been a photographer as well as a writer.

The most recent *Paris Review* interview that I've consulted was with Jeanette Winterson, whose responses on the question of audience are of two minds. First, she declares: "I simply do the work that I need to do without imagining an audience at all" (*Paris Review* 145:98). She directs her responsiveness instead to the body of literature already in existence: "I cannot do my own work without known work" (82). The latter position is one with which I think all mature writers would agree. Yet Winterson also admits a desire to challenge readers with the possibility of change—of being, as she puts it, "the hero in their own lives" (99). And her account of herself as a precocious child evangelist—a background she shared with James Baldwin—continually writing and delivering sermons, shows that she acquired hands-on early experience in how to hold and persuade an audience. Which means, I would guess, that she no longer has to figure out those angles; instead, she's free to focus on the demands of her secular vocation—in which, as she still says, "You really have to have faith . . . and you do have to believe, because there is no other way" (84).

Winterson speaks of these matters in a way not so far from Flannery O'Connor's, in *Mystery and Manners*. O'Connor, asked why she wrote, answered candidly, "Because I'm good at it." She was right—and also right in adding that the gift required a submission of the self: "In art, the self becomes self-forgetful in order to meet the demands of the thing seen and the thing being made."

Looking back over the diversity of writers' sense of how they connect with the world out there, it seems that for some the awareness of *performance,* that raising of the voice, however subtle, that marks all style in writing, is practiced essentially as a mystery or a birthright ritual. For others, by contrast, it represents a more conscious challenge, a stimulus toward competition. Gaining experience in writing means, among other things, understanding our own temperament in this regard. For that will substantially determine the individual range of voice a writer best commands—something not always intuitively recognized.

Here I want to consider the second stage: the encounter between writer and reader *after* the work is complete in draft and receives its first outside exposure. This is a much more familiar subject of discussion, given the widespread workshop culture to which most young writers have been exposed, and I have less to add to it. But, whether the early audience of the fictional work consists of random friends, workshop leaders and participants, literary agents or editors, our first realization must be that no writer can expect to please all possible readers. (And that goes double for fellow writers, having their own stake in the art.) The task then is to experiment, test our limits as well as our preferences, feeling for the zone of connection.

In the process apprentice writers often hit against difficulties that can direct them toward what they'll do best. For instance, a writer who pitches the voice so quietly that the story just murmurs from the page can learn from specialists in the intimate voice. It might be Marcel Proust or Virginia Woolf or Colette, alternatively Alice Munro or Andre Dubus—but the choices are many, for learning the best strategies of overcoming distance, of tuning the resonance. There are some common mistakes of diffident writing—such as dutifully tracking through an everyday routine, where the mind needs to take charge and *perform* the vital meanings, the dynamic shape of the story; or "losing" a character along the way (especially that essential antagonist figure); or else letting an ending just fade away. The example of first-rate writers of one's own kind is absolutely the place to go for help in these situations.

Alternatively, the writer who "overpitches"—working the voice so hard that the story drowns in performance noise or is hung up on self-consciously looking over the shoulder for an effect—that kind of writer could profit from close study of the practitioners of more overt fictional authority. I've named some of these already, and we could include Toni Morrison among them, of course, and Angela Carter, for instance.

Over time, then, it's been my experience that writers themselves, by discovering what fiction they're especially drawn to read, can identify their best allies and teachers in the art. This is not to say that one would hope or even want one's range as a writer to equal the range of one's reading enjoyment. For instance, I have a great admiration and love for the work of the late Donald Barthelme, yet I'm acutely conscious of the ways in which it can resist me as a reader, let alone as a potential colleague. Barthelme's most deeply understood theme was the relations between men, and especially those between son and father, as in "Views of My Father Weeping" and his finest novel, *The Dead Father*. Perhaps because of this I can't always be sure of my foothold in his "universe of discourse" (as he calls it in *Snow White*). Even so, what I can do with my admiration, as a writer, is to make occasional pleasurably covert borrowings and to learn from the acute discipline in Barthelme's work as a checking device for my own.

Apprentice writers in workshop often find themselves, as we know, writing "for" a teacher whose aesthetic they find less than congenial and who may indeed not be an ideal reader for their work. But, again, I've known a few people whose writing life seemed to wither after the apparently wonderful experience of having a strong mentor. It should be clear, in any case, that, even with the best of luck in the matchmaking process, the workshop experience remains just a fractional stage in the writer's education. We take from it what we can, and afterwards we do the essential thing—go on teaching ourselves through continuous practice in the art and through reading in literature at large.

Finally, a very brief and partial note on the treacherous issue of the unknown editor out there, as audience. Here are some telling lines from the preface to *American Stories II* (1991), an anthology drawn from the *Atlantic Monthly,* by C. Michael Curtis: "Among other things, successful stories remind us of *our own* moral uneasiness, the difficulty of *our own life choices*. We like finding characters who seem to us 'realistic' because they are afflicted with uncertainties *like our own*" (xii, italics added). The repeated emphasis has to raise a chilling question in any writer's mind: who is meant by the "us" implicit in this emphatically repeated *our own*—and what accompanying agenda and baggage? Absent a naively wholehearted Enlightenment view of one universal human nature, across gender and racial divides and discrimination, how can we others (the writers) deal with the inevitability of warps in the way reading is conducted?

Perhaps, on this score, what we can mostly guess is that it makes sense to cast our net as widely as possible: to send the work out in search of those editors who may be receptive to what we're doing, to pursue the leads, and to take whatever good advice we can get under advisement. And we can look one more time at the writing we've done, to be sure it shows confidence in itself, given that whatever is seen intensely and valued strongly makes a fair claim on the human world. If we find any doubt, we go back—or forwards—and perform the work, *da capo,* with even more reckless confidence.

MARGOT LIVESEY

How to Tell a True Story

Nine years ago I was teaching summer school at a university outside of Boston when in a small Scottish town my stepmother died. Her death was, from my perspective, sudden. On my way to class I found a letter in the mailbox from Aunt Marian; I read it on the bus. Janey, my stepmother, had had a fall and was in hospital but not to worry she was making good progress. I don't remember what I taught that day but I do recall my anger. Her accident, I foresaw, would mean new problems, new difficulties, for me. I was still angry when the chairman came into my office with a message that Janey was very ill. I hurried home immediately and made arrangements to fly to Glasgow. Then I phoned the hospital, Perth Infirmary, only to discover she was already dead. A week later a birthday card arrived. A nurse had written the address and a joke about Janey's many gentlemen visitors. She herself had signed the card, shakily, "love M."

I did not go to her funeral. I knew I would have to return later to deal with her possessions, and I was too poor to make two transatlantic trips and too young to understand the complex reasons for which one might attend a funeral where no other mourner would be offended by one's absence. Instead, I decided to write a story about her. The question was how? She was almost fifty when she married my father, and I knew only snatches about that large part of her life that had already occurred. I wanted to honor her memory, to be faithful to the facts, as I understood them, including our deep estrangement, and yet to do merely that would have resulted in a skinny, parsimonious, undignified story. I needed imagination as well as memory.

Over the course of a difficult autumn I wrote the story, "Learning by Heart." It was a long story, a hundred pages, with two braided narratives. One strand of the narrative was what I remembered of my childhood and adolescence with my stepmother, and I wrote the material as if I were writing an essay. Although I was presenting it as a story, I wanted readers to think, oh yes, this really did happen. The other strand was my imagining of Janey's life. The life I did not know and had no

First published in the *AWP Chronicle* 26, no. 3 (December 1993).

means to discover, I dreamed up on the page. And in a number of ways I signaled to the reader that this part of the narrative had a different onto-logical status, was true in a different way. I wrote it as fiction.

I am not sure how well "Learning by Heart" succeeds, but since then, in and out of the classroom, I have pondered how the intuitive choices I made in writing that story might be refined. I began to notice that I often gave my students conflicting advice. A student would bring me a story about a family with three children. Sometimes I would say, why do you need Edwina, Margaret, and Theo? It just confuses your reader. Why don't you collapse Edwina and Margaret into a single character and just have two children? Sometimes, however, I found myself saying the opposite. Why only have three children? I would ask. Why not have five? Or go for broke—have seven?

In the first case I was advising the student along the traditional lines of story writing. Be expedient. As Sydney Cox says in his opinionated book *Indirections,* every sentence, every detail, should reveal character, deepen the theme, and advance the plot. The pleasure of this kind of narrative is not that we think we are reading about the real world but, rather, that the wings of symmetry are unfolding around us; briefly, we are on a planet where human behavior makes sense. I call this fiction.

In the second case I was clearly suggesting an alternative strategy. The authority of the story was coming, in part, from the degree to which it made the reader feel that the events described really had occurred. And the way to strengthen the story was to increase this effect. Rather than expediency, I urged the student to make the story messier, more con-fusing, in other words more lifelike. I call this anti-fiction.

Throughout this century it seems to me an increasing number of authors have been choosing to have five children rather than two. We can find story after story, novel after novel, where the boundaries between author and character, real and imagined, are blurred and our experience is closer to reading autobiography or history. I do not mean to suggest that there are simply two, exclusive choices. Rather, I see a continuum, stretching from tales beginning "Once upon a time . . ." where we are blithely expected to believe that a wolf can pass for a grandmother, to the most explicit anti-fiction, works whose authors bla-tantly encourage what Sartre might have termed a hemorrhaging between fiction and reality. In Joan Didion's *Democracy* and Tim O'Brien's *The Things They Carried* characters share the names and occu-pations of their creators.

Once I got a glimpse of the continuum I wondered what lay behind these alternatives and how the signals were given to the reader. The first question invites a comet's tail of speculations. My suspicion is that most authors make these choices unconsciously, as I did, because of their prior relationship with the material. But at a deeper level, farther into the astral debris, lurks the demon of how to give our work authority. By the end of her life my stepmother had very few visitors. What right had I to ask my readers to be among them? To endure the wallpaper and the antimacassars and, worst of all, my stepmother's boring, tyrannical conversation.

In a recent fit of homesickness I reread *Dr. Jekyll and Mr. Hyde,* a novel I think of as essentially Scottish that happens to be set in London. As usual, I was consoled by the darkness and fog, but this time I was also struck by Stevenson's use of documents: letters and Dr. Jekyll's confession. Looking at other nineteenth-century novels—*Wuthering Heights, Dracula, The Woman in White*—I discovered a startling number of interlocking narrators, diaries found in locked boxes, death-bed confessions, and, of course, letters. These authors knew that their incredible tales needed authenticating, and they approached their readers like a prosecutor a jury, bombarding us with testimonials from expert witnesses.

In this century such devices have fallen out of fashion but not because we have become more credulous as readers. If anything, our credulity has declined, and we are liable to read a letter in fiction as yet more fiction. There are gorgeous counterexamples. Part of the brilliance of Nathaniel West's *Miss Lonelyhearts* is the inclusion of letters from Miss Lonelyhearts's constituents that are absolutely integral to the plot and to the anguished voice of the novel. More recently, A. S. Byatt paid homage to the nineteenth century in her novel *Possession* by including a fabricated poem. The novel captivated many readers, but most I suspect soon realized that they could follow the plot without reading the poem and turned those pages with increasing speed.

Not only have we grown wary of devices, but we have decided to privilege memory over imagination, or so it seems to me. In the current climate a novel set in Vietnam, written by someone who had not been there, would be unlikely to meet with the rapturous reception of *The Red Badge of Courage.* Certain experiences—war, other races, some illnesses, perhaps other sexual orientations—are no longer deemed appropriate territory for the imagination. We want the author to be writing out of memory. Even a kind of impersonal memory—the American-born, Jewish author writing about the Holocaust—is preferable to none. The long tradition of the amateur writer is under siege. Authors, along with other people, are now expected to have credentials.

We are even reluctant to permit an author to write fully about a character of the opposite sex, as witness our overwhelming assumption that first-person narrators are the same gender as their authors. In "Learning by Heart" I did not bother for many pages to identify the narrator as a young woman, a version of myself; I knew the reader would think that anyway. These assumptions, which can do so much for our work when we follow them, become problematic if we want to contradict them, especially I think for women writing about men. A dozen great fictional heroines—Pamela, Moll Flanders, Molly Bloom, Emma Bovary, Anna Karenina—sidle out of my bookcase, swishing their skirts courtesy of their male authors, but not a single man, suited by a woman's pen, steps forward to keep them company. Perhaps writing about men, like the ascent of K7, is something that most women are not interested in, but one would like to feel sure that it is a genuine choice, rather than a constraint.

Optimistically, I like to think that this narrowing of authorial authority has as one of its main origins the widening of the canon and the general recognition that minorities are willing and able to speak for themselves. But I also wonder if it might not be linked to the surge of anti-fiction. Authors have been encouraging readers to map fiction onto the real world, and even when we want to we may have trouble now in reversing that trend. Perhaps Lewis Carroll's "Sylvie and Bruno Concluded" might serve as a cautionary tale. In this story Carroll describes Sylvie and Bruno's attempts to find an accurate map. Eventually, the two children end up with a one-to-one map and wreak havoc among the local farmers by blocking out the sun.

Putting aside these vexed matters of authority and autobiography, I want to explore in a little more detail what makes readers think, just from reading, that some stories really happened and in others that the question is irrelevant. As with the job interview, first impressions are vital, so a good place to look is the openings of a few familiar works.

Here is Joyce embarking on his great voyage:

Stately, plump Buck Mulligan came from the stairhead, bearing a bowl of lather on which a mirror and a razor lay crossed. A yellow dressing-gown, ungirdled, was sustained gently behind him on the mild morning air. He held the bowl aloft and intoned:

—*Introibo ad altare Dei.*

Halted, he peered down the dark winding stairs and called out coarsely:

—Come up, Kinch! Come up, you fearful jesuit!

There is nothing in these events that renders them immediately fictional. In fact, the quotidian subject matter could easily find a place in an essay, but Joyce gives us unmistakable signals that we are on the planet of fiction. There is no visible narrator. The act of writing is concealed. We are made to believe that the words sprang up on the page without effort. Characters are shown to us through action and dialogue. There is no initial attempt at explanation. There is considerable specificity of detail and a kind of heightened density to the style. From our earliest listening and reading we have learned to understand these as the hallmarks of fiction. We are not, I think, allowed for a moment to take this as biography or history.

Here, on the other hand, is Proust:

> For a long time I used to go to bed early. Sometimes, when I had put out my candle, my eyes would close so quickly that I had not even time to say "I am going to sleep." And half an hour later the thought that it was time to go to sleep would awaken me; I would try to put away the book which, I imagined, was still in my hands, and to blow out the light; I had been thinking all the time, while I was asleep, of what I had just been reading, but my thoughts had run into a channel of their own, until I myself seemed actually to have become the subject of my book: a church, a quartet, the rivalry between François I and Charles V.

The paragraph continues to explore this confusion between waking and sleeping, book and self. In his dreamlike state the narrator ponders the act of writing: "the subject of my book would separate itself from me, leaving me free to choose whether I would form part of it or no." There is an absence of dialogue and a lack of immediacy; right away we are being told that events are remembered. Most noteworthy of all, we are in the presence of a narrator who is not immediately distinguished from the author. Crucial to *Remembrance of Things Past* is the narrator's situation as an only child, and such is the autobiographical force of the writing, that I think almost all readers are amazed to discover that Proust had a brother. Surely we can be forgiven our confusion when Proust not merely tolerates but encourages it. The narrator of this novel is not named for many hundreds of pages, but, when at last he is, his name is Marcel.

Over and above all this the basic difference between *Ulysses* and *Remembrance of Things Past* is between the third person and the first. The third person is the "once upon a time" voice that signals we are being told a story. In "Learning by Heart" I was being absolutely conventional when I put the parts about Janey's life that I was largely inventing in the third person and the part that I had actually experienced in the first person. But the way in which I used the first person would not have been possible without the example of Proust. There were, after all, plenty of first-person novels prior to *Remembrance,* but reading, for example, *Tristram Shandy, Robinson Crusoe, Jane Eyre,* we have, I think, no impulse to confuse author and narrator. For one thing, these authors carefully separate themselves from the narrator. Look at the opening paragraph of *Great Expectations.*

> My father's family name being Pirrip, and my Christian name Philip, my infant tongue could make of both names nothing longer or more explicit than Pip. So I called myself Pip, and came to be called Pip.

Could Dickens have mentioned Pip's name a little more often in the first paragraph? Reading on, we find in Pip's fanciful description of the tombstones of his relatives the density and the unnatural specificity of fiction, and, although events are clearly in the past, neither the act of remembering nor writing is invoked. My first thought was that even a reader who knows nothing of Dickens's early life would suspect that more than the name of the narrator is being fictionalized. But that is the wrong way round. We are being so clearly signaled that this is fiction that the question, "Did these things really happen?" does not occur, anymore than we ask if a wolf in a nightgown would really make a convincing grandmother. This kind of opening was later passionately subverted by Salinger's Holden Caulfield, who announces that he is not going to tell us "where I was born, and what my lousy childhood was like, and . . . all that David Copperfield kind of crap."

In shifting the boundaries between the self and the book, Proust, I would argue, has had a far greater influence than Joyce. A host of fictional memoirs has been published since *Remembrance of Things Past,* some of which have sought to extend the continuum of anti-fiction even further. How far this can be done without the reader wondering why this material is being called fiction is a question to ponder. A few years ago the French writer Marguerite Duras, after a long silence, published a short novel, *The Lover.* The novel centers on the relationship between a fifteen-and-a-half-year-old French girl and her Chinese lover. The American edition had a photograph of the young Duras on the front cover, and it was widely mentioned in reviews that this novel was heavily, if not entirely autobiographical.

Putting aside these marketing techniques, one of the most obvious things about reading the opening pages of Duras's novel is the way she shuttles back and forth between France and Indochina, between her fifteen-year-old and her present self. It could, I suppose, give the effect of muddle or disorganization, but in fact it strengthens our sense that the events described have really occurred. Duras is simply remembering and picking out what she wants to tell us. When I went back to "Learning by Heart" I realized I had done the same thing. Janey's story moved steadily forward with the occasional memory embedded in the flow; it was hard enough to make things up without skipping around. But in the part that I was remembering I found it almost impossible to progress chronologically. Describing Janey's marriage to my father, I skipped a quarter of a century to report my reading of the letters she had received at that time. Not one of the twenty-odd letters referred to me. The only reason for such an omission could surely be Janey's failure to mention that she was acquiring not only a husband but a stepdaughter.

In the nineteenth century Duras would probably have used letters or a sensational secret diary to support her story. Late in the twentieth century, however, she relies upon a heavy hemorrhaging between reality and fiction. No one could attack the plot because she was telling us that these events really happened, but, if pressed too closely, she could protest that this was fiction. Several times in *The Lover* the narrator claims that she has never written about this material before, and, now that she is, she plans to tell the whole truth and nothing but the truth. Even fairly soon after publication, however, astute critics were diagnosing a hole in the heart of the novel. And now Duras is agreeing with them. She is advertised as being at work on a new book that will reveal what the scandalous relationship in *The Lover* concealed—namely her incestuous relationship with her brother.

I do not mean to sound as if I am taking Duras to task for mendacity per se. My concern is not whether the events described in a work of fiction occurred but, rather, the techniques by which an author might make a reader believe they did. All authors omit and select. When I discover that Proust has a brother, it does not detract from the beauty and authenticity of his portrayal of an only child. In "Learning by Heart" I described at length my loneliness and isolation. The truth is that for a good part of my childhood we lived near a family with four children who frequently took me in, but I never mention them. I like to think that this omission was not merely a bid for reader sympathy but also a way to clarify the story, to allow Janey and my relationship with her to emerge more clearly. No, my charge against Duras is not the omission but the way in which the omission distorts the material, as, for instance, Dickens's attempt at a happy ending to *Great Expectations* seems to distort all that the novel has been moving toward.

Besides the techniques I've already suggested—vagueness, the invocation of remembering and writing, shuttling, hemorrhaging, the absence of dialogue—I've discovered three more techniques that help to create the illusion of anti-fiction. One, which I do not advocate to my students, is what I'm rather nervously going to call "bad writing." Fiction tends to be well written. A surprising number of characters and narrators reach what, if one stops to think, are quite unrealistic heights of eloquence. It follows, then, that one way for authors to make their work seem real is by the judicious use of bad writing.

I was a little hard-pressed to find an example of this outside of my own work, but I think you can glimpse what I'm talking about in the opening of Camus's novel *The Stranger,* a novel for which I have great admiration.

> Maman died today. Or yesterday maybe, I don't know. I got a telegram from the home: "Mother deceased. Funeral tomorrow. Faithfully yours." That doesn't mean anything. Maybe it was yesterday.
>
> The old people's home is at Marengo, about fifty kilometers from Algiers, I'll take the two o'clock bus and get there in the afternoon. That way I can be there for the vigil and come back tomorrow night. I asked my boss for two days off and there was no way he was going to refuse me with an excuse like that.

I am playing the devil's advocate, of course, in suggesting that this is bad writing, but what I'm getting at is obvious. The prose is painfully flat, almost to the point of being simplistic. Even though these sentences demonstrate what Carver called "fundamental accuracy of detail," many writers would hesitate to write them. They seem too unadorned, too unliterary, to transport the reader, but at least in *The Stranger* they effectively create a narrator in whose capacity for violence and lack of self-analysis we come to vividly believe. The anti-fiction quality is further strengthened by the uncertainty: "Maman died today. Or yesterday maybe." After all, if it's fiction, there is no reason for any vagueness. We can just decide whatever we want.

From these opening sentences Camus leads us forward to the moment of murder. And this is another technique of anti-fiction I want to suggest, although *technique* may not be the correct term. Fiction tends to offer us conventional post-Freudian psychology. Motivation is one of the principle ways in which fiction makes sense. Readers as well as writers are deeply committed to this, and, even when a writer tries to prevent us from making certain connections, we often insist on doing so anyway. In *Aspects of the Novel* Forster describes plot as the causal relation between events: the king died, and then the queen died because of grief.

What he did not say was that if the king dies and then a little later the queen dies, the reader will, willy-nilly, link the two events, even if the author tells us firmly that they have nothing to do with each other.

One of the most frightening things about the world, however, is that action and motivation are often not so neatly connected. I would argue that part of what Camus accomplishes is the creation of a much more complex psychological model, a model that partakes not so much of the glibness with which we too often analyze others but of the mystery with which we speak of ourselves. In writing about Janey, I felt reluctant to the point of paralysis to attribute motivation to her. She was a giant of my childhood, and neither time nor mortality can dwarf her. This was one of the major reasons I wanted my account of our relationship to sound true; I wanted to block both my own and the reader's easy attempts at psychoanalysis.

Lastly, as an anti-fictional technique I want to point to what I call the use of history. It is surprising how many stories and novels contain absolutely minimal references to current events, to anything beyond the characters and their relationships. Jane Austen, as has often been remarked, makes no reference to the Battle of Waterloo. This exclusion seems to suggest that both readers and writers yearn in art for a certain kind of transcendence of the everyday. It also means that, as soon as we start to connect the lives of our characters with the real world, we are taking a step toward making our fiction sound like anti-fiction. For four years of my childhood I attended a girls' school, which I prayed nightly would be closed down or burned to the ground. But, as I explain in "Learning by Heart," the major fact in bringing about the closure of the school was not my prayers but the shrinking of British colonies, which led to fewer people working abroad who needed to send their daughters home to be educated.

All these techniques I've been listing, except bad writing, can be found to gorgeous effect in Tim O'Brien's *The Things They Carried*. This book, dedicated to its characters, takes as one of its main themes the connection between fact and fiction. In "How To Tell a True War Story" the narrator says, if you ask whether a story is true and the answer matters, you've got your answer.

> For example, we've all heard this one. Four guys go down a trail. A grenade sails out. One guy jumps on it and takes the blast and saves his three buddies.
> Is it true?
> The answer matters.
> You'd feel cheated if it never happened. Without the grounding

reality, it's just a trite bit of puffery. . . . Yet even if it did happen . . . you know it can't be true, because a true war story does not depend upon that kind of truth. Absolute occurrence is irrelevant. A thing may happen and be a total lie; another thing may not happen and be truer than the truth.

Here I think O'Brien delineates the dilemma of all serious fiction writers. However we approach our work and the world, we are trying to get at that truth that lies beyond absolute occurrence.

Most of the examples I've offered demonstrate the strength of anti-fiction, but one of the major hazards of the enterprise can be seen, I think, in the experiences of a friend who wrote a series of personal essays about Israel. "Very nice," responded an editor, "but who would want to read about you?"

I immediately applied this chilling question to myself. When I stopped to think, it seemed at first glance very odd that, on the one hand, it would never occur to me to write my autobiography because my life is so pedestrian and, on the other hand, I persist in writing stories that are more or less autobiographical. As the editor says, why should anyone be interested in reading about me?

I think the answer lies in the nature of fiction and art in general. Art has the power to transform the world, and nowhere is that power more evident than when applied to the unpromising material of the everyday. In the hands of Flaubert the relationship between a poorly educated serving woman and her parrot becomes a subject of resonance and beauty.

In the case of Janey, however, I lacked confidence in my ability to transform, and there were too many suitcases of truth that I wanted to smuggle into the story. I would never have got them all onto the planet of fiction. Instead, I tried to create the illusion that Janey had lived and died in the way I described. I knew that this illusion could be immensely seductive but if I failed to rise above the anecdotal then the reader would balk and say, but why should I want to read about Janey and you?

Machiavelli urged the Prince in the service of the state to become a great liar. In the service of truth writers, I think, need to follow this advice. I may not be able to control my autobiographical impulses, but there is a measure of control to be gained over the way in which I reveal my secrets. Will I send them forth into the world as fiction? or anti-fiction? or some mixture of the two? As Proust so simply and elegantly says, "the subject of my book would separate itself from me, leaving me free to choose whether I would form part of it or no." Writers are always present in their work. The question is how.

Contributors

Charles Baxter is the author of four books of stories and three novels, most recently *The Feast of Love,* nominated for the National Book Critics Circle Award. He is also the author of a book of essays on fiction, *Burning Down the House,* and has edited a volume of essays, *The Business of Memory.* He lives in Ann Arbor and teaches at the University of Michigan as well as in the Warren Wilson MFA Program for Writers.

Robert Boswell is the author of seven books of fiction: *The Sorrow Pageant, American Owned Love, Living to Be 100, Mystery Ride, The Geography of Desire, Dancing in the Movies,* and *Crooked Hearts.* He has received two National Endowment for the Arts Fellowships, a Guggenheim Fellowship, the Iowa School of Letters Award for Fiction, the 1995 PEN West Award for Fiction, and the 1996 Evil Companions Award. His stories have appeared in the *New Yorker, Best American Short Stories, O'Henry Prize Stories, Best Stories from the South, TriQuarterly,* the *Georgia Review,* and many other magazines. He teaches at New Mexico State University and in the Warren Wilson MFA Program for Writers and resides with his wife, the writer Antonya Nelson, and their two children in Las Cruces, New Mexico, and Telluride, Colorado.

Karen Brennan is the author of *Here on Earth* and *Wild Desire.* A memoir based on her daughter's brain injury, *Being with Rachel,* is forthcoming. She teaches in the Warren Wilson MFA Program for Writers and is an associate professor at the University of Utah.

Judith Grossman was born in a nonscenic area of London, England, and graduated from Somerville College, Oxford. After moving to the United States, she studied at Brandeis University and has since taught at the University of California, Irvine, and in the Writing Seminars at Johns Hopkins University as well as in the MFA Program for Writers at Warren Wilson College. Her previous publications include critical essays and a novel, *Her Own Terms* (1988), listed by the *New York Times* among the Notable Books of the Year. Her first story collection, *How Aliens Think,* was published in 1999.

Ehud Havazelet is the author of two collections, *What Is It Then Between Us?* (1988) and *Like Never Before* (1998). He is a recipient of fellowships from Stanford University and the Whiting and Rockefeller foundations. He teaches in the University of Oregon Creative Writing Program and in the Warren Wilson MFA Program for Writers. He lives in Corvallis, Oregon.

C. J. Hribal is the author of *The Clouds in Memphis* (2000), which won the AWP Award in Short Fiction. He is also the author of *Matty's Heart* (1984), a collection of short fiction; and *American Beauty* (1987), a novel. He edited and wrote the introduction for *The Boundaries of Twilight: Czecho-Slovak Writing from the New World* (1991). The recipient of a National Endowment for the Arts Fellowship and a Bush Foundation Fellowship, he is Associate Professor of English at Marquette University, where he teaches creative writing and English. He is also a member of the fiction faculty in the Warren Wilson MFA Program for Writers.

Margot Livesey was born and grew up in Scotland and now divides her time between London and Massachusetts, where she presently teaches at Emerson College; she is also a member of the fiction faculty in the Warren Wilson MFA Program for Writers. She is the author of a collection of stories, *Learning by Heart,* and of three novels, *Homework, Criminals,* and *The Missing World.*

Michael Martone's *The Blue Guide to Indiana* is forthcoming in the fall of 2001. *The Flatness and Other Landscapes* won the AWP Prize for Creative Nonfiction. He is the author of several books of fiction, including *Seeing Eye, Fort Wayne Is Seventh on Hitler's List,* and *Pensées: The Thoughts of Dan Quayle.* He lives in Tuscaloosa, Alabama, with the poet Theresa Pappas and their two children.

Kevin McIlvoy has taught creative writing for twenty years at New Mexico State University, where he has also been editor-in-chief of the national literary magazine *Puerto del Sol.* He received his MFA degree from the University of Arizona, his master's degree from Colorado University, and his bachelor's degree from the University of Illinois. He is the coordinator of the Senior Writing Outreach Project (funded by NMSU and the McCune Foundation), which establishes creative writing workshops in senior centers throughout New Mexico. For eighteen years he has been volunteer instructor at the Munson Senior Center in Las Cruces, New Mexico, and he has been editor and publisher of the annual *Serape* anthology, which publishes the work of New Mexico writers over fifty-five. His short fiction has appeared in the *Southern Review, TriQuarterly, Chelsea, Ploughshares, Missouri Review,* and other magazines. Two of his novels, *Little Peg* and *Hyssop,* have recently been published in paperback. He has taught in the Warren Wilson MFA Program for Writers for over ten years.

Cuban-born **Pablo Medina** is the author of several works of poetry and prose, most recently, *The Floating Island* (poems) and *The Return of*

Felix Nogara (novel). His work has appeared in numerous periodicals and anthologies, and he has lectured and read widely throughout the United States, Latin America, and the Middle East. Currently, he teaches in the Warren Wilson MFA Program for Writers and at the New School University, where he also directs the Writing Program at Eugene Lang College. He resides in Montclair, New Jersey.

Antonya Nelson has taught in the Warren Wilson MFA Program for Writers since 1993. She is the author of three story collections and three novels, the most recent of which is *Living to Tell.* She lives in Las Cruces, New Mexico, and Telluride, Colorado.

Susan Neville is the author of the story collections *In the House of Blue Lights, Indiana Winter,* and *Invention of Flight.* She has won the Flannery O'Connor Award for Short Fiction, the Richard Sullivan Prize, and the Pushcart Prize. A collection of essays, *Fabrication,* will be published 1 March 2001. She lives in Indianapolis and is the Demia Butler Professor of English at Butler University.

Novelist and screenwriter **Richard Russo** is the author of the novels *Mohawk, The Risk Pool, Nobody's Fool, Straight Man,* and *Empire Falls,* scheduled for publication May 2001. He lives in Maine.

Steven Schwartz is the author of two story collections, *To Leningrad in Winter* (1985) and *Lives of the Fathers* (1991); and two novels, *Therapy* (1994) and *A Good Doctor's Son* (1998), which received the 1999 Colorado Book Award for Fiction. His fiction has appeared in many publications, including the *Chicago Tribune,* the *San Francisco Chronicle, Tikkun, Redbook, Antioch Review,* and *Ploughshares.* He has received the Nelson Algren Award, a National Endowment for the Arts Fellowship, and two O'Henry Awards. A professor of English at Colorado State University, he also teaches in the Warren Wilson College MFA Program for Writers and has been an associate faculty member at the Bread Loaf Writers' Conference, where he was the John Gardner Fellow in Fiction.

Jim Shepard is the author of a short story collection, *Batting Against Castro,* and five novels, *Flights, Paper Doll, Lights Out in the Reptile House, Kiss of the Wolf,* and, most recently, *Nosferatu.* He teaches film and literature at Williams College and fiction writing in the Warren Wilson MFA Program for Writers.

Joan Silber is the author of the novels *Household Words,* which won the PEN/Hemingway Award, and *In the City.* Her most recent book is the story collection *In My Other Life.* Her short fiction has appeared in the *New Yorker, Ploughshares, Voice Literary Supplement, Paris Review, Boulevard,* and other magazines. She has received grants from the Guggenheim Foundation, the National Endowment for the Arts, and the New York Foundation on the Arts. She lives in New York and teaches at Sarah Lawrence College and in the Warren Wilson MFA Program for Writers.

Debra Spark is the author of the novels *Coconuts for the Saint* (1994) and *The Ghost of Bridgetown* (2001). She directs the Creative Writing Program at Colby College in Maine and has taught in the Warren Wilson MFA Program for Writers for four years.

Peter Turchi is the author of three books, including a novel (*The Girls Next Door*), a collection of stories (*Magician*), and a work of nonfiction. His stories have appeared in *Ploughshares, Story, Alaska Quarterly Review,* and *Puerto del Sol,* among other magazines. The recipient of an NEA Fellowship, an Illinois Arts Council Literary Award, and North Carolina's Sir Walter Raleigh Award, Turchi has taught at the University of Arizona, Northwestern University, and Appalachian State University. Since 1993 he has taught in and served as Director of Warren Wilson College's MFA Program for Writers.

Chuck Wachtel's books include the novels, *Joe the Engineer,* winner of the PEN/Hemingway Citation, and *The Gates;* a collection of stories and novellas, *Because We Are Here;* and two collections of poems and short prose, *The Coriolis Effect* and *What Happens to Me.* His work has appeared in the *Nation, Pequod, Village Voice, Western Humanities Review, Witness, World,* and in dozens of other literary magazines both here and abroad. He teaches in the Graduate Program in Creative Writing at New York University as well as in the MFA Program for Writers at Warren Wilson College.